The Twentieth-Century Composer Speaks

An Index of Interviews

Mari Nishimura

The Twentieth-Century Composer Speaks cites over a thousand interviews with composers of our century. The people whose interviews are indexed here discuss not only their compositions and musical style, but also their roles as conductors, performers, teachers, authors, and observers of the contemporary scene. Hans Werner Henze looks at musical life in Cuba, Olivier Messiaen discusses religion, Peter Maxwell Davies speaks about fourteenth-century English music. Other composers speak on topics ranging from Ghanian music to film scores, from politics and sociology to Zen Buddhism, from neoclassicism to post minimalism, from opera to player-piano music.

Each entry gives concise information, including the name and dates of the composer interviewed, the date and place of the interview, the name of the interviewer, topics discussed, and a full citation of the source of the interview. The work is arranged by composers' names, and there are indexes by interviewers' names and by subjects.

By providing access to these primary sources, in which composers talk to us in their own words, Ms. Nishimura has enriched the knowledge of anyone interested in the musical life of our time.

The Twentieth-Century
Composer Speaks

The Twentieth-Century Composer Speaks

An Index of Interviews

Mari Nishimura

FALLEN LEAF PRESS
BERKELEY
in association with the
KUNITACHI COLLEGE OF MUSIC, LIBRARY
TOKYO

Published by Fallen Leaf Press
P.O. Box 10034
Berkeley, CA 94709 USA

in association with the

Kunitachi College of Music, Library
5-5-1 Kashiwa, Tachikawa
Tokyo, 190 Japan

Library of Congress Cataloging–in–Publication Data

Nishimura, Mari, 1962–
    The twentieth-century composer speaks: an index of interviews
/ Mari Nishimura.
        p. cm. -- (Fallen Leaf reference books in music; no. 28)
    Includes bibliographical references (p.) and indexes.
    ISBN 0-914913-29-8
    1. Composers--Interviews--Indexes. 2. Music--20th century
--History and criticism--Indexes. I. Title. II. Title: 20th-cen-
tury composer speaks. III. Series.
ML118.N57 1993
780'.92'2--dc20   93-29548
                                             CIP
                                            MN

Contents

Preface

"How wonderful it would be if we could talk to Mozart via time machine and tape recorder!" In this fervent wish, Barry Brook[1] neatly summarizes the importance of a composer's spoken words to music scholars and historians.

Although extensive quotations jotted down from the conversation of others have survived the centuries (Boswell's "interviews" of Dr. Johnson being only one of many examples), oral history as an organized discipline did not develop until the mid-twentieth century and the advent of the tape recorder. In 1948, Allan Nevins established the Oral History Research Office at Columbia University. By 1967 the discipline had grown sufficiently to require its own organization–the Oral History Association (OHA).

The procedures and results of oral history have not been fully accepted by scholars even today, however, and the very nature of the activity causes much debate among historians. Some believe that transcripts of interviews are simply raw materials, constructed by the active intervention of the interviewer. Others find that oral history is history itself–"filtered through a particular individual experience at a particular moment in time."

This debate has let to concerns about what properly comprises an interview and how it should be conducted. In 1979, the OHA established guidelines defining the roles of interviewers and interviewees, and calling on those who produced oral history to create source material that would be authentic, useful, and reliable.

Interviewing–at least scholarly interviewing–has thus become more systematic. Oral history can be seen to fall into three categories[2]: 1) autobiographical, in which interviewees reminisce about themselves; 2) biographical, in which interviewees talk about someone else; and 3) group interviews, in which people of similar backgrounds or interests address the same subject and answer the same questions.

In the case of music, autobiographical interviews uncover information not only about composers' lives but also about techniques involved in their compositions and about influences on their work. Most of the interviews cited in the present book are autobiographical. Among biographical interviews are those of Paul Pisk speaking on Schoenberg, Leonard Bernstein on Herbert von Karajan, John Cage on Satie, Morton Feldman on Cage. Group interviews are epitomized by *The Black Composer Speaks*[3], by David N. Baker et al., in which a group of African-American composers answer the same questions in their individual ways.

The people who have conducted the interviews noted here are variously journalists and other writers; performers, composers, and other musicians; and teachers, scholars, and technical specialists. The composers who are the subjects of these interviews discuss not only their compositions and style, but also their roles as conductors, performers, teachers, authors, and observers of the contemporary scene. They speak on topics ranging from Ghanian music to film scores, from politics and sociology to Zen Buddhism, from neo-classicism to post-minimalism, from opera to player-piano music. Hans Werner Henze looks at musical life in Cuba, Olivier Messiaen discusses religion, Peter Maxwell Davies considers fourteenth-century English music. Krzystof Penderecki talks about his *St. Luke Passion*, Steve Reich his *Desert Music*, Ernst Křenek his *Karl V.* In short, these interviews unearth a wealth of firsthand information about twentieth-century composers. The present book, which cites over a thousand interviews with twentieth-century composers, will enrich the research of students, historians, and all others interested in the musical life of our time. These interviews have provided the time machine that enables composers to talk to us in their own words.

---

1. Deena Rosenberg and Bernard Rosenberg, *The Music Makers*, (N.Y.: Columbia University Press, 1979), pp. x-xi.
2. Norman Hoyle, "Oral History," *Library Trends* 21 (July 1972): 64-65.
3. For its imprint information, see SOURCES section.

序

　第二次世界対戦後まもなく、米国でアラン・ネヴィンズ Allan Nevins によってコロンビア大学に口述記録リサーチのための事務局 Oral History Research Office が設立され、口述記録は組織化された学問の 1 分野として確立された。以後、コーネル大学、ハーヴァード大学、ハリウッド博物館、プリンストン大学等で、口述作業による様々なプロジェクトが進められてきた。音楽学者のみならず演奏者にとっても、ある作品を究めようとするならば、音符に託されたその作曲家の創作の意図をより深く理解しようと努めるであろう。眼前にある作品だけではない。その作品を取り巻く様々な環境、また作曲家の音楽経験やその時代の文化的状況を包括的に捉えて行かねばならない。非常に限られた乏しい情報しか今日の我々に残されていないような過去の音楽を探っていく場合において、口述記録による文献資料の重要性は顕著である。18世紀音楽の専門である音楽学者バリー・ブルックBarry Brookをして、「もしタイム・マシンがあったなら、テープ・レコーダーを携えてモーツァルトに会いに行けるだろうに。そうであれば、何と素晴らしいことか。」と言わしめたのは、もっともなこととうなづかざるを得ない。様式的にも形式的にも或る程度の規範を持っていた時代の音楽に比べ、今日では、更に"音楽"それ自体の領域が拡がり、語法が多様化してきており、個々の作曲家は独自の考え方に基づいて創作活動を行っている態がある。そうした状況においては、まさにインタヴュアーとの"知のパフォーマンス"の形式を通して[1]、作曲家自身の口から出る言葉の一つ一つが重みを帯びてくるのである。

　ノーマン・ホイル Norman Hoyle[2] は、対談を次の 3 つのタイプに分類している。1）自伝的、2）第三者に関する伝記的、3）或るグループに共通のテーマを持つもの、である。第 1 のタイプは、特定の作曲家の自身による生涯または思い出話といった事柄から、作曲技法や創作活動における外的影響にいたる様々な側面を語ってもらうものである。第 2 は本人自身についてではなく、第三者に焦点を当てており、『記念論文集』などでよくみられる型である。第 3 はデヴィド・ベイカー他著『黒人作曲家は語る』[3]にみられるように、或る基準で集められたグループを対象として、個々に同一の質問を投げかけることに依ってそのグループの共通した傾向などを探っていこうとするものである。このように、対談は、より組織化され、信憑性の高い学術的に裏打ちされた情報として取り扱われるようになってきた。研究者や学生が何を求めているかによって、異なるタイプのインタヴューが選択され得るであろう。これは、口述記録というまだ歴史の浅い、しかしながら現代の科学の発展によってのみ成し得ることの出来た一つの方法論なのである。現在では、無視することの出来ないほど相当数の対談による出版物が生み出されていることをみれば、これらが学術的資料として耐え得ると認められる。ここにまとめた現代作曲家へのインタヴューの索引の利用を通じて、利用者の研究・調査に少しでも役立つことを願っている。

脚注
1. 『身体の想像力　山口昌男対談集』（岩波書店、1987年）、p. 29。
2. Norman Hoyle, "Oral History," *Library Trends* 21 (July 1972) : 64- 65.
3. 詳細は、SOURCESの"BAKER B"を参照。

Introduction

SCOPE

This book indexes interviews of twentieth-century composers of "serious" music. It cites interviews published in music journals (and in a very few non-music journals), as well as in books and in sound recordings, between 1949 and 1987. It is limited to works in Western European languages.

Almost all of the interviews were conducted orally, but a few were written by the interviewee. (These are clearly indicated in the index.) Discussions involving more than one composer are also included, as long as they were conducted informally and contain substantial dialog.

Because of their relative inaccessibility, I have excluded materials in archival collections, such as the Oral History: American Music project at Yale University that contains valuable material on Ives and Hindemith, among others, or the large series of transcripts dealing with dance, music, and other topics collected by the Regional Oral History Office at the University of California at Berkeley.

SOURCES

I gathered data for this book from music periodical indexes (*Music Index* and *RILM Abstracts*); published library catalogs, such as those of the Boston Public Library, the New York Public Library, and the Library of Congress; the *New York Times Index*; and two online services, RLIN and DIALOG. I also systematically searched all of the relevant periodicals in the Music Library at the State University of New York, Buffalo. I personally examined about 25% of the sources.

ARRANGEMENT

The book contains a main section, COMPOSERS, and two indexes, one to INTERVIEWERS and one to SUBJECTS.

COMPOSER INDEX

The COMPOSERS section contains full entries for the interviews, with complete citations; it is arranged alphabetically by composers' names. In the case of a composer with more than one interview, the entries for that composer are subarranged chronologically.

Each complete citation contains the following information, as available:

Distinctive entry number. The indexes refer the user to these numbers.

Name and date(s) of the composer(s) interviewed. If more than one composer took part in a conversation, the full citation for the interview appears under the name of the composer filing earliest in the alphabet. *See* references direct the user from the other interviewees' names to the name under which the citation is entered.

Date of the interview. Dates of interviews are those provided in the source, if noted. If an interview lacks a definitive date, I have used the publication date of the source. When an interview was conducted on different dates, the dates are separated by a semicolon. Such interviews are filed under the latest date.

Place of the interview (city, state for the United States, country).

Name of the interviewer(s). Names of up to two interviewers are entered in the complete citation. Additional names that do not appear in the COMPOSERS section are indexed in the INDEX OF INTERVIEWERS (see below).

Topics discussed. Topics are listed alphabetically, regardless of the order in which they were discussed or the weight given them in the interview. Often composers spoke about a broad range of topics, even in brief interviews. Some interviewers changed topics with each question; others stayed with a single topic throughout. I did not index topics touched upon but not discussed in depth. I have selected and modified subject terms from a variety of lists, including the *Library of Congress Subject Headings*, the *Music Index* and the *RILM Author-Subject Index*. Topics are indexed in the SUBJECT INDEX (see below).

Specific works by the interviewee. Whenever composers discussed their own works (rather than merely mentioning them in passing), I listed the titles of the works in the entry. The form of the entry follows standard library practice: for example, *Concerto, piano*, rather than *Piano Concerto*. Names of prose writings by the interviewee discussed in the interview are listed in italics after the list of musical compositions.

Presence of an appended list of the interviewee's works, indicated by (Y) or (N).

Presence of appended biographical information about the interviewee, indicated by (Y) or (N).

Source (publication in which the interview appeared); title and location of article. The name of the publication is indicated by an abbreviation. Complete titles of journals and publication information for books are given in the LIST OF SOURCES. This field also contains the title of the interview and the specific citation (pagination, issue, etc.). The source cited may not be the original version of an interview transcript but rather only the one available to me.

Language in which the interview was published. The language code (see LIST OF ABBREVIATIONS) refers to the language in which the interview is published, not necessarily that used in the actual interview. If other versions of the interview are available, they are mentioned in the NOTES.

Notes. Miscellaneous information of any type is noted here, including variant versions of sources, as well as *see-* and *see also* references.

Sample entry:

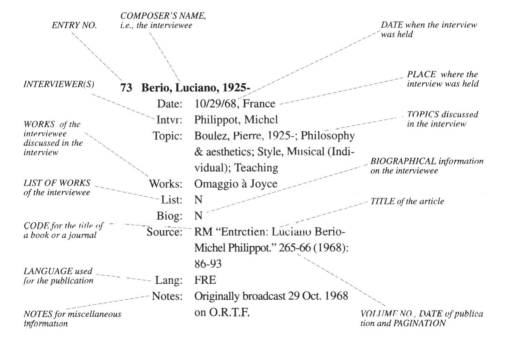

Entry number 73: Michel Philippot interviewed composer Luciano Berio, who discussed his own musical style, and his contemporary, Pierre Boulez, and so on. The interview took place on October 29, 1968, in France. The article appears in French on pages 86-93 of *La Revue Musicale*, and contains neither a list of Berio's works nor a biography of the composer.

INTERVIEWER INDEX

The Index is arranged alphabetically by interviewers' names, and in the case of multiple interviewers includes names that do not appear in the COMPOSERS section. Transcribers of interviews are not indexed unless they actually conducted the interview. Numbers refer the user to entry numbers in the COMPOSERS section.

SUBJECT INDEX

The SUBJECT INDEX is arranged alphabetically by topic. Subdivisions of single-word entries and compound-word entries are indented under their headings.

Sample entries:

> Composers
> > Economic conditions, 16, 58
> > Influences, 11, 142
> > Political conditions, 33, 130
> > 20th-century, 49, 296
> > > Europe, 46
> > > Influences, 970, 1032

Numbers refer the user to entry numbers in the COMPOSERS section.

Abbreviations

DAN	Danish	NOR	Norwegian
ENG	English	POR	Portuguese
FRE	French	SPA	Spanish
GER	German	SWE	Swedish
ITA	Italian		

Sources

ACA   American Composers Alliance. *ACA Bulletin*. New York: American Composers Alliance, 1938-1965.

ACCENT   *Accent: A Magazine for Young Musicians*. Evanston, Ill.: Accent Publishing, 1975-1982.

ALBET M   Albet, Montserrat. *Moderne Musik. Von den Regeln der Klassik zum freien Experiment. Interviewpartner: Karlheinz Stockhausen.* Translated by Christina Mailla. Reinbek bei Hamburg: Rowohlt, 1977.

AM   *American Music*. Champaign, Ill.: Sonneck Society and the University of Illinois Press, 1983-. Quarterly

ANGELES M   Angeles Gonzáles, María, and Saavedra, Leonora. *Musica Mexicana Contemporánea*. México: Fondo de Cultura Económica, 1982.

AR   *American Recorder*. New York: The American Recorder Society, 1960-. Quarterly

ARNOLD W   Arnold, Heinz Ludwig, ed. *Wolf Biermann*. München: Edition Text und Kritik, 1975

ARTES   *Artes* (Stockholm). Stockholm: Forum, 1975-. Bimonthly

ARTFORUM   *Artforum*. New York: Artforum, 1962-. Monthly

ASCAP   *ASCAP in Action*. New York: American Society of Composers, Authors and Publishers, 1979-. 3 times a year; formerly *ASCAP Today* (1967-1979).

ASO   *L'Avant-Scène Opéra*. Paris: L'Avant Scène, 1976 1982; 1986-. Monthly

ASTERISK   *Asterisk: A Journal of New Music*. Ann Arbor, Mich.: C. P. Phrogge & Associates, 1974-. (Ceased publication)

AUDEL P   Audel, Stéphane, ed. *My Friends and Myself: Conversations with Francis Poulenc*. Translated by James Harding. London: Dobson, 1978.

BAILEY M   Bailey, Derek. *Musical Improvisation*. Englewood Cliffs, N.J.: Prentice-Hall, 1980.

BAKER B Baker, David N., et al., ed. *The Black Composer Speaks*. Metuchen, N.J.: Scarecrow Press, 1978.

BERIO T *Two Interviews, Luciano Berio with Rossana Dalmonte and Bálint András Varga*. New York: M. Boyars, 1984. Translation of *Intervista sulla Musica* (Roma; Bari: Laterza, 1981).

BMSJ *British Music Society Journal*. Andover, England: British Music Society, 1979-. Annually

BOIS I Bois, Mario. *Iannis Xenakis: The Man and His Music*. Westport, Conn.: Greenwood Press, 1980. Reprint of the edition published by Boosey & Hawkes Music Publishers, London, 1967.

BOULEZ C Boulez, Pierre. *Conversations with Célestin Deliège*. London: Eulenburg Books, 1976. Translation of *Par volonté et par hasard: Entretiens avec Célestin Deliège*. (Paris: Seuil, 1975); German translation as *Wille und Zufall: Gespräche mit Célestin Deliège und Hans Mayer*. (Stuttgart: Belser, 1977).

BP *Boston Phoenix*. Boston, Mass.: N.p., 1972-. Weekly

BPM *Black Perspective in Music*. New York: The Foundation for Research in the Afro-American Creative Arts, 1973-. Semiannually

BRAVO *Bravo*. (Lack of imprint information)

BROCK H Brockmeier, Jens, ed. *Hans Werner Henze: Musik und Politik. Schriften und Gespräche*. München: Deutscher Taschenbuch, 1984.

BUNGE H Bunge, Hans. *Hanns Eisler, Gespräche mit Hans Bunge: Fragen Sie mehr über Brecht*. Hanns Eisler: Gesammelte Werke, Serie III, Bd. 7. Leipzig: VEB Deutscher Verlag für Musik, 1975.

CAGE F Cage, John. *For the Birds*. Boston: M. Bovars, 1981. Translation of *Pour les Oiseaux: Entretiens avec Daniel Charles* (Paris: P. Belfond, 1976).

CAR *Cahiers Albert Roussel*. Bruxelles: Les Amis belges d'Albert Roussel, 1978-1981.

CARNOVALE G Carnovale, Norbert. *Gunther Schuller, A Bio-Bibliography*. Bio-bibliographies in Music, no. 6. Westport, Ct.: Greenwood Press, 1987.

CBDNA *CBDNA Journal.* Columbus, Ohio: College Band Directors National Association, 1984-. Semiannually

CC *Canadian Composer/Le Compositeur Canadien.* Toronto: Creative Arts, 1965-. Monthly

CHOT L Chotzinoff, Samuel. *A Little Nightmusic.* New York: Harper & Row, 1964.

CJ *Choral Journal.* Tampa, Fla.: American Choral Directors Association, 1959-. 9 times a year

CK *Contemporary Keyboard.* Saratoga, Calif.: Keyboard Players International, 1975-1981.

CM *Church Music.* St. Louis: Concordia Publishing, 1966-1980.

CMF *Le Courrier musical de France.* Paris: L'Association pour la Diffusion de la Pensée Française, 1963-1980.

CMJ *Computer Music Journal.* Cambridge, Mass.: MIT Press, 1977-. Quarterly

COMP(CA) *Composer Magazine.* Redondo Beach, Calif.: Composers' Autograph Publications, 1969-1981.

COMP(GA) *Composer!* Atlanta, Ga.: Composers' Resources, 1986-. 3 times a year

COMP(LONDON) *Composer.* London: Composers' Guild of Great Britain, 1959-1974; British Music Information Centre, 1974-1987. 3 times a year.

CONTACT *Contact: A Journal of Contemporary Music.* London. Contact, 1971-. 3 times a year

CONTRECHAMPS *Contrechamps.* Lausanne: L'Age d'Homme, 1983-. Semiannually

COP Copland, Aaron. *El Salón México....* RCA Red Seal ARL 1-2862, 1978. Sound recording. (The interview between the composer and Philip Ramey on the record jacket)

COTT S Cott, Jonathan. *Stockhausen, Conversations with the Composer.* New York: Simon & Schuster, 1973.

CRUMB D *Un Dialogo: George Crumb con José Antonio Alcaraz.* Mexico City: Ediciones de la Biblioteca Benjamin Franklin, 1977; reprint ed., Bogotá: Centro Colombo-Americano, 1983.

CSM *Christian Science Monitor.* Boston: Christian Science Publishing, 1908-. Daily

CULTURES *Cultures.* Paris: Unesco, 1973-1985.

DB *Down Beat.* Elmhurst, Ill.: Maher Publications, 1934-. Monthly

DICKINSON T Dickinson, Peter, ed. *Twenty British Composers.* London: J & W Chester, 1975.

DISCOTECA *Discoteca.* Milan: N.p., 1960-1972.

DM *Dansk Musiktidsskrift.* Copenhagen: G. E. C. Gad, 1925-. Bimonthly

DOCUMENTS *Documents [Reproduced from Autobiographies, Interviews, Lectures, Writings, etc.].* N.p.: The Open University Press, 1978.

EAR *Ear Magazine.* New York: New Wilderness Foundation, 1973-80. Irregularly

EDWARDS F Edwards, Allen. *Flawed Words and Stubborn Sounds; A Conversation with Elliott Carter.* New York: W. W. Norton, 1972.

EISLER S *Hanns Eisler sprich über Hölderlin.* Wergo 60064/III. Sound recording of the publication titled *Fragen Sie mehr über Brecht, Hanns Eisler im Gespräch* by Hans Bunge (München: Rogner & Bernhard, 1970).

EM *Electronic Musician.* Berkeley, Calif.: Electronic Musician, 1985-. Monthly

ENTRETEMPS *Entretemps* (Paris). Paris: Entretemps, 1986-. Quarterly

ETHMUS *Ethnomusicology.* Ann Arbor, Mich.: Wesleyan University Press, 1953-. 3 times a year

ETUDE *Etude.* Philadelphia: T. Presser, 1833-1957.

EWJ *East West Journal.* Brookline, Mass.: Kushi Foundation, 1971-1986.

EXPRESS   *L'Express*. Paris: Groupe Express, 1953-. Irregularly

FAILLA M   Failla, Salvatore Enrico. *Musicisti Italiani d'oggi*. Catania: La Goliardica, 1984.

FANFARE   *Fanfare*. Tenafly, N.J.: Fanfare, 1977-. Bimonthly

FMQ   *Finnish Music Quarterly*. Helsinki: Sibelius Academy, 1985-. Quarterly

FP   *Feedback Papers: Informationen, Berichte, Ideen, Projekte, Dokumente und Aufsätze*. Köln: Feedback Studio Verlag, 1971-1983.

FTM   *Film and TV Music*. New York: National Film Music Council, 1956-1958. 5 times a year

GAGNE S   Gagne, Cole, and Caras, Tracy. *Soundpieces: Interviews with American Composers*. Metuchen, N.J.: The Scarecrow Press, 1982.

GARLAND L   Garland, Peter, ed. *A Lou Harrison Reader*. Santa Fe, N.M.: Soundings, 1987.

GENA J   Gena, Peter, and Brent, Jonathan, eds. *A John Cage Reader: In Celebration of His 70th Birthday*. New York: C. F. Peters, 1982.

GILLESPIE G   Gillespie, Don, ed. *George Crumb, Profile of a Composer*. Composer Profiles, 2. New York: C. F. Peters, 1985.

GOLEA B   Goléa, Antoine. *Rencontres avec Pierre Boulez, avec trois horstexte*. Paris: R. Julliard, 1958.

GOLEA M   Goléa, Antoine. *Rencontres avec Olivier Messiaen*. Paris: R. Julliard, 1960.

GRABS H   Grabs, Manfred, ed. *Hanns Eisler Heute: Berichte-Probleme-Beobachtungen*. Forum: Musik in der DDR: Arbeitsheft, 19. Berlin: Akademie der Kunste der DDR, 1974.

GRIFFITHS G   Griffiths, Paul. *György Ligeti*. The Contemporary Composers Series. London: Robson Books, 1983.

GRIFFITHS N   Griffiths, Paul. *New Sounds, New Personalities: British Composers of the 1980s in Conversation with Paul Griffiths*. London: Faber, 1985.

HANSEN A Hansen, Mathias, and Müller, Christa, eds. *Forum: Musik in der DDR: Arnold Schönberg, 1874 bis 1951; zum 25. Todestag des Komponisten.* Berlin: Akademie der Künste der DDR, 1976.

HARMONIE *Harmonie: Catalogue générale classique.* Paris: Harmonie, 1976-1979. Annually

HARVITH E Harvith, John, and Harvith, Susan Edwards, eds. *Edison, Musicians, and the Phonograph.* New York: Greenwood Press, 1987.

HEISTER K Heister, Hanns-Werner, and Sparrer, Walter-Wolfgang, eds. *Der Komponist Isang Yun.* München: Edition Text-Kritik, 1987.

HETEROFONIA *Heterofonía; Revista Musical.* Mexico: Conservatorio Nacional de Musica, 1968-. Quarterly

HF *High Fidelity.* Great Barrington, Mass.: Audiocom, 1951-1958.

HF/MA *High Fidelity/Musical America.* Marion, Ohio: ABC Leisure Magazines, 1979-1980.

HP *High Performance.* Los Angeles, Calif.: Astro Artz, 1978-. Quarterly

HUOT E Huot, Cécile. *Entretiens avec Omer Létourneau.* Montréal: Quinze, 1979.

HYMN *Hymn.* New York: Hymn Society of America, 1949-. Quarterly

IAIMR Tulane University of Louisiana. Inter-American Institute for Musical Research. *Anuario/Yearbook.* New Orleans: Tulane University of Louisiana, 1965-1969; Anuario interamericano de investigación musical, 1970-1975.

INTERFACE *Interface: Journal of New Music Research.* Amsterdam: Swets & Zeitlinger, 1972-. 4 times a year

JACOB R Jacobson, Robert. *Reveberations: Interviews with the World's Leading Musicians.* N.Y.: W. Morrow, 1974.

JM *Jounal of Musicology.* St. Joseph, Mich.: Imperial Printing, 1982-. Quarterly

JUNG L Jungheinrich, Hans-Klaus. *Lust am Komponieren. Musikalische Zeitfragen 16.* Kassel: Bärenreiter, 1985.

KAC C   Kaczynski, Tadeusz. *Conversations with Witold Lutoslawski*. London: Chester Music, 1984; German translation published as *Gespräche mit Witold Lutoslawski; mit einem Anhang, Balint Andras Varga.* (Leipzig: P. Reclam, 1976).

KEELE F   *First American Music Conference, Keele University, England, April 18-21, 1975.* Keele: University of Keele, 1977.

KELEMEN L   Kelemen, Milko. *Labyrinthes sonores*. Paris: Champion, 1985. Previously published as *Klanglabyrinthe* (München: Piper, 1981) and as *Labirinti zvuka* (Zagreb, 1982).

KEYBD   *Keyboard*. Cupertino, Calif.: GPI Publications, 1981-. Monthly

KLUP W   Klüppelholz, Werner. *Was ist musikalische Bildung?* Musikalische Zeitfragen 14. Kassel: Bärenreiter, 1984.

KN   *Key Notes: Musical Life in the Netherlands*. Amsterdam: Donemus, 1975-. Annually

KOK J   *Joonas Kokkonen–ja Timo Mäkinen Keskustelevat Musiikista ja Elämästä.* [Savonlinna: Savonlinnan Kirjapaino Osakeyhtiö], 1979.

KOST A   Kostelanetz, Richard. *American Imaginations*. Berlin: N.p., 1983.

KOST J   Kostelanetz, Richard, ed. *John Cage: Documentary Monographs in Modern Art*. N.Y.: Praeger Publishers, 1970.

KOST O   Kostelanetz, Richard. *The Old Poetries and the New*. Ann Arbor: Univ. of Michigan Press, 1981.

KOST T   Kostelanetz, Richard. *The Theatre of Mixed Means*. New York: Dial Press, 1968.

LAND B   Landowski, Marcel. *Batailles pour la Musique*. Paris: Seuil, 1979.

LIGETI G   *Gyorgy Ligeti in Conversation with Péter Várnai, Josef Hausler, Claude Samuel, and himself*. London: Eulenburg, 1983.

LOM C   Lombardi, Luca. *Conversazioni con Petrassi*. Milano: Suvini Zerboni, 1980.

LUCK C   Lück, Rudolf. *Cesar Bresgen*. Österreichische Komponisten des XX. Jahrhunderts, Bd. 21. Wien: Österreichischer Bundesverlag, 1974.

M AGO   *Music, The American Guild of Organists Magazine.* New York: American Guild of Organists, 1967-1978.

M ART   *Music and Artists.* New York: The Music Journal, 1968-1972.

M JEU   *Musique en Jeu.* Paris: Seuil, 1970-1978.

M MAG   *Music Magazine.* Toronto: Music Magazine, 1978-. Quarterly

M MED   *Musik und Medizin.* Neu-Isenburg: JMP Verlag, 1974-. Monthly

MA   *Musical America.* New York: ABC Consumer Magazine, 1898-. Bimonthly

MADERNA D   *Bruno Maderna, Documenti.* Milano: Suvini Zerboni, 1985.

MAINKA S   Mainka, Annelore, and Mainka, Jürgen, eds. *Situationen, Reflexionen, Gespräch, Erfahrungen, Gedanken.* Berlin: Neue Musik Berlin, 1986.

MB   *Musik und Bildung.* Mainz: B. Schott, 1969-. Monthly

MBR   *Conversations [with] Earle Brown, John Cage, Morton Feldman, Hans G. Helms, Heinz-Klaus Metzger, and Christian Wolff.* EMI Electrola C165-289547, 1972. Sound recording.

MC   *Musical Courier.* New York, 1883-1961.

MDB   *Musikrat der DDR, Bulletin.* Berlin-East, Musikrat der Deutschen Demokratischen Republik, 1963-. 3 times a year

MEJ   *Music Educators Journal.* Reston, Va.: Music Educators National Conference, 1914-. Monthly

MELOS   *Melos.* Mainz: Schott, 1920-. Quarterly; Jahrg. 42-45, 1975-78 merged to *Neue Zeitschrift für Musik* (Jahrg. 136-139) and formed *Melos/NZ* (Jahrg. 1-4, 1975-78).

MELOS/NZ   *Melos/NZ.* See **MELOS**

MESSIAEN M   Olivier Messiaen. *Musique et couleur. Nouveaux entretiens avec Claude Samuel.* Paris: P. Belfond, 1986.

MESSINIS M   Messinis, Mario, and Scarnecchia, Paolo, eds. *Musica e politica. Teoria e critica della contestualità sociale della musica, Voci sull'est,* *testimonianze e letture di contemporanei.* Venezia: La Biennale di Venezia, 1977.

MET I Metzger, Heinz-Klaus, and Riehn, Rainer, eds. *Iannis Xenakis.* Musik-Konzepte, Heft 54/55. München: Edition Text und Kritik, 1987.

MET J Metzger, Heinz-Klaus, and Riehn, Rainer, eds. *John Cage.* Musik-Konzepte, Sonderband. München: Edition Text und Kritik, 1978.

MET R Metzger, Heinz-Klaus, and Riehn, Rainer, eds. *Rückblick auf die Zukunft.* Musik-Konzepte, Heft 6. München: Edition Text und Kritik, 1978.

MG *Musik und Gesellschaft.* Berlin: Henschelverlag, 1951-1990. Monthly

MJ *Music Journal.* New York: Elemo Publishing, 1943-. Bimonthly

MM *Music and Musicians.* London: Filmtax, 1952-. Monthly

MN *Music News.* Wilmington, Vt.: Keyboard Press, 1984-. Monthly

MQ *Musical Quarterly.* New York: Macmillan, 1915-. Quarterly

MR *Musica/Realtà, Rivista Quadrimestrale.* Milano: Edizioni Unicopli, 1980-. 3 times a year

MT *Musical Times.* Kent, England: Novello, 1844-. Monthly

MU *Music in the USSR.* Moscow: VAAP-INFORM, 1981-. Quarterly

MUSCAN *Musicanada.* Ottawa: The Canadian Music Council, 1967- Quarterly

MUSICA *Musica.* Kassel: Bärenreiter-Verlag, 1947-. Bimonthly

MUSTEXTE *Musiktexte.* Köln: Musiktexte, 1983-. 5 times a year

MUSWORKS *Musicworks.* Toronto: Only Paper Today, 1978-. 3 times a year

MZ *Musik der Zeit.* Bonn: Boosey & Hawkes, 1958-1960.

N. O. A. Journal See **OJ**

NATTIEZ P Boulez, Pierre. *Points de repère*, ed. Jean-Jacfues Nattiez. Paris: C. Bourgois, 1981; 2d rev. ed.: Paris: C. Bourgois; Seuil, 1985.

NEULAND *Neuland Jahrbuch.* Köln: H. Henck, 1980-1985. Annually

NHQ   *New Hungarian Quarterly*. Budapest: Lapkiadó Publishing House, 1960-. Quarterly

NMA   *NMA* [New Music Article]. Brunswick, Victoria: NMA Publications, 1982-. Annually

NORTH M   Northcott, Bayan, ed. *The Music of Alexander Goehr: Interviews and Articles*. London: Schott, 1980.

NOTOWICZ W   Notowicz, Nathan. *Wir reden hier nicht von Napoleon. Wir reden von ihren! Gespräch mit Hanns Eisler und Gerhart Eisler*. Translated by Jürgen Elsner. Berlin: Neue Musik, 1971.

NUTIDA   *Nutida Musik*. [Stockholm]: Sveriges Radio, 1957/58-. Bimonthly

NYB   *New York Berlin*. New York: Sound Art Foundation, 1985-1986.

NYT   *New York Times*. New York: H. J. Raymond, 12 May 1834-. Daily

NZ   *Neue Zeitschrift für Musik*. Bonn: Schott, 1834-1974; 1979-. Monthly. See also **MELOS**.

OB   *Ord och Bild*. Stockholm: Tryckeri AB Federativ, 1892-. Monthly

OJ   *Opera Journal*. Miss.: National Opera Association, 1968-. Quarterly

ON   *Opera News*. New York: Metropolitan Opera Guild, 1936-. Irregularly

ONE   *1/1 [i.e., One/one] the Quarterly Journal of the Just Intonation Network*. San Francisco, Calif.: The Just Intonation Network, 1985-. Quarterly

OPTION   *Option*. Los Angeles, Calif.: Sonic Options Network, 1985-. Bimonthly

PAC   *Performing Arts in Canada*. Toronto: Performing Arts Magazine, 1963-. Quarterly

PALMER H   Palmer, Christopher. *Herbert Howells: A Study*. Sevenoaks: Novello, 1978.

PAULI F   Pauli, Hansjörg. *Für Wen komponieren Sie eigentlich?* Frankfurt am Main: S. Fischer, 1971.

PIERRET E   Pierret, Marc. *Entretiens avec Pierre Schaeffer*. Paris: P. Belfond, [1969]

PINZAUTI M Pinzauti, Leonardo. *Musicisti d'oggi: Venti colloqui.* Musica e Musicisti, 2. Torino: ERI, 1978.

PM *Polish Music/Polnische Musik.* Warsaw: Ars Polona Foreign Trade Krakowskie Przedmiescie, 1966-. Quarterly

PN *Percussive Notes.* Urbana, Ill.: Percussive Arts Society, 1963-. 5 times a year

PNM *Perspectives of New Music.* Seattle: University of Washington, 1962-. Semiannually

PR *Paris Review.* Flushing, N.Y.: Paris Review, 1953-. Quarterly

RASS MC *Rassegna musicale Curci.* Milano: Edizioni Curci, 1956-. 3 times a year

RAYNER D Rayner, Sheila Finch, ed. *Dane Rudhyar interviewed by Sheila Finch Rayner, Clare G. Rayner and Rob Newell.* Long Beach,Calif.: University Library, California State University, Long Beach, 1977.

RE *Revue d'esthétique.* Paris: Union Générale d'Edition, 1948-. Semiannually

RES *Res.* Cambridge, Mass.: Peabody Museum of Archaeology and Ethnology, Harvard University, 1981-. Semiannually

REX K Rexroth, Dieter, ed. *Der Komponist Hans Werner Henze.* Mainz: Schott, 1986.

RICCI V Ricci, Franco Carlo. *Vittorio Rieti.* La Musica e la Danza, 2. Napoli: Edizioni Scientifiche Italiane, 1987.

RINSER V Rinser, Luise. *Der verwundete Drache.* [Frankfurt am Main]: S. Fischer Verlag, 1977.

RISEN A Risenhoover, Morris. *Artists as Professors: Conversations with Musicians, Painters, Sculptors.* Urbana: University of Illinois Press, [1976]

RM *La Revue musicale.* Paris: Editions de la Nouvelle Revue Française, 1920-.

RMC *Revista Musical Chilena.* Santiago, Chile: Universidad de Chile, 1945-. Semiannually

RMI   *Nuova rivista musicale italiana*. Torino: Edizioni RAI Radiotelevisione italiana, 1967-. Quarterly

ROSEN M   Rosenberg, Bernard, and Rosenberg, Deena. *The Music Makers.* New York: Columbia University Press, 1979.

RS   *Rolling Stone*. New York: Straight Arrow Publishers, 1967-. Biweekly

RUFER B   Rufer, Josef. *Bekentnisse und Erkenntnisse. Komponisten über Ihr Werk*. Frankfurt am Main: Propylaen, 1979.

S MAG   *Symphony Magazine*. Washington, D.C.: American Symphony Orchestra League, 1980-. Bimonthly

SAMSON C   Samson, Helen F. *Contemporary Filipino Composers: Biographical Interviews.* Quezon City: Monlapaz Publishing, 1976.

SAMUEL C   Samuel, Claude. *Conversations with Olivier Messiaen.* London: Stainer & Bell, 1976.

SBC   *Sounding Brass and the Conductor*. London: Novello, 1972-1980.

SCHAFER B   Schafer, Raymond Murray. *British Composers in Interview.* London: Faber & Faber, [1963]

SCHERZO   *Scherzo*. Paris: Vie Musicale, 19??-1975.

SCHMIDT J   Schmidt-Miescher, Marianne, and Gachnang, Johannes, eds. *Jenseits von Ereignissen: Texte zu einer Heterospektive von George Brecht.* Bern: Kunsthalle, 1978.

SCHMIDT M   Schmidt, Felix. *Musikerportraits: Impressionen aus den Werkstätten von Komponisten und Interpreten.* Hamburg: Hoffmann und Campe, 1984.

SCHMIDT T   Schmidt, Felix, ed. *Tamtam: Monologe und Dialoge zur Musik.* München: R. Piper Co. Verlag, 1975.

SCHON G   *Arnold Schönberg. Gedenkausstellung 1974*. Wien: Universal Edition, 1974.

SCHON R   Schönberg, Klaus, ed. *Roaratorio, ein Irischer Circus über Finnegans Wake.* 2nd ed. Köningstein: Athenäum, 1986. Accompanied by cassette recording.

SCHONING B   Schöning, Klaus. *Das Buch der Hörspiele*. Frankfurt am Main: Suhrkamp Verlag, 1982.

SCHRADER I   Schrader, Barry. *Introduction to Electro-Acoustic Music*. Englewood Cliffs, N.J.: Prentice-Hall, 1982.

SCHWARTZ C   Schwartz, Elliott, and Childs, Barney, eds. *Contemporary Composers on Contemporary Music*. New York: Da Capo Press, 1978.

SESSION T   Sessions, Roger. *The Three Piano Sonatas*. Opus One no. 56/57. Sound recording

SHUFFETT M   Shuffett, Robert. "The Music, 1971-75, of George Crumb: A Style Analysis." Ph. D. dissertaion, Peabody Institute, 1979.

SI   *Studio International: Journal of Modern Art*. London: National Magazine, 1893-. Bimonthly

SILENCES   *Silences*. Paris: Editions de la Différence/Silences, 1985-. Quarterly

SIMON C   Simon, Douglas. *Chambers/Scores by Alvin Lucier. Interviews with the Composer*. Middletown, Conn.: Wesleyan University Press, 1980.

SL   *Soviet Life*. Washington: N.p., 1956-. Monthly

SM   *Schweizerische Musikzeitung*. Zürich: Gesellschaft Schweizerische Musikzeitung, 1861-1983.

SMITH S   Smith, Joan Allen. *Schoenberg and His Circle, A Viennese Portrait*. New York: Schirmer Books, 1986.

SONNTAG A   Sonntag, Brunhilde, and Matthei, Renate, eds. *Annäherung, an Sieben Komponistinnen: Mit Berichten, Interviews und Selbst-darstellungen*. Kassel: Furore-Verlag, 1987-1989. 2 vols.

SONUS   *Sonus*. Cambridge, Mass.: Sonus, 1980-. Semiannually

SOUNDINGS   *Soundings: A Music Journal*. Cardiff, Calif.: University College Cardiff Press, 1972-. Annually

SOURCE   *Source: Music of the Avant Garde*. Davis, Calif.: Composer/Performer Edition, 1967-1973.

SPEER M   Speer, Gotthard, and Winterhoff, Hans-Jürgen, eds. *Meilensteine eines Komponistenlebens. Kleine Festschrift zum 70. Geburtstag von Günter Bialas.* Kassel: Bärenreiter, 1977.

STOCK G   *Gespräch in Kürten, am 2. Juni 1973, zwischen Karlheinz Stockhausen und Hugo Pits Gruppe "Kunstkring voor Onkonventionele Muziek en Klankenkonfiguraties".* Kunstkreis für Unkonventionelle Musik und Klangkonfigurationen aus Sterksel, Holland. [N.p., n.d.]

STRA C   Stravinsky, Igor. *Conversations with Igor Stravinsky.* Berkeley, Calif.: University of California Press, 1959, 1980.

STRA D   Stravinsky, Igor. *Dialogues: Igor Stravinsky and Robert Craft.* Berkeley, Calif.: University of California Press, 1982.

STRA E   Stravinsky, Igor. *Expositions and Developments: Igor Stravinsky and Robert Craft.* London: Faber Music; Garden City, NJ: Doubleday, 1962, 1981.

STRA M   Stravinsky, Igor. *Memories and Commentaries by Igor Stravinsky and Robert Craft.* Berkeley, Calif.: University of California Press, 1981.

STRA R   Stravinsky, Igor. *Retrospectives and Conclusions: Igor Stravinsky and Robert Craft.* N. Y.: Alfred A. Knopf, 1969.

STRA T   Stravinsky, Igor. *Themes and Episodes [by] Igor Stravinsky and Robert Craft.* N.Y.: Alfred A. Knopf, 1966.

STURZ K   Stürzbecher, Ursula. *Komponisten in der DDR: 17 Gespräche.* Hildesheim: Gerstenberg, 1979.

SUDER G   Suder, Alexander L., ed. *Günther Bialas.* Komponisten in Bayern, Bd. 5. Tutzing: Verlegt bei Hans Schneider, 1984.

SWN   *Soho Weekly News.* New York: J. Leese, 1973-1982.

SWOM   *Sadler's Wells Opera Magazine.* London: Sadler's Wells Opera. (Ceased publication)

SYNAPSE   *Synapse: The Electronic Music Magazine.* Los Angeles, Calif.: Synapse Publishing, 1966-. Bimonthly

TANNEN C   Tannenbaum, Mya. *Conversations with Stockhausen*. Translated by David Butchart. Oxford: Clarendon Press, 1987.

TDR   *Tulane Drama Review*. New York: New York University, 1955/56-. Quarterly

TEMPO   *Tempo*. London: Boosey & Hawkes, 1939-1946; 1946-. Quarterly

THOM J   Thomerson, Kathleen. *Jean Langlais, A Bio-bibliography*. Bio-bibliographies in Music, no. 10. New York: Greenwood Press, 1987.

THOMSON V   *A Virgil Thomson Reader*. Boston: Houghton Mifflin, 1981.

TR   *Transatlantic Review*. London: Transatlantic Review, 1959-1977.

TW   *Totally Wired: Artists in Electronic Sound*. Philadelphia, Pa.: Pennsylvania Public Radio Associates, 1983-1985. Sound recording

ULRICH A   Ulrich, Allan. *Art of Film Music: A Tribute to California's Film Composers, the Oakland Museum, March 12, 13 & 14, 1976*. Oakland, Calif.: The Museum, 1976.

VALENTIN H   Valentin, E., et al. *Harald Genzmer*. Komponisten in Bayern, Bd. 1. Tutzing: H. Schneider, 1983.

VARGA L   Varga, Bálint András. *Lutoslawski Profile*. London: Chester Music, 1976.

VH   *VH 101*. Paris: F. Essellier, 1970-. Quarterly

VV   *Village Voice*. New York: Village Voice, 1955-. Weekly

WM   *The World of Music*. Wilhelmshaven, Germany: Heinrichshofen, 1957-. 3 times a year

WORDS M   *Words and Music*. New York: Poetry in Review Foundation, 1983.

WOUTERS F   Wouters, Jos. *Fifteen Years Donemus; Conversations with Dutch Composers*. Amsterdam: Donemus Foundation, 1964.

XENAKIS E   Xenakis, Iannis. *Entretien avec Jacques Bourgeois*. Paris: Boosey & Hawkes, [1970?]

Yearbook for Inter-American Musical Research See **IAIMR**

ZIMMER D   Zimmermann, Walter. *Desert Plants*: *Conversations with 23 American Musicians*. Vancouver: A. R. C. Publications, 1976. English texts followed by German texts in Walter Zimmermann, *Insel Musik*, pp. 519-46.

ZIMMER I   Zimmermann, Walter. *Insel Musik*. Köln: Beginner Press, 1981.

ZMP   *Zeitschrift für Musikpädagogik*. Regensburg: Erhard Friedrich Verlag, 1976-. 5 times a year

Composers

1   Abejo, Maria Rosalina, 1922-
Intvr: Samson, Helen F.
Topic: Style, (Individual)
List: Y
Biog: N
Source: SAMSON C, pp. 1-9
Lang: ENG

2   Adaskin, Murray, 1906-
Topic: Canada
List: Y
Biog: Y
Source: MUSCAN "Portrait of ... Murray Adaskin." 1 (May 1967): 8-9
Lang: ENG, FRE

3   Adler, Samuel, 1928-
Intvr: McCray, James
Topic: Composition–Influences; Education; Philosophy & aesthetics
Works: We are the echoes
List: N
Biog: N
Source: CJ "An interview with Samuel Adler." 18/9 (May 1978): 16-18
Lang: ENG

4   Agostini, Lucio
Intvr: McNamara, Helen
Topic: Creativity; Television music
List: N
Biog: N
Source: CC "Lucio Agostini: Amazing productivity, enthusiasm." 92 (June 1974): 4-9, 45
Lang: ENG, FRE

5   Alain, Olivier, 1918-
Date: 10/30/68, France
Topic: Electronic music; Henry, Pierre–Style; Henry, Pierre. *L'Apoca-*
lypse de Jean; Musique concrète; Radio broadcasting–Programs; Schaeffer, Pierre, 1910-
List: N
Biog: N
Source: RM "Pierre Henry: Entretien avec Olivier Alain, François Bayle, Martine Cadieu, Maurice Fleuret, Jacques Lonchampt." 265-66 (1968): 115-28
Lang: FRE
Notes: Originally broadcast 30 Oct. 1968 on O.R.T.F. François Bayle, Martine Cadieu, Maurice Fleuret and Jacques Lonchampt also participated in the interview.

6   Amu, Ephraim, 1899-
Date: 8/16/86, Ghana
Intvr: Agawu, V. Kofi
Topic: African music; Composition–Technique; Ghanaian music
Works: Yen ara asase nis; Bonwere kentenwene
List: N
Biog: N
Source: BPM "Conversation with Ephraim Amu: The making of a composer." 15 (Spr. 1987): 50-63
Lang: ENG

7   Amy, Gilbert, 1936-
Intvr: Jameux, Dominique
Topic: Composers–Relations with audiences; Europe; Schools of music
List: N
Biog: N
Source: M JEU "Entretien avec Gilbert Amy." 3 (1971): 72-84
Lang: FRE

1

8 Amy, Gilbert, 1936-
Date: 1/72
Intvr: Mâche, François-Bernard
Topic: Music & science; Sociology
List: N
Biog: Y
Source: RM "Les mal entendus. Compositeurs des années 70." 314-315 (1978): 25-35
Lang: FRE

9 Anderson, Beth, 1950-
Intvr: Tuynman, Carol E.
Topic: *Ear Magazine*
List: N
Biog: N
Source: EAR "Talking about the early years: Interview with Beth Anderson." 8/1-2 (Feb.-May 1983): 4-10
Lang: ENG

10 Anderson, T. J. (Thomas Jefferson), 1928-
Intvr: Hunt, Joseph
Topic: Black composers; Black music
List: N
Biog: Y
Source: BPM "Conversation with .... Thomas J. Anderson: Blacks and the classics." 1 (Feb. 1973): 157-65
Lang: ENG
Notes: Reprinted from the *Real Paper* (Cambridge, Mass.), 16 May 1973, pp. 26-32.

11 Anderson, T. J. (Thomas Jefferson), 1928-
Intvr: Baker, David N., et al.

Topic: Black composers; Composers–Influences; Composition–Technique; Performance; Style (Individual)
Works: Horizon '76
List: Y
Biog: N
Source: BAKER B, pp. 1-14
Lang: ENG

12 Andriessen, Hendrik, 1892-1981.
Intvr: Jurres, André; Wouters, Jos
Topic: Pijper, Willem, 1894-1947
List: N
Biog: Y
Source: WOUTERS F, pp. 6-21
Lang: ENG, GER
Notes: Daniël Ruyneman also participated in the interview.

13 Andriessen, Louis, 1939-
Intvr: Koopmans, Rudy
Topic: Performance practice
List: N
Biog: N
Source: KN "We don't mess around with minor details: Interviews with Louis Andriessen, Reinbert de Leeuw and Misha Mengelberg on the occasion of a concert tour by Phil Glass." 4 (Dec. 1976): 34-36
Lang: ENG
Notes: Reinbert de Leeuw and Misha Mengelberg also participated in the interview.

14 Andriessen, Louis, 1939-
Date: 1/81
Intvr: Schönberger, Elmer

Topic: Composition–Technique; Creative process; Text setting
Works: Time; Republic
List: N
Biog: N
Source: KN "Louis Andriessen on the conceiving of time." 13 (June 1981): 5-11
Lang: ENG
Notes: Previously published in *De Revisor* (1981-82).

15 Andriessen, Louis, 1939-
Intvr: Haakman, Anton
Topic: Composers as authors; Stravinsky, Igor, 1882-1971
List: N
Biog: N
Source: KN "Identifying Igor Stravinsky: The Apollonian clockwork by Louis Andriessen and Elmer Schönberger." 18 (Dec. 1983): 23-26
Lang: ENG
Notes: Elmer Schönberger also participated in the interview.

16 Anhalt, István, 1919-
Topic: Composers–Economic conditions; Canada
List: Y
Biog: Y
Source: MUSCAN "István Anhalt, a portrait." 13 (Aug. 1968): [8-9]
Lang: ENG, FRE

17 Antoniou, Theodor, 1935-
Date: 8/75, Mass.
Intvr: Rosenberg, Bernard; Rosenberg, Deena

Topic: Composition–Influences
Works: Protest I, II; Events I, II, III
List: N
Biog: N
Source: ROSEN M, pp. 71-78
Lang: ENG

18 ApIvor, Denis, 1916-
Intvr: Routh, Francis
Topic: Composers, English–20th-century; Style (Individual)
List: Y
Biog: N
Source: COMP(LONDON) "The avant-garde: Then and now." 59 (Wint. 1976-77): 19-23
Lang: ENG

19 Applebaum, Louis, 1918-
Intvr: Flohil, Richard; Schulman, Michael
Topic: Composers–Social conditions; Government & arts; Television music
List: N
Biog: Y
Source: CC "Interview! A new Canadian composer feature: Lou Applebaum." 87 (Jan. 1974): 10-19
Lang: ENG, FRE

20 Appleton, Jon Howard, 1939-
Topic: Electronic music synthesizers
List: N
Biog: N
Source: TW "I sing the body electric." 1/1 (1983)
Lang: ENG

21 Appleton, Jon Howard, 1939-
Topic: Audiences; Computers; Electronic music; Musique concrète
List: N
Biog: N
Source: TW "Computer synthesis: Jon Appleton." 1/7 (1983)
Lang: ENG

22 Arapov, Boris Aleksandrovich, 1905-
Intvr: Lobanov, Mikhail
List: N
Biog: Y
Source: MU "In search of high spiritual values: An interview with Boris Arapov." July-Sept. 1986, pp. 20-21
Lang: ENG

23 Archer, Violet, 1913-
Topic: Canada
Works: Cantata sacra; Concerto, piano; Concerto, violin; Prelude-incantation; Sonata, horn, piano
List: Y
Biog: Y
Source: MUSCAN "Violet Archer, a portrait." 14 (Sept. 1968): [8-9]
Lang: ENG, FRE

24 Archer, Violet, 1913-
Intvr: Rosen, Robert
Topic: Commissions; Composition–Influences
Works: Sganarelle
List: N
Biog: Y
Source: MUSCAN "Words about music: A series of ...." 38 (Mar. 1979): 18-19
Lang: ENG, FRE

25 Arma, Paul, 1905-1988.
Intvr: Beaufils, Marcel
Topic: Creativity; War songs
List: N
Biog: Y
Source: HETEROFONIA "Entrevista con Paul Arma." 11 (Mar.-Apr. 1970): 12-15
Lang: SPA

26 Arnell, Richard, 1917-
Intvr: Orr, Buxton
Topic: Composition–Technique; Electronic music
Works: Astronauts; Combat zone; I think of all soft limbs; Nocturne, Prague, 1968
List: N
Biog: N
Source: COMP(LONDON) "The composer speaks–7: Richard Arnell in conversation with Buxton Orr." 53 (Wint. 1974-75): 17-20
Lang: ENG

27 Arnold, Malcolm, 1921-
Intvr: Schafer, Raymond Murray
Topic: Composers–Relations with performers; Harmony; Motion picture music; Orchestras; Revisions of music
List: N
Biog: Y
Source: SCHAFER B, pp. 147-54
Lang: ENG

28 Arseneault, Raynald, 1945-
Date: 12/76
Intvr: Proulx, Michelle
Topic: Performance practice; Style (Individual)

Works: Canzoni; Concerto de chambre; Ode pour la mort d'un ami; Pâques; Quatre miniatures; Recueil pour piano; Sept pièces; Sonate
List: N
Biog: Y
Source: MUSCAN "Words about music: A series of .... " 32 (May 1977): 18-19
Lang: ENG, FRE

29 Ashley, Robert, 1930-
Date: 11/9/66, Davis, Calif.
Topic: Composers–Relations with performers; Time
Works: In memoriam ... Esteban Gomez
List: N
Biog: N
Source: SOURCE "Robert Ashley, Larry Austin, Karlheinz Stockhausen: Conversation." 1/1 (Jan. 1967): 104-7
Lang: ENG
Notes: Conversation with Larry Austin and Karlheinz Stockhausen. Swedish translation also published in *Nutida Musik* 10/8 (1966-67): 16-22.

30 Ashley, Robert, 1930-
Intvr: Zimmermann, Walter
Works: Your move, I think; *Music with roots in the aether*
List: N
Biog: N
Source: ZIMMER D "Robert Ashley." pp. 121-35
Lang: ENG

31 Ashley, Robert, 1930-
Intvr: Anson, Peter; Sokol, Casey
Works: *Music with roots in the aether*
List: N
Biog: N
Source: MUSWORKS "A conversation with Robert Ashley." 5 (Fall 1978): 16-18
Lang: ENG

32 Ashley, Robert, 1930-
Date: 7/7/80, New York City, N.Y.
Intvr: Caras, Tracy; Gagne, Cole
Topic: Creative process; Performance practice
Works: Automatic writing; "In memoriam" set; Maneuvers for small hands; Perfect lives; Sonata, piano (1959); Title withdrawn; Trios; The Wolfman tape
List: Y
Biog: Y
Source: GAGNE S, pp. 15-34
Lang: ENG

33 Asriel, André, 1922-
Date: 1973
Intvr: Lippmann, Günter
Topic: Composers–Political conditions; Eisler, Hanns, 1898-1962
List: Y
Biog: N
Source: GRABS H "Interviews mit Eisler-Schülern." pp. 207-8
Lang: GER

Austin, Larry, 1930-
See no. 29.

5

34 Austin, Larry, 1930-
Intvr: Zimmermann, Walter
Topic: Ives, Charles Edward. *The Universe Symphony*; Realizations and reconstructions
List: N
Biog: N
Source: ZIMMER D, pp. 207-220
Lang: ENG

35 Austin, Larry, 1930-
Topic: Electronic music; Improvisation
List: N
Biog: N
Source: PNM "Forum: Improvisation." 21 (Fall-Spr. 1982-83): 26-33
Lang: ENG

36 Avelino, Ariston, 1911-
Intvr: Samson, Helen F.
Topic: Careers in music; Motion picture music
List: Y
Biog: N
Source: SAMSON C, pp. 10-17
Lang: ENG

37 Avril, Edwin, 1920-
Intvr: Barron, James
Works: Cantata 1040
List: N
Biog: N
Source: NYT "The 1040 blues." 12 June 1977, sec. 11, p. 2
Lang: ENG

38 Baaren, Kees van, 1906-1970.
Intvr: Jurres, André; Wouters, Jos
Topic: Pijper, Willem, 1894-1947; Stravinsky, Igor, 1882-1971; 12-tone system

List: N
Biog: Y
Source: WOUTERS F, pp. 40-59
Lang: ENG, GER
Notes: Hans Henkemans also paticipated in the interview.

39 Babbitt, Milton, 1916-
Intvr: Fowler, Charles Bruner
Topic: Electronic music; Electronic musical instruments; Musique concrète
List: N
Biog: N
Source: MEJ "An interview with Milton Babbitt." 55 (Nov. 1968): 56-61, 127-33
Lang: ENG
Notes: Also published in *Electronic Music* (Washington, D.C.: Music Educators National Conference, 1968), pp. 22-27, 79-80; excerpted in *American Musical Digest* (Prepublication issue): 43.

40 Babbitt, Milton, 1916-
Intvr: Peyser, Joan
Topic: Performance practice
Works: Relata II
List: N
Biog: N
Source: NYT "The affair proved traumatic." 12 Jan. 1969, sec. 2, p. 17
Lang: ENG

41 Babbitt, Milton, 1916-
Date: 8/24/75, New York City, N.Y.
Intvr: Caras, Tracy; Gagne, Cole
Topic: Audiences–20th-century music;

Composers–Relations with audiences; Electronic music

Works: All set; Du; Vision and prayer
List: Y
Biog: Y
Source: GAGNE S, pp. 35-52
Lang: ENG

42 Babbitt, Milton, 1916-
Date: 5/76, New York City, N.Y.
Intvr: Rosenberg, Bernard; Rosenberg, Deena
Topic: Composers–Social conditions; Electronic music; Music publishing; Performance
Works: Du; Four canons; Into the good grond; A solo requiem; Three compositions for piano
List: N
Biog: N
Source: ROSEN M, pp. 39 59
Lang: ENG

43 Babbitt, Milton, 1916-
Intvr: Hirschfeld, Jeffrey G.
Topic: Composers–Relations with audiences; Composition Influences; Composition–Technique; Music & science; 20th-century music
List: N
Biog: N
Source: HF/MA "Milton Babbitt: A not-so-sanguine interview." 32 (June 1982): 16-18, 40
Lang: ENG

44 Babbitt, Milton, 1916-
Intvr: Varga, Bálint András
Topic: Composition–Influences; Sound; Style (Individual)

List: N
Biog: N
Source: NHQ "Three questions on music: Extracts from a book of interviews in the making." 93 (Spr. 1984): 197-202
Lang: ENG

45 Babbitt, Milton, 1916-
Intvr: Grimes, Ev
Topic: Audiences; Electronic music; Philosophy & aesthetics; Teaching
List: N
Biog: N
Source: MEJ "Conversations with American composers." 72 (May 1986): 52-53, 58-65
Lang: ENG

46 Babbitt, Milton, 1916-
Intvr: Blaustein, Susan; Brody, Martin
Topic: Composers–20th-century–Europe; Teaching
List: N
Biog: N
Source: CONTRECHAMPS "Création d'une culture musicale: Milton Babbitt se souvient." 6 (Apr. 1986): 35-49
Lang: FRE
Notes: Translated from English into French by Jacques Demierre.

47 Babbitt, Milton, 1916-
Intvr: Karpman, Laura
Topic: Mathematics; Music & science; Teaching; 12-tone system
List: N
Biog: N

Source: PNM "An interview with Milton Babbitt." 24 (Spr.-Sum. 1986): 81-87

Lang: ENG

48 Bäck, Sven-Erik, 1919-
Intvr: Hellquist, Per-Anders
Topic: Form
Works: Concerto, violin
List: N
Biog: N
Source: NUTIDA "Dialog kring en fiolkonsert." 2/5 (1958-59): 15-16
Lang: SWE

49 Bäck, Sven-Erik, 1919-
Topic: Composers–20th-century; Electronic music; Music & religion; Serial music
List: N
Biog: N
Source: NUTIDA "Östen Sjöstrand/Sven-Erik Bäck/Bengt-Emil Johnson." 10/3-4 (1966-67): 2-15
Lang: SWE
Notes: Conversation with Östen Sjöstrand.

50 Bäck, Sven-Erik, 1919-
Intvr: Rying, Matts
Topic: Culture; Style (Individual); Sweden
List: N
Biog: N
Source: NUTIDA "Konst är kommunikation [Art is communication]." 15/4 (1971-72): 29-34
Lang: SWE

51 Bainbridge, Simon, 1952-
Intvr: Griffiths, Paul
Topic: Creative process; Revisions of music
List: Y
Biog: Y
Source: GRIFFITHS N, pp. 39-45
Lang: ENG

52 Balingit, Jose, 1926-
Intvr: Samson, Helen F.
Topic: Careers in music; Jazz & popular music
List: Y
Biog: N
Source: SAMSON C, pp. 18-26
Lang: ENG

53 Barber, Samuel, 1910-1981.
Intvr: Gruen, John
Topic: Composers–Relations with performers
Works: Antony and Cleopatra
List: N
Biog: N
Source: NYT "And where has Samuel Barber been ...?" 3 Oct. 1971, sec. 2, pp. 15, 21, 30
Lang: ENG

54 Barber, Samuel, 1910-1981.
Intvr: Henahan, Donal
Topic: Sound recordings
List: N
Biog: N
Source: NYT "I've been composing all my life, off and on." 28 Jan. 1979, sec. 2, pp. 19, 24
Lang: ENG

55 Barlow, Clarence, 1945-
Date: 8/11/84, Munich, Germany
Intvr: Kaske, Stephan
Topic: Composition–Technique; Computer music
Works: Çoğluotobüsisletmesi; January at the Nile
List: N
Biog: Y
Source: CMJ "A conversation with Clar-ence Barlow." 9/1 (Spr. 1985): 19-28
Lang: ENG

56 Barrio Moreno, Adelino
Intvr: Pulido, Esperanza
Topic: Educational materials–Harmonics
Works: Tríptico
List: N
Biog: Y
Source: HETEROFONIA "Entrevista de Adelino Barrio con Esperanza Pulido." 67 (Sept.-Dec. 1979): 15-17
Lang: SPA
Notes: The interview was based on questions sent by Esperanza Pulido to Adelino Barrio.

57 Bassett, Leslie Raymond, 1923-
Topic: Audiences–20th-century music; Style (Individual)
List: N
Biog: N
Source: ASTERISK "An interview with Leslie Bassett." 2/2 (May 1976): 11-15
Lang: ENG

58 Bassett, Leslie Raymond, 1923-
Intvr: Blackburn, Robert T.; Risenhoover, Morris
Topic: Colleges & universities; Composers–Economic conditions; Teaching
List: N
Biog: Y
Source: RISEN A, pp. 31-36
Lang: ENG

59 Bassett, Leslie Raymond, 1923-
Date: 9/84, Ann Arbor, Mich.
Intvr: Rachleff, Larry
Topic: Wind band music
List: Y
Biog: Y
Source: CBDNA "An interview with Leslie Bassett." 2/1 (Wint. 1985): 1-4
Lang: ENG

60 Bauckholt, Carola, 1959-
Date: 8/9/83
Intvr: Shaked, Yuval
Topic: Incidental music
List: Y
Biog: N
Source: NEULAND "7 Fragen aus einem Interview von Yuval Shaked mit Carola Bauckholt am 9. August 1983." 4 (1983-84): 194-96
Lang: GER

61 Bauckholt, Carola, 1959-
Intvr: Leukert, Bernd; Lüdenbach, Clair
Topic: Women composers
List: Y
Biog: Y

Source: NZ "Frau und Musik: Qual-
itäts-fragen und Ängste Weg-
schieben .... Gespräch mit der
Kölner Komponistin Carola
Bauckholt." 145/9 (Sept. 1984):
12-15

Lang: GER

62 Baur, Jürg, 1918-
Intvr: Lang, Klaus
Topic: Composition–Technique; Quota-
tions, Musical
List: Y
Biog: Y
Source: NZ "Gespräch mit Jürg Baur."
144/10 (Oct. 1983): 18-20
Lang: GER

Bayle, François, 1932-
See no. 5.

63 Beckwith, John, 1927-
Topic: Canada; Composition–Influences
Works: A Chaucer suite; Circle with tan-
gents; Great Lakes suites; Jonah;
Sharon fragments; Three stud-
ies for string trio
List: Y
Biog: Y
Source: MUSCAN "John Beckwith, a
portrait." 6 (Nov. 1967): [8-9]
Lang: ENG, FRE

64 Beecroft, Norma, 1934-
Topic: Canada; Composition–Influences
List: Y
Biog: Y
Source: MUSCAN "Norma Beecroft, a
portrait." 19 (May 1969): [10-11]
Lang: ENG, FRE

65 Benhamou, Maurice Piere, 1936-
Works: Kaddish
List: N
Biog: N
Source: M JEU "Dix jeunes composi-
teurs." 1 (Nov. 1970): 82-83
Lang: FRE

66 Benjamin, Arthur, 1893-1960.
Intvr: Schafer, Raymond Murray
Topic: Form; Opera; Text setting
List: N
Biog: Y
Source: SCHAFER B, pp. 47-52
Lang: ENG

67 Benjamin, George, 1960-
Intvr: Griffiths, Paul
Topic: Creative process; Quotations,
Musical; Sound
Works: Ringed by the flat horizon
List: Y
Biog: Y
Source: GRIFFITHS N, pp. 22-30
Lang: ENG

68 Bennett, Richard Rodney, 1936-
Intvr: Tracey, Edmund
Topic: Composers–Relations with audi-
ences; Composers–Relations
with librettists; Creative process;
Opera; Performance; Style (Indi-
vidual)
Works: The mines of sulphur; A penny
for a song
List: N
Biog: N
Source: SWOM "Richard Rodney Ben-
nett talks to Edmund Tracey."
[1967]: [3-5]
Lang: ENG

69 Benson, Warren, 1924-
Date: 9/83-10/83
Intvr: Hunsburger, Donald Ross
Topic: Band music–Analysis
Works: The leaves are falling
List: Y
Biog: Y
Source: CBDNA "A discussion with Warren Benson: The leaves are falling." 1/1 (Spr. 1984): 7-17
Lang: ENG

70 Bentzon, Niels Viggo, 1919-
Intvr: Dirckinck-Holmfeld, Gregers
Topic: Existentialism; Philosophy & aesthetics
List: N
Biog: N
Source: NUTIDA "Kald mig bare eksistentialist [Just call me an existentialist]." 6/5 (1962-63): 49-50
Lang: DAN, SWE
Notes: Questions written in Swedish.

71 Berger, Arthur, 1912-
Date: Fall/78
Intvr: Coppock, Jane
Topic: Boulanger, Nadia, 1887-1979; Colleges & universities; Concerts & recitals; *Perspectives of New Music*; Teaching
List: N
Biog: N
Source: PNM "Conversation with Arthur Berger." 17 (Fall-Wint. 1978): 40-67
Lang: ENG

72 Berger, Arthur, 1912-
Topic: *Perspectives of New Music*

List: N
Biog: N
Source: PNM "Arthur Berger and Benjamin Boretz: A conversation about *Perspectives*." 25 (1987): 592-607
Lang: ENG
Notes: Conversation with Benjamin Boretz.

73 Berio, Luciano, 1925-
Date: 10/29/68, France
Intvr: Philippot, Michel
Topic: Boulez, Pierre, 1925-; Philosophy & aesthetics; Style (Individual); Teaching
Works: Omaggio à Joyce
List: N
Biog: N
Source: RM "Entretien: Luciano Berio–Michel Philippot." 265-66 (1968): 86-93
Lang: FRE
Notes: Originally broadcast 29 Oct. 1968 on O.R.T.F.

74 Berio, Luciano, 1925-
Date: 1/69, Milan, Italy
Intvr: Pinzauti, Leonardo
Topic: Electronic music; Italy; Opera
Works: Folk songs
List: N
Biog: N
Source: PINZAUTI M, pp. 95-106
Lang: ITA
Notes: Previously published in *Nuova Rivista Musicale Italiana* 3 (Mar.-Apr. 1969): 265-74; also German translation in *Melos* 37 (May 1970): 177-81.

75 Berio, Luciano, 1925
Date: 7/72, Caserta, Italy
Intvr: Bornoff, Jack
Topic: Communications industries
List: N
Biog: N
Source: CULTURES "Music, musicians, and communication–five interviews: 1. Luciano Berio, with the participation of Vittoria Ottolenghi, Baia Domizia." 1/1 (1973): 113-22
Lang: ENG

76 Berio, Luciano, 1925-
Intvr: Emmerson, Simon
Topic: Creative process
Works: A-Ronne; O King
List: N
Biog: N
Source: MM "Luciano Berio talks to Simon Emmerson." 282 (Feb. 1976): 26-28
Lang: ENG

77 Berio, Luciano, 1925-
Date: 4/20/76, Cleveland, Ohio
Intvr: Felder, David
Topic: Electronic music; Style (Individual)
List: N
Biog: N
Source: COMP(CA) "An interview with Luciano Berio." 7 (1975-76): 9-15
Lang: ENG

78 Berio, Luciano, 1925-
Date: 1980-81
Intvr: Dalmonte, Rossana
Topic: Careers in music; Composition–Technique; Creative process; Education; Electronic music; Institut de Recherche et de Coordination Acoustique-Musique (IRCAM); Italy; Philosophy & aesthetics; Serial music
Works: Sequenzas; Sinfonia
List: Y
Biog: Y
Source: BERIO T, pp. 15-137
Lang: ENG
Notes: Originally published as Luciano Berio, *Intervista sulla Musica, a cura di Rossana Dalmonte* (Roma: Bari Laterza, 1981).

79 Berio, Luciano, 1925-
Date: 1980-81
Intvr: Varga, Bálint András
Topic: Incidental music; Vocal music
List: Y
Biog: Y
Source: BERIO T, pp. 139-67
Lang: ENG
Notes: Originally published as Luciano Berio, *Bészelgetések Luciano Berióval* (Budapest: Editio Musica, 1981).

80 Berio, Luciano, 1925-
Intvr: Schrader, Barry
Topic: Creative process; Electronic music; Music & literature
Works: Omaggio à Joyce
List: N
Biog: N
Source: SCHRADER I "16. Interview with Luciano Berio: 'Thema: Omaggio à Joyce.'" pp. 179-83
Lang: ENG

81 Berio, Luciano, 1925-
Date: 1983
Intvr: Albèra, Philippe; Demierre, Jacques
Topic: Composition–Technique; Text setting
Works: Coro
List: N
Biog: N
Source: CONTRECHAMPS "Entretien avec Luciano Berio." 1 (Sept. 1983): 60-66
Lang: FRE

82 Berkeley, Lennox, 1903-1989.
Intvr: Schafer, Raymond Murray
Topic: Composers–Relations with audiences; Creative process; Criticism; Music & literature; Style (Individual)
List: N
Biog: Y
Source: SCHAFER B, pp. 83-91
Lang: ENG

83 Berkeley, Lennox, 1903-1989.
Date: 1973, England
Intvr: Dickinson, Peter
Topic: Composers, French–Influences; Style (Individual); 20th-century music
List: N
Biog: N
Source: DICKINSON T, pp. 23-29
Lang: ENG

84 Bernier, René, 1905-
Intvr: Peeters, André
Topic: Roussel, Albert, 1869-1937; Schools of music
List: N
Biog: Y
Source: CAR "Entretien avec René Bernier, rousselien de la première heure." 1 (1978): 19-26
Lang: FRE

85 Bernstein, Elmer, 1922-
Intvr: Ulrich, Allan
Topic: Motion picture music; Philosophy & aesthetics
Works: The magnificent seven; Toccata for toy trains
List: Y
Biog: N
Source: ULRICH A, pp. 8-11
Lang: ENG

86 Bernstein, Leonard, 1918-1990.
Intvr: Wagner, Walter
Topic: Composers as conductors; Concerts & recitals; Orchestral music; Teaching
List: N
Biog: N
Source: NYT "Bernstein–a teacher, too." 11 June 1972, sec. 2, pp. 15, 18
Lang: ENG
Notes: Also published in *ASCAP Today* 6 (July 1972): 6-11.

87 Bernstein, Leonard, 1918-1990.
Intvr: Corry, John
Topic: Performance practice
Works: Mass
List: N
Biog: N
Source: NYT "Bernstein alters Mass for opening here tonight." 28 June 1972, sec. 1, p. 47
Lang: ENG

88 Bernstein, Leonard, 1918-1990.
Intvr: Reichen, Manfred
Topic: Composers as conductors; Conductors–Relations with audiences
List: N
Biog: N
Source: NZ "Ich muß alles teilen: Ein Gespräch mit Leonard Bernstein." 133/11 (1972): 634-36
Lang: GER

89 Bernstein, Leonard, 1918-1990.
Intvr: Willis, Thomas
Topic: Conducting–Symphony orchestras
List: N
Biog: N
Source: ACCENT "Leonard Bernstein: America's music man." 2 (Mar.-Apr. 1977): 10-13
Lang: ENG

90 Bernstein, Leonard, 1918-1990.
Date: 9/77, Vienna, Austria
Intvr: Schmidt, Felix
Topic: Conducting; Karajan, Herbert von, 1908-1989; Style (Individual); United States
List: N
Biog: N
Source: SCHMIDT M, pp. 26-33
Lang: GER

91 Bernstein, Leonard, 1918-1990.
Intvr: Ardoin, John
Topic: Composers as conductors; Israel Philharmonic Orchestra
List: N
Biog: N

Source: NYT "Israel gives Bernstein a 30-year retrospective." 17 Apr. 1977, sec. 2, pp. 1, 15
Lang: ENG

92 Bernstein, Leonard, 1918-1990.
Date: 1/84, N.Y.
Intvr: Wegner, Josef U.
Topic: Music & literature; Music & religion
List: N
Biog: Y
Source: NZ "Das aktuelle Porträt: Bald wieder Opernkomponist? Sinfonie, Musical, Oper–Leonard Bernstein im Gespräch." 147/10 (Oct. 1986): 29-31
Lang: GER

93 Bernstein, Leonard, 1918-1990.
Intvr: Page, Tim
Topic: Concerts & recitals
List: N
Biog: N
Source: NYT "At 67, Bernstein comes home to Carnegie Hall." 20 Sept. 1985, sec. 3, p. 3
Lang: ENG

94 Betts, Lorne M., 1918-
Topic: Canada
List: Y
Biog: Y
Source: MUSCAN "Lorne M. Betts, a portrait" 28 (Apr. 1970): [8-9]
Lang: ENG, FRE

95 Bialas, Günter, 1907-
Date: 1972
Intvr: Haffner, Gerhard

Topic: Education; Gebrauchsmusik; Teaching
List: Y
Biog: N
Source: SPEER M "Ein Interview mit Günter Bialas anlässlich seines 65. Geburtstages", pp. 81-83
Lang: GER

96 Bialas, Günter, 1907-

Date: Good Fri/84 Salzburg, Austria
Intvr: Keller, Wilhelm
Topic: Composition–Technique; Libretto; Opera
List: N
Biog: N
Source: SUDER G, pp. 14-18, 28-38
Lang: GER

97 Bialas, Günter, 1907-

Date: 5/84
Intvr: Weis, Günther
Topic: Choral music; Composition–Technique; Style (Individual)
List: Y
Biog: N
Source: SUDER G, pp. 47-58
Lang: GER

98 Biel, Michael von, 1937-

Date: Spr/77 Cologne, Germany
Intvr: Zimmermann, Walter
Topic: Creativity; Electronic music; Form; Guitar music; Keyboard instrument music; Philosophy & aesthetics; Popular music; Spatiality in composition; Violoncello music
List: Y
Biog: Y

Source: FP "Gespräch mit Michael von Biel." 13 (June 1977): 2-11
Lang: GER
Notes: Also published in Walter Zimmermann, *Insel Musik* (Köln: Beginner Press, 1981), pp. 123-33.

99 Biermann, Wolf, 1936-

Date: 1974, Berlin, Germany
Intvr: Antes, Klaus
Topic: Composers–Social conditions; Folk music; Music & politics; Songs; Songwriting; Text setting
List: Y
Biog: N
Source: ARNOLD W, pp. 15-29
Lang: GER
Notes: Compiled by the interviewer after the conversation.

100 Biermann, Wolf, 1936-

Intvr: Reininghaus, Frieder
Topic: Classicism; Text setting
List: N
Biog: N
Source: NZ "Rameaus Grossneffe: Ein Gespräch mit Wolf Biermann über Musik." 148/3 (Mar. 1987): 15-18
Lang: GER

101 Birnstein, Renate, 1946-

Date: 6/83
Intvr: Schulze, Brigitte
Topic: Creative process; Minimal music; Philosophy & aesthetics; Women composers
Works: In terra; IDEM
List: Y

15

Biog: Y
Source: NEULAND "Renate Birnstein: Ein Portrait; Gespräch mit Renate Birnstein." 4 (1983-84): 159-70
Lang: GER

102 Birtwistle, Harrison, 1934-
Intvr: Griffiths, Paul
Topic: Composers as performers; Composition–Technique; Creative process
Works: Punch and Judy; Verses for ensembles
List: Y
Biog: Y
Source: GRIFFITHS N, pp. 186-94
Lang: ENG

103 Blacher, Boris, 1903-1975.
Intvr: Burde, Wolfgang
Topic: Composition–Technique
Works: Yvonne, Prinzessin von Burgund
List: N
Biog: N
Source: NZ "Interview mit Boris Blacher." 134/1 (1973): 20-23
Lang: GER

104 Blacher, Boris, 1903-1975.
Intvr: Lewinski, Wolf-Eberhard von
List: N
Biog: N
Source: MUSICA "Die Zeit–das unbarmherzig Mass: Ein Gespräch, das Wolf-Eberhard v. Lewinski führte." 29 (May-June 1975): 216-18
Lang: GER

105 Bliss, Arthur, 1891-1975.
Intvr: Milner, Donald
Topic: Philosophy & aesthetics
List: N
Biog: N
Source: DICKINSON T, pp. 6-7
Lang: ENG
Notes: Originally broadcast 4 May 1970 on BBC.

106 Bodin, Lars-Gunnar, 1935-
Topic: Cage, John, 1912-1992; Electronic music; I-Ching
List: N
Biog: N
Source: OB "Semikolon; John Cage; Musical Pleasure" 74 (1965): 142-49
Lang: SWE
Notes: Conversation with Bengt Emil Johnson. Not printed in conversational style.

107 Bodin, Lars-Gunnar, 1935-
Intvr: Rying, Matts
Topic: Electronic music
Works: Arioso; My world is your world; Winters events
List: N
Biog: N
Source: NUTIDA "Vår musikkritik är meningslös." 16/2 (1972-73): 24-28
Lang: SWE

108 Boehmer, Konrad, 1941-
Intvr: Wijtman, Barend
Topic: The Netherlands Association of Composers; Societies, associations, etc.

List: N
Biog: Y
Source: KN "Interview with Konrad Boehmar." 5 (June 1977): 41-43
Lang: ENG

109 Boerman, Jan, 1923-
Intvr: Beer, Roland de
Topic: Composition–Technique; Electronic music
Works: Alchemie; De zee; Ontketening; Weerstand
List: N
Biog: Y
Source: KN "The voltage-controlled emotions of Jan Boerman." 18 (Dec. 1983): 12-19
Lang: ENG

110 Börtz, Daniel, 1943-
Intvr: Rying, Matts
Topic: Creativity; Critics; Sweden
List: N
Biog: N
Source: NUTIDA "Vi skrattar åt kritikernas artiklar." 17/2 (1973-74): 37-41
Lang: SWE

111 Bolcom, William, 1938-
Date: 6/24/77, Ann Arbor, Mich.
Intvr: Harvith, John; Harvith, Susan Edwards
Topic: Live performances; Sound recording & reproduction
List: N
Biog: Y
Source: HARVITH E, pp. 291-309
Lang: ENG
Notes: Joan Morris also participated in the interview.

112 Borden, David, 1938-
Topic: Composition–Technique; Electronic music; Electronic music synthesizers; Polyphony; Tonality
List: N
Biog: N
Source: TW "The new polyphony: Philip Glass and David Borden." 1/16 (1983)
Lang: ENG

Boretz, Benjamin A., 1934-
See no. 72.

113 Boucourechliev, André, 1925-
Date: 1/74
Intvr: Mâche, François-Bernard
Topic: 20th-century music
Works: Archipels
List: N
Biog: Y
Source: RM "Les mal entendus. Compositeurs des années 70." 314-15 (1978): 37-45
Lang: FRE

114 Boucourechliev, André, 1925-
Intvr: Artaud, Alain
Topic: Notation; Orchestras, Text setting
Works: Archipels
List: N
Biog: N
Source: SCHERZO "André Boucourechliev." 45 (June-July 1975): 8-10
Lang: FRE

115 Boulez, Pierre, 1925-
Intvr: Goléa, Antoine

Topic: Composition–Technique; Philosophy aesthetics; Style (Individual)
List: N
Biog: N
Source: GOLEA B
Lang: FRE

116 Boulez, Pierre, 1925-
Topic: Audiences–20th-century music
List: N
Biog: N
Source: MELOS "Zwei Komponisten geben Auskunft." 28/3 (March 1961): 65-68
Lang: GER
Notes: Conversation with Heinrich Sutermeister.

117 Boulez, Pierre, 1925-
Intvr: Hall, Barrie
Topic: Composers as conductors; Concerts & recitals–20th-century music
List: N
Biog: N
Source: MM "Boulez ... talks to Barrie Hall." 14/1 (Sept. 1965): 18, 25
Lang: ENG

118 Boulez, Pierre, 1925-
Intvr: Bužga, Jaroslav
Topic: Composers as conductors; Ethnic music; 20th-century music
List: N
Biog: N
Source: MELOS "Interview mit Pierre Boulez in Prag." 34/5 (May 1967): 162-64
Lang: GER

119 Boulez, Pierre, 1925-
Intvr: Hohmeyer, Jürgen; Schmidt, Felix
Topic: Opera–20th-century; Opera audiences; Opera composers
List: N
Biog: N
Source: MELOS "Pierre Boulez: Sprengt die Opernhäuser in die Luft!" 34/12 (Dec. 1967): 429-37
Lang: GER
Notes: First published in *Spiegel*, 25 Sept. 1967.

120 Boulez, Pierre, 1925-
Intvr: Henahan, Donal
Topic: Audiences
List: N
Biog: N
Source: NYT "Tables are turned on avant-garde composer." 5 Dec. 1967, sec. 1, p. 56
Lang: ENG

121 Boulez, Pierre, 1925-
Date: 2/69
Intvr: Cope, David Howell; Wilson, Galen
Topic: Composers–Relations with audiences; Electronic music; Music & science; Performance practice; Sound recordings
List: N
Biog: N
Source: COMP(CA) "An interview with Pierre Boulez." 1/2 (Fall 1969): 78-85
Lang: ENG

122 Boulez, Pierre, 1925-
Intvr: Peyser, Joan
Topic: Electronic music; Philosophy &
       aesthetics
List: N
Biog: N
Source: NYT "A fighter from way back."
       9 Mar. 1969, sec. 2, pp. 19, 32
Lang: ENG

123 Boulez, Pierre, 1925-
Date: 6/12/69, Vienna, Austria
Topic: Composers as conductors
List: N
Biog: N
Source: NYT "Pierre Boulez starts plans
       for 1971." 13 June 1969, sec. 1,
       p. 39
Lang: ENG

124 Boulez, Pierre, 1925-
Date: 3/20/70, Montréal, Canada
Intvr: Kendergi, Maryvonne
Topic: Composers as conductors; Con-
       cert halls–Design & construction;
       Mathematics; Sociology; 20th-
       century music–Analysis
List: N
Biog: N
Source: RMC "Se interroga a Pierre
       Boulez." 118 (Apr.-July 1972):
       22-35
Lang: SPA
Notes: Previously published in French
       in *The Canada Music Book* 2
       (Spr.-Sum. 1971): 31-48.

125 Boulez, Pierre, 1925-
Intvr: Cotta, Michèle; Nussac, Sylvie de

Topic: France; Opera; Theater–Design
       & construction
List: N
Biog: N
Source: EXPRESS "L'Express va plus
       loin avec Pierre Boulez." 979
       (13-19 Apr. 1970): 66-75
Lang: FRE

126 Boulez, Pierre, 1925-
Date: 11/70, Germany
Intvr: Tomek, Otto
Topic: Audiences; Symphony orchestras
List: N
Biog: N
Source: NZ "Lösungen für unsere Zeit
       finden! Ein Gespräch zwischen
       Pierre Boulez und Otto Tomek."
       132/2 (1971): 62-68
Lang: GER
Notes: Originally broadcast Nov. 1970
       on West Germany Radio Station.

127 Boulez, Pierre, 1925-
Topic: Improvisation; Interpretation
List: N
Biog: N
Source: VH "Pierre Boulez." 4 (Wint.
       1970-71). 6-15
Lang: FRE

128 Boulez, Pierre, 1925-
Date: London, England
Intvr: Heyworth, Peter
Topic: Audiences; Composers as con-
       ductors; Concerts & recitals;
       Stockhausen, Karlheinz, 1928-
List: N
Biog: N

Source: NYT "What is Boulez up to with the Philharmonic?" 14 Nov. 1971, sec. 2, pp. 15, 26
Lang: ENG

129 Boulez, Pierre, 1925-
Date: 8/72, Baden-Baden, Germany
Intvr: Bornoff, Jack
Topic: Community relations; Concert halls; Electronic music; Performance practice–20th-century music
List: N
Biog: N
Source: CULTURES "Music, musicians, and communication–five interviews: 2. Pierre Boulez." 1/1 (1973): 123-35
Lang: ENG

130 Boulez, Pierre, 1925-
Date: 5/16/73, Firenze, Italy
Intvr: Pinzauti, Leonardo
Topic: Composers–Political conditions; Composers, Italian–20th-century; Interpretation; Italy
List: N
Biog: N
Source: PINZAUTI M, pp. 213-19
Lang: ITA
Notes: Previously published in *Nuova Rivista Musicale Italiana* 7 (Apr.-June 1973): 226-30

131 Boulez, Pierre, 1925-
Date: 8/73
Intvr: Jack, Adrian
Topic: Composers as conductors; Electronic music; Performance–20th-century music

List: N
Biog: N
Source: MM "Boulez answers some questions: Adrian Jack poses them." 255 (Nov. 1973): 32-36
Lang: ENG

132 Boulez, Pierre, 1925-
Intvr: Peskó, Zoltán
Topic: Incidental music; Opera
List: N
Biog: N
Source: MELOS "Gespräch mit Pierre Boulez." 40/5 (Sept.-Oct. 1973): 274-79
Lang: GER

133 Boulez, Pierre, 1925-
Date: 11/8/73, N.Y.
Intvr: Henahan, Donal
Topic: Careers in music
List: N
Biog: N
Source: NYT "Boulez ending exile with post in Paris." 9 Nov. 1973, sec. 1, p. 28
Lang: ENG

134 Boulez, Pierre, 1925-
Date: 8/72, London, England; 8/74, Baden-Baden, Germany
Intvr: Deliège, Célestin
Topic: Berg, Alban, 1885-1935; Char, René, 1907-1988; Composers as conductors; Composition–Technique; Education; Electronic music; Form; Harmony; Poetry; Schoenberg, Arnold, 1874-1951; Serialism

Works: Domaines; e.e.cummings ist der Dichter; Eclat; ... explosante/ fixe ... ; Figures, doubles, prismes; Livre pour quatuor; Le marteau sans maître; Pli selon pli; Poésie pour pouvoir; Polyphonie X; Le soleil des eaux; Sonatas, piano; Structures

List: N

Biog: N

Source: BOULEZ C

Lang: ENG

Notes: This is an English translation of *Par Volonté et Par Hasard: Entretiens avec Célestin Deliège* (Paris: Les Editions du Seuil, 1975); German translation in *Wille und Zufall* (1977), pp. 9-139; Italian translation in *Per volontà e per caso, Conversazioni con Célestin Deliège* (Torino: Einaudi, 1977). also excerpted in *Musica e Politica* (Venice: La Biennale di Venezia, 1977), pp. 442-43.

135 Boulez, Pierre, 1925-

Intvr: Jameux, Dominique

Topic: Electro-acoustics; Revisions of music; Serialism

Works: Polyphonie X; Poésie pour pouvoir; Structures

List: N

Biog: N

Source: M JEU "Pierre Boulez: Sur 'Polyphonie X' et 'Poésie pour pouvoir.'" 16 (Nov. 1974): 33-35

Lang: FRE

Notes: Also published in *Points de repère* (Paris: Christian Bourgois, 1981; rev. ed. 1985), pp. 201-5.

136 Boulez, Pierre, 1925-

Intvr: Jacobson, Robert

Topic: Audiences; Composition–Influences; Serial music; Style (Individual)

List: N

Biog: N

Source: JACOB R "Pierre Boulez." pp. 21-33

Lang: ENG

137 Boulez, Pierre, 1925-

Date: 2/76, London, England

Intvr: Liebert, Georges

Topic: Composers as conductors; Performance practice; Wagner, Richard, 1813-1883

List: N

Biog: N

Source: ASO "Entretien avec Pierre Boulez." 6-7 (Nov.-Dec. 1976): 144-58

Lang: FRE

Notes: Excerpts from the interview.

138 Boulez, Pierre, 1925-

Date: 12/30/76, Baden-Baden, Germany

Intvr: Mayer, Hans

Topic: Composers–Relations with performers; Conducting; Interpretation; Wagner, Richard. *Der Ring des Nibelungen*

List: N

Biog: N

Source: BOULEZ W "Der Interpret vor der Objektivität der Partitur." pp. 141-71

Lang: GER

Notes: Translated from French into German by Hans Mayer.

139 Boulez, Pierre, 1925-
Intvr: Oesch, Hans
Topic: Composers as conductors; Form
List: N
Biog: N
Source: MELOS/NZ "Interview mit Pierre Boulez." 2/4 (1976): 293-96
Lang: GER

140 Boulez, Pierre, 1925-
Intvr: Peskó, Zoltán
Topic: Experimental music theater; Music theater
List: N
Biog: N
Source: TEMPO "Musical aspects in today's musical theatre: A conversation between Pierre Boulez and Zoltán Peskó." 127 (Dec. 1978): 2-9
Lang: ENG

141 Boulez, Pierre, 1925-
Date: 6/3/84, Ojai, Calif.
Intvr: Gable, David
Topic: Europe; Opera; United States
Works: Répons; Soleil des eaux; Sonata, piano, no. 2; Visage nuptial
List: N
Biog: N
Source: JM "Ramifying connections: An interview with Pierre Boulez." 4 (1985-86): 105-13
Lang: ENG

142 Boulez, Pierre, 1925-
Intvr: Schmidt, Felix
Topic: Aleatory music; Composers–Influences; Composers as conductors; Composition–Technique; France; Philosophy & aesthetics; Style (Individual)
List: N
Biog: N
Source: SCHMIDT M, pp. 169-88
Lang: GER

143 Boulez, Pierre, 1925-
Date: 3/86, Boston, Mass.
Intvr: Schaefer, John
Topic: Electronic music; Institut de Recherche et de Coordination Acoustique-Musique (IRCAM)
List: N
Biog: N
Source: EAR "Meet The Composer: Pierre Boulez." 11/1 (Aug.-Sept. 1986): 22-23
Lang: ENG

144 Branca, Glenn, 1948-
Topic: Composers–Influences; Composition–Technique; Electronic music; Electronic musical instruments; Popular music; Tonality
Works: Symphony, no. 3 ("Gloria")
List: N
Biog: N
Source: TW "Post-minimalism: Glenn Branca and Paul Dresher." 2/13 (1985)
Lang: ENG

145 Brant, Henry, 1913-
Date: Wint/64, Bennington, Vt.
Topic: Community relations
List: N
Biog: N
Source: ACA "Composers on Main street." 12/1 (Spr. 1964): 1-6

Lang: ENG
Notes: Conversation with Lionel Nowak, edited by Theodore Strongin.

146 Brant, Henry, 1913-
Intvr: Everett, Thomas G.
Topic: Composition–Technique; Performance practice
List: N
Biog: N
Source: COMP(CA) "Interview with Henry Brant." 7 (1975-76): 29-38
Lang: ENG

147 Brant, Henry, 1913-
Intvr: Somer, Hilde
Topic: Audiences
List: N
Biog: N
Source: EAR "Conversation with Henry Brant." 3/1 (Feb. 1977): [6]
Lang: ENG

148 Brant, Henry, 1913-
Date: 11/20/80, New York City N.Y.
Intvr: Caras, Tracy; Gagne, Cole
Topic: Composers–Relations with performers; Philosophy & aesthetics
Works: Immortal combat; Rural antiphonies; Symphony for percussion
List: Y
Biog: Y
Source: GAGNE S, pp. 53-68
Lang: ENG

149 Brecht, George, 1925-
Date: 1965
Intvr: Alocco, Marcel; Vautier, Ben

Topic: Composers–Influences; Creativity; Philosophy & aesthetics
List: Y
Biog: N
Source: SCHMIDT J, pp. 149-63
Lang: FRE
Notes: Previously published in *Identités* (Summer-Autumn, 1965): 6-7.

150 Brecht, George, 1925-
Date: 4/15/67, Milan, Italy
Intvr: Martin, Henry
Topic: Creative process; Culture–Europe; Duchamp, Marcel, 1887-1968; Experimental music; Philosophy & aesthetics
List: Y
Biog: N
Source: SCHMIDT J, pp. 131-47
Lang: GER
Notes: Translated into German by Max Wechsler. Previously published in *Art International* (Lugano, Nov. 1967): 20-24.

151 Brecht, George, 1925-
Date: 1972
Intvr: Page, Robin
Topic: Experimental music; Fluxus; Maciunas, George, 1931-1978; *V Tre Flux-Newspaper*; Yam Festival
List: Y
Biog: N
Source: SCHMIDT J, pp. 119-29
Lang: GER
Notes: Translated into German by Max Wechsler. Previously published in *Art and Artists* (Oct. 1972): 29-32.

152 Brecht, George, 1925-
Date: 1973
Intvr: Lebeer, Irmeline
Topic: Cage, John–Influences; Creative process; Experimental music; Fluxus; Performance practice–20th-century music; Philosophy & aesthetics
List: Y
Biog: N
Source: SCHMIDT J, pp. 101-17
Lang: FRE
Notes: Previously published in *L'art Vivant* 39 (May 1973): 16-19.

153 Brecht, George, 1925-
Date: 1974
Intvr: Nabakowski, Gislind
Topic: Audiences–20th-century music; Experimental music; Fluxus; Happenings; Yam Festival
List: Y
Biog: N
Source: SCHMIDT J, pp. 85-99
Lang: GER

154 Brecht, George, 1925-
Date: 7/30/76-7/31/76, 8/2/76, Cologne, Germany
Intvr: Nyman, Michael
Topic: Cage, John–Influences; Creativity; Experimental music; Fluxus; Incidental music; Notation; Performance; Philosophy & aesthetics
List: N
Biog: N
Source: SI "George Brecht." 984 (Nov.-Dec. 1976): 256-66
Lang: ENG

Notes: Also published in Marianne Maiescher-Schmidt, ed., *Jenseits von Ereignissen* (Bern: Kunsthalle, 1978), pp. 35-83.

155 Brecht, George, 1925-
Date: 6/24/78-6/25/78
Intvr: Martin, Henry
Topic: Artists–20th-century; Arts–20th-century; Arts & science; Criticism; Culture; Duchamp, Marcel, 1887-1968; Philosophy & aesthetics
List: Y
Biog: N
Source: SCHMIDT J "Ein Gespräch mit George Brecht", pp. 5-33
Lang: GER

156 Bredemeyer, Reiner, 1929-
Date: 2/77; 4/77
Intvr: Stürzbecher, Ursula
Topic: Composition–Technique; Style (Individual); Theater
Works: Kontakte suchen
List: Y
Biog: Y
Source: STURZ K, pp. 268-92
Lang: GER

157 Bresgen, Cesar, 1913-1988.
Intvr: Lück, Rudolf
Topic: Children, Music for; Creative process; Folk music; Gebrauchsmusik; Keyboard instrument music; Opera; Sociology; Teaching; Vocal music
Works: Impressionen; Der Mann im Mond; Totentanz; Visiones amantis

List: Y
Biog: Y
Source: LUCK C
Lang: GER
Notes: Excerpts are published in
Rudolf Lück, "Gespräch mit
Cesar Bresgen," *Musik und
Bildung* 5/12 (1973): 682-85.

158 Bresgen, Cesar, 1913-1988.
Intvr: Lück, Rudolf
Topic: Children, Music for; Style (Individual)
List: N
Biog: N
Source: NZ "NZ-Serie: Komponieren
heute. Cesar Bresgen: Ein Werk–
Stadtgespräch anlässlich seines
siebzigsten Geburtstags." 144/12
(Dec. 1983): 14-17
Lang: GER

159 Brief, Todd, 1953-
Intvr: Goldstein, Perry
Topic: Style (Individual)
Works: Cantares; Slow lament
List: N
Biog: N
Source: EAR "Todd Brief: Emotion within form." 10/2 (Nov.-Dec. 1985): 6
Lang: ENG

160 Britten, Benjamin, 1913-1976.
Intvr: Schafer, Raymond Murray
Topic: Auden, Wystan Hugh, 1907-
1973; Creative process; Libretto;
Opera; Vocal music
Works: Peter Grimes
List: N
Biog: N
Source: SCHAFER B, pp. 113-24
Lang: ENG

161 Britten, Benjamin, 1913-1976.
Intvr: Warrack, John
Topic: Composers–Social conditions;
Opera
List: N
Biog: N
Source: MA "Benjamin Britten: Musician of the year, in conversation
with John Warrack." 84/10
(Dec. 1964): 20-21, 272-4
Lang: ENG

162 Broman, Sten, 1902-1983.
Intvr: Sjögren, Henrik
Topic: Composition–Influences; Symphony
Works: Musica cathedralis; Symphony,
no. 7
List: N
Biog: N
Source: NUTIDA "Se jag gör allting
nytt." 15/4 (1971-72): 36-39
Lang: SWE

163 Brott, Alexander, 1915-
Topic: Canada; Composers–Economic
conditions
Works: Concerto, violin; Critic's corner;
Songs of contemplation; Spheres
in orbit; V-niet (Vignettes)
List: Y
Biog: Y
Source: MUSCAN "Alexander Brott, a
portrait." 17 (Mar. 1969): 10-11
Lang: ENG, FRE

164 Brown, Earle, 1926-
Intvr: Henahan, Donal
Topic: Composers–Relations with per-
formers; Europe; United States
List: N
Biog: N
Source: NYT "Earle Brown: They love
him in Baden-Baden." 21 June
1970, sec. 2, pp. 15, 18
Lang: ENG

165 Brown, Earle, 1926-
Intvr: Metzger, Heinz-Klaus
Topic: Composers–Relations with audi-
ences; Music & politics; Philos-
ophy & aesthetics; Popular mu-
sic; Sociology; Style (Individual)
List: N
Biog: N
Source: MBR "Morton Feldman, Earle
Brown and Heinz-Klaus Metz-
ger in discussion." Side 8
Lang: ENG

166 Brown, Earle, 1926-
Date: 8/75, Lenox, Mass.
Intvr: Rosenberg, Bernard; Rosenberg,
Deena
Topic: Electronic music; Performance
practice; Philosophy & aesthet-
ics
Works: Available forms I, II; Folio;
Time spans
List: N
Biog: N
Source: ROSEN M, pp. 79-91
Lang: ENG

167 Brown, Earle, 1926-
Intvr: Bailey, Derek

Topic: Aleatory music; Improvisation
List: N
Biog: N
Source: BAILEY M, pp. 77-83
Lang: ENG

168 Brün, Herbert, 1918-
Date: 1975, Ill.
Intvr: Smith, Stuart
Topic: Composers–Social conditions;
Jazz & popular music; Wolpe,
Stefan, 1902-1972
List: N
Biog: N
Source: PNM "A portrait of Herbert
Brün." 17/2 (Sum. 1979): 61-75
Lang: ENG

169 Brün, Herbert, 1918-
Intvr: Siwe, Thomas
Topic: Composers–Relations with per-
formers; Percussion instruments;
Style (Individual)
Works: At loose ends; Plot; Stalks and
trees and drops and clouds;
Touch and go
List: N
Biog: N
Source: PN "An interview with Herbert
Brün." 22/3 (Mar. 1984): 4-15
Lang: ENG

170 Bruins, Theo, 1929-
Intvr: Calis, Hein
Topic: Sound recordings
Works: Concerto, piano
List: N
Biog: Y
Source: KN "Theo Bruins: A selection

purely on the basis of intrinsic quality." 10 (Dec. 1979): 64-65

Lang: ENG

171 Bryars, Gavin, 1943-

Intvr: Griffiths, Paul

Topic: Cage, John, 1912-1992; Composers–Relations with performers; Creativity; Satie, Erik, 1866-1925; 20th-century music

Works: The sinking of the Titanic

List: Y

Biog: Y

Source: GRIFFITHS N, pp. 148-59

Lang: ENG

172 Budd, Harold, 1936-

Topic: Improvisation; Jazz

List: N

Biog: N

Source: PNM "Forum: Improvisation." 21 (Fall 1982-Sum. 1983): 53-62

Lang: ENG

173 Buenaventura, Alfredo Santos, 1929-

Intvr: Samson, Helen F.

List: Y

Biog: N

Source: SAMSON C, pp. 27-36

Lang: ENG

174 Buenaventura, Antonino, 1904-

Intvr: Samson, Helen F.

Topic: Composers as conductors

List: Y

Biog: N

Source: SAMSON C, pp. 37-48

Lang: ENG

175 Burton, Jim

Intvr: Zimmermann, Walter

Topic: Experimental music; Kitchen; Meet The Composer; Performance practice

Works: Mail order preacher

List: N

Biog: N

Source: ZIMMER D, pp. 93-102

Lang: ENG

176 Bush, Alan Dudley, 1900-

Intvr: Schafer, Raymond Murray

Topic: Composers–Political conditions; Form; Music & politics; 12-tone system

Works: Dialectic; Symphony

List: N

Biog: N

Source: SCHAFER B, pp. 53-63

Lang: ENG

177 Bussotti, Sylvano, 1931-

Intvr: Capponi, Piero

Topic: Composers as performers

List: N

Biog: N

Source: NUTIDA "Dialog om den otidsliga konsten." 11/1 (1967-68): 56-58

Lang: SWE

Notes: Translated into Swedish by Giorgio Padoan.

178 Bussotti, Sylvano, 1931-

Date: 8/70

Intvr: Pinzauti, Leonardo

Topic: Boulez, Pierre, 1925-; Dallapiccola, Luigi, 1904-1975; Opera; Philosophy & aesthet-

ics; Scherchen, Tona, 1938-;
Style (Individual); Theater
List: N
Biog: N
Source: PINZAUTI M, pp. 161-73
Lang: ITA
Notes: Previously published in *Nuova Rivista Musicale Italiana* 4 (Sept.-Oct. 1970): 898-909; also German translation in *Melos* 38/7-8 (June-Aug. 1971): 284-91.

179 Bussotti, Sylvano, 1931-
Date: 6/22/82
Intvr: Failla, Salvatore Enrico
Topic: Audiences; Composers as theater directors; Incidental music; 20th-century music
List: N
Biog: N
Source: FAILLA M "Intervista a Sylvano Bussotti: Note a correnti alternative." pp. 73-84
Lang: ITA

180 Bussotti, Sylvano, 1931-
Intvr: Scherzer, Ernst
Topic: Composers as theater directors
List: Y
Biog: N
Source: NZ "Komponieren heute: Sylvano Bussotti. Ein Gespräch." 145/4 (Apr. 1984): 17-18
Lang: GER

181 Cacioppo, George, 1927-
Topic: Concerts & recitals–20th-century music; ONCE Group
List: N

Biog: Y
Source: ASTERISK "The ONCE Group." 2/1 (Dec. 1975): 8-15
Lang: ENG

182 Cacioppo, George, 1927-
Intvr: Brown, Anthony
Topic: Education; ONCE Group
List: N
Biog: N
Source: COMP(CA) "An interview with George Cacioppo." 8 (1976-77): 31-35
Lang: ENG

183 Cage, John, 1912-1992.
Date: 1961
Intvr: Ashley, Robert; Reynolds, Roger
Topic: Creativity; Philosophy & aesthetics; Sound; Zen Buddhism
Works: *Silence*
List: N
Biog: N
Source: SCHWARTZ C "Interview with Roger Reynolds, 1962." pp. 335-48
Lang: ENG
Notes: Originally published in *Generation Magazine*(Ann Arbor, Mich., 1962).

184 Cage, John, 1912-1992.
Intvr: Kirby, Michael; Schechner, Richard
Topic: Philosophy & aesthetics; Sound, Environmental; Teaching; Theater–Design & construction
Works: Eighteen happenings in six parts; Fontana mix; Theatre piece; Water music

List: N
Biog: N
Source: TDR "An interview with John Cage." 10/2 (Wint. 1965): 50-72
Lang: ENG

185 Cage, John, 1912-1992.
Intvr: Mimaroglu, Ilhan
Topic: Composition–Technique; Style (Individual)
Works: Cartridge music; Fontana mix; Williams mix
List: N
Biog: N
Source: DISCOTECA "John Cage: In una intervista di Ilhan Mimaroglu." Nov. 1965, pp. 29-30
Lang: ITA

186 Cage, John, 1912-1992.
Intvr: Zwerin, Michael
Topic: Jazz; Popular music
List: N
Biog: N
Source: VV "A lethal measurement." 6 Jan. 1966, pp. 13, 19
Lang: ENG

187 Cage, John, 1912-1992.
Date: Sum/66, N.Y.
Intvr: Kostelanetz, Richard; Opper, Susanna
Topic: Aleatory music; Philosophy & aesthetics; Zen Buddhism
Works: Rozart mix; Theatre piece; Variations V; Williams mix
List: Y
Biog: Y
Source: KOST J "Conversation with John Cage." pp. 6-35

Lang: ENG
Notes: Some passages were reprinted from Richard Kostelanetz, *The Theatre of Mixed Means* (RK Editions, 1968).

188 Cage, John, 1912-1992.
Date: 6/19/68, Urbana, Ill.
Intvr: Austin, Larry; Johnston, Benjamin Burwell
Topic: Computer music; Computers
Works: HPSCHD
List: N
Biog: N
Source: SOURCE "John Cage, Lejaren Hiller: HPSCHD." 2/2 (July 1968): 10-13
Lang: ENG

189 Cage, John, 1912-1992.
Intvr: Kostelanetz, Richard
Topic: Criticism; Theater
Works: Rozart mix; Variations V
List: N
Biog: Y
Source: KOST T "Conversations–John Cage." pp. 50-63
Lang: ENG

190 Cage, John, 1912-1992.
Date: 1968, 1970-71
Intvr: Charles, Daniel
List: N
Biog: N
Source: CAGE F
Lang: ENG
Notes: Interviews began in 1968 as a series in *La Revue d'Esthetique* 21/2-4 (Apr.-Dec. 1968) by Daniel Charles.

191 Cage, John, 1912-1992.
Date: 4/7/72, N.Y.
Intvr: Helms, Hans Günter
Topic: Aleatory music; China; I-Ching;
         Performance practice; Politics
Works: Credo in us; HPSCHD; 34'46.
         776"; *Silence*
List: Y
Biog: Y
Source: MET J "John Cage; Gedanken
         eines progressiven Musikers über
         die beschädigte Gesellschaft."
         pp. 18-40
Lang: ENG, GER
Notes: Previously published in *Pro-
         tokolle* 30 (Mar. 1974).

192 Cage, John, 1912-1992.
Date: 5/72, Bremen, Germany
Intvr: Gligo, Nikša
Topic: Composers–Social conditions;
         Philosophy & aesthetics
List: N
Biog: N
Source: MELOS "Ich traf John Cage in
         Bremen." 40/1 (Jan.-Feb. 1973):
         23-29
Lang: GER

193 Cage, John, 1912-1992.
Intvr: Henahan, Donal
Topic: Performance practice;
         Thomson, Virgil, 1896-1989
List: N
Biog: N
Source: NYT "Who throws dice, reads
         I-Ching, and composes?" 3 Sept.
         1972, sec. 2, p. 9
Lang: ENG

194 Cage, John, 1912-1992.
Intvr: Helms, Hans Günter
Topic: Aleatory music; Education–
         United States; Mao, Tsetung,
         1893-1976; Philosophy &
         aesthetics; Sound recordings
List: N
Biog: N
Source: MBR "Conversation with John
         Cage, Christian Wolff, Hans G.
         Helms." Side 7, Bd. 1 (1972)
Lang: ENG

195 Cage, John, 1912-1992.
Date: 7/14/73, Stony Point, N.Y.
Intvr: Gillmor, Alan
Topic: Philosophy & aesthetics; Style
         (Individual)
List: N
Biog: N
Source: CONTACT "Interview with
         John Cage." 14 (Fall 1976): 18-25
Lang: ENG
Notes: Also published in *Nutida Musik*
         21/1 (1977-78).

196 Cage, John, 1912-1992.
Date: 7/14/73, Stony Point, N.Y.
Intvr: Gillmor, Alan; Shattuck, Roger
Topic: Satie, Erik, 1866-1925; Thoreau,
         Henry David, 1817-1862
List: N
Biog: N
Source: CONTACT "Erik Satie: A con-
         versation." 25 (Fall 1982): 21-26
Lang: ENG

197 Cage, John, 1912-1992.
Intvr: Kostelanetz, Richard

Topic: Composers–Relations with audi-
ences; Composers as authors;
Composers as poets; I-Ching
Works: Mureau; *Empty words*
List: N
Biog: N
Source: KOST A, pp. 54-86
Lang: GER
Notes: Reprinted from Richard Koste-
lanetz, *John Cage* (Köln, 1973).

198 Cage, John, 1912-1992.
Intvr: Goldberg, Jeff
Topic: Lennon, John, 1940-1980;
Schoenberg, Arnold, 1874-
1951; Sound recordings;
Stravinsky, Igor, 1882-1971;
Style (Individual)
Works: 4'33"
List: N
Biog: N
Source: SWN "John Cage interview:
Cage on everything." 12 Sept.
1974, sec. Art
Lang: ENG

199 Cage, John, 1912-1992.
Intvr: Davies, Dennis Russell
Topic: Performance practice–20th-cen-
tury music
Works: Score
List: N
Biog: N
Source: ASTERISK "An interview with
Dennis Russell Davies and John
Cage." 1/1 (Dec. 1974): 20-25
Lang: ENG

200 Cage, John, 1912-1992.
Intvr: Brown, Anthony

Topic: Performance practice; Thoreau,
Henry David, 1817-1862
Works: *Empty words*
List: N
Biog: N
Source: ASTERISK "An interview with
John Cage." 1/1 (Dec. 1974):
26-32
Lang: ENG

201 Cage, John, 1912-1992.
Intvr: Goldberg, Jeff
Topic: Philosophy & aesthetics
List: N
Biog: N
Source: TR "John Cage. Interviewed by
Jeff Goldberg." 55-56 (May
1976): 103-110
Lang: ENG

202 Cage, John, 1912-1992.
Intvr: Zimmermann, Walter
Topic: Arts & politics; Nature; Philos
ophy & aesthetics; Thoreau,
Henry David, 1817-1862; Zen
Buddhism
List: N
Biog: N
Source: ZIMMER D, pp. 47-68
Lang: ENG

203 Cage, John, 1912-1992.
Date: 8/28/77
Intvr: Reynolds, Roger
Topic: Dance music; Improvisation;
Nancarrow, Conlon, 1912-; Phi-
losophy & aesthetics; Sound
Works: Branches; Child of tree; Lecture
on the weather
List: N

Biog: N
Source: MQ "John Cage and Roger Reynolds: A conversation." 65 (Oct. 1979): 573-94
Lang: ENG
Notes: Excerpts from an interview (Aug. 1977) that continues an interview made in 1961.

204 Cage, John, 1912-1992.
Date: Spr/78
Intvr: Kostelanetz, Richard
Topic: Composers as poets; Creative process
Works: *Writing Through Finnegans Wake*
List: N
Biog: N
Source: KOST A, pp. 87-102
Lang: GER
Notes: Originally made for SoHo Television. Previously published in *New York Arts Journal* 19 (Nov. 1980), and in Richard Kostelanetz, *The Old Poetries and the New* (Ann Arbor: Univ. of Michigan Press, 1981).

205 Cage, John, 1912-1992.
Intvr: Furman, Maureen
Topic: Electronic music; Philosophy & aesthetics; Zen Buddhism
Works: Music of the spheres
List: N
Biog: Y
Source: EWJ "Zen composition: An interview with John Cage." (May 1979): 42-46
Lang: ENG

206 Cage, John, 1912-1992.
Date: 8/15/79, Paris, France
Intvr: Schöning, Klaus
Topic: Computers; Joyce, James, 1882-1941
Works: Roaratorio, an Irish circus on Finnegans Wake
List: N
Biog: N
Source: SCHON R "John Cage/Klaus Schöning: Laughtears, conversation on 'Roaratorio.'" pp. 72-115
Lang: ENG, GER
Notes: Recorded on a tape which matches the text of pp. 107-13.

207 Cage, John, 1912-1992.
Date: 1979
Intvr: Kostelanetz, Richard
Topic: Aleatory music; I-Ching; Joyce, James, 1882-1941; Poetry; Thoreau, Henry David, 1817-1862
Works: Mureau; *Empty words*
List: N
Biog: N
Source: KOST O, pp. 247-73
Lang: ENG

208 Cage, John, 1912-1992.
Date: 3/30/80, New York City, N.Y.
Intvr: Caras, Tracy; Gagne, Cole
Topic: Creative process; Philosophy & aesthetics
List: Y
Biog: Y
Source: GAGNE S, pp. 69-86
Lang: ENG

209 Cage, John, 1912-1992.
Intvr: Cope, David Howell
Topic: Aleatory music; Nancarrow, Conlon, 1912-; Performance practice; Philosophy & aesthetics
List: N
Biog: N
Source: COMP(CA) "An interview with John Cage." 10-11 (1978-80): 6-22
Lang: ENG

210 Cage, John, 1912-1992.
Date: 4/3/81
Intvr: Timar, Andrew, et al.
Topic: Computers; Performance–20th-century music; Sound, Environmental
Works: Roaratorio, an Irish circus on Finnegans Wake; 30 pieces for 5 orchestras
List: N
Biog: N
Source: MUSWORKS "A conversation with John Cage." 17 (Fall 1981): 10-15
Lang: ENG

211 Cage, John, 1912-1992.
Date: 1981, London, Canada
Intvr: Behrens, Jack
List: N
Biog: Y
Source: M MAG "A celebration: John Cage at 75." 10/4 (Dec. 1987): 10-13
Lang: ENG
Notes: Interviews are inserted throughout the article.

212 Cage, John, 1912-1992.
Date: 3/31/82, N.Y.
Intvr: Gena, Peter
Topic: Composition–Influences; Education; Philosophy & aesthetics
List: Y
Biog: Y
Source: GENA J "After antiquity. John Cage in conversation with Peter Gena." pp. 167-83
Lang: ENG
Notes: Reprinted from the catalogue, Major Byrne, *New Music America '82* (Chicago).

213 Cage, John, 1912-1992.
Intvr: Sterritt, David
Topic: Performance; Sound
List: N
Biog: N
Source: CSM "Composer John Cage, master of notes–and sounds." 4 May 1982, p. 19
Lang: ENG

214 Cage, John, 1912-1992.
Date: 3/18/82, N.Y.; 5/29/82, London, England
Intvr: Montagne, Stephen
Topic: Composers–Political conditions; Thoreau, Henry David, 1817-1862
Works: 4'33"
List: N
Biog: N
Source: AM "John Cage at seventy: An interview." 3/2 (Sum. 1985): 205-16
Lang: ENG

Notes: Excerpts from this interview were previously published in *Classical Music* (22 May 1982): 11, and in *Contact* (Autumn 1982): 30.

215 Cage, John, 1912-1992.
Date: 11/82
Intvr: Fletcher, Laura; Moore, Thomas
Topic: Composers–Relations with audiences; Composers–Relations with performers; Performance–20th-century music
Works: Branches
List: N
Biog: N
Source: SONUS "John Cage: An interview, by Laura Fletcher and Thomas Moore." 3/2 (Spr. 1983): 16-23
Lang: ENG

216 Cage, John, 1912-1992.
Intvr: Kostelanetz, Richard
Topic: I-Ching; Poetry
Works: *Writings through Finnegans Wake*
List: Y
Biog: Y
Source: GENA J "Talking about 'Writings through Finnegans Wake.'" pp. 142-50
Lang: ENG

217 Cage, John, 1912-1992.
Intvr: Smith, Stuart
Topic: Aleatory music; Percussion instruments
List: N
Biog: N

Source: PN "Interview with John Cage." 21/3 (Mar. 1983): 3-7
Lang: ENG

218 Cage, John, 1912-1992.
Intvr: Schöning, Klaus
Topic: Drama
Works: Roaratorio, an Irish circus on Finnegans Wake
List: N
Biog: N
Source: NEULAND "Gespräch über 'James Joyce, Marcel Duchamp, Erik Satie: Ein Alphabet' zwischen John Cage und Klaus Schöning." 5 (1984-85): 375-81
Lang: GER
Notes: Originally broadcast 6 July 1983 at WDR3-Radio Studio.

219 Cage, John, 1912-1992.
Date: 11/19/83, N.Y.
Intvr: Marcus, Bunita; Pellizzi, Francesco
Topic: Philosophy & aesthetics; Sound
Works: Ryoanji
List: N
Biog: N
Source: RES "Conversation with Morton Feldman (Bunita Marcus and Francesco Pellizzi)." 6 (Fall 1983): 112-36
Lang: ENG
Notes: Morton Feldman also participated in the interview. Excerpts in German published in *Musiktexte* 5 (July 1984): 21-27.

220 Cage, John, 1912-1992.
Date: 5/80; 4/84, N.Y.

Intvr: Varga, Bálint András
Topic: Style (Individual)
List: N
Biog: N
Source: NZ "Komponieren heute: These, Antithese, Syntheses. Ein Doppelgespräch mit John Cage und Morton Feldman." 147/1 (Jan. 1986): 25-27
Lang: GER
Notes: This includes extracts from Cage's comments (1 & 22 May 1980) and the interview with Feldman in Apr. 1984.

221 Cage, John, 1912-1992.
Intvr: Varga, Bálint András
Topic: Composition–Influences; Sound; Style (Individual)
List: N
Biog: N
Source: NIIQ "Three questions on music: Extracts from a book of interviews in the making." 93 (Spr. 1984): 197-202
Lang: ENG

222 Cage, John, 1912-1992.
Intvr: Sommers, Scott
Topic: Creative process; Electronic music
Works: Ryoanji
List: N
Biog: N
Source: MUSTEXTE "'I'd like to be surprised.' John Cage im Gespräch." 15 (July 1985): 23-26
Lang: GER
Notes: Also published in the weekly paper *Public News (Houston, Texas),* 10 (Apr. 1986): 1, 8-9.

223 Cage, John, 1912-1992.
Intvr: Shapiro, David, et al.
Topic: Music & art; Sound; Zen Buddhism
Works: Cantos; Cheap imitation; Double music; Dream; Music for carillon, no. 5
List: N
Biog: N
Source: RES "On collaboration in art: A conversation with David Shapiro." 10 (Fall 1985): 103-116
Lang: ENG

224 Cage, John, 1912-1992.
Intvr: Wulffen, Thomas
Topic: Audiences–Germany, West (former); Computers; Critics; Philosophy & aesthetics
List: N
Biog: N
Source: NYB "An interview with John Cage." 1/1 (1985): 92-94
Lang: ENG
Notes: German translation published in *Zitty* (Mar. 1985).

225 Cage, John, 1912-1992.
Intvr: Grimes, Ev
Topic: Composers–Relations with audiences; Composition–Influences; Style (Individual)
List: N
Biog: Y
Source: MEJ "Conversations with American composers." 73/3 (Nov. 1986): 47-49, 58-59
Lang: ENG

226 Cage, John, 1912-1992.
Intvr: Kostelanetz, Richard
Topic: Electronic music; Notation; Radio broadcasting
Works: Branches; HPSCHD; Imaginary landscapes; Music for; Radio music; Speech, five radios, news-reader; 30 pieces for string quartet; Williams mix
List: N
Biog: Y
Source: MQ "John Cage and Richard Kostelanetz: A conversation about radio." 72 (1986): 216-27
Lang: ENG

227 Cage, John, 1912-1992.
Topic: Performance practice
List: N
Biog: N
Source: HP "John Cage." 38 (1987): 20-29
Lang: ENG
Notes: Summary of interviews held during past 22 years, compiled by Richard Kostelanetz.

228 Caltabiano, Ronald, 1959-
Intvr: Schneider, Steve
Topic: Creative process
List: N
Biog: N
Source: NYT "Awards galore for a young composer." 15 Apr. 1984, sec. 21, p. 17
Lang: ENG

229 Cardew, Cornelius, 1936-1981.
Date: 10/21/74
Intvr: Potter, Keith
Topic: Communism; Composers–Political conditions
List: N
Biog: N
Source: CONTACT "Some aspects of a political attitude: Cornelius Cardew interviewed." 10 (Wint. 1974-75): 22-27
Lang: ENG

230 Cardew, Cornelius, 1936-1981.
Intvr: Jack, Adrian
Topic: Composers–Relations with audiences
List: N
Biog: Y
Source: MM "Cornelius Cardew interviewed by Adrian Jack." 273 (May 1975): 30-34
Lang: ENG

231 Carlstedt, Jan, 1926-
Intvr: Johnson, Bengt Emil
Topic: Creativity; Music & art
Works: Quartet, string
List: N
Biog: N
Source: NUTIDA "Den process som avsätter betydande konstverk är hos oss mycket långsam!" 20/3 (1976-77): 32-35
Lang: SWE

232 Carter, Elliott, 1908-
Topic: Composition–Technique; Ives, Charles Edward, 1874-1954; Performance
Works: Quartet, string, no. 1
List: N
Biog: N
Source: MQ "Shop talk by an American

composer." 46 (Apr. 1960):
189-201

Lang: ENG

233 Carter, Elliott, 1908-

Date: 9/68

Intvr: Boretz, Benjamin A.

Topic: Composition–Technique; Philosophy & aesthetics; Pitch; Tone color

Works: Double concerto; Variations for orchestra

List: N

Biog: N

Source: PNM "Conversation with Elliott Carter." 8/2 (Spr.-Sum. 1970): 1-22

Lang: ENG

234 Carter, Elliott, 1908-

Intvr: Peyser, Joan

Topic: Composers–Relations with performers; United States

List: N

Biog: N

Source: NYT "Acclaim for a musical loner." 2 Mar. 1969, sec. 2, pp. 21, 35

Lang: ENG

235 Carter, Elliott, 1908-

Date: 1968-70

Intvr: Edwards, Allen

Topic: Boulanger, Nadia, 1887-1979; Composers–Influences; Composition–Technique; Europe; Philosophy & aesthetics; Sociology; 20th-century music; United States

List: N

Biog: N

Source: EDWARD F

Lang: ENG

236 Carter, Elliott, 1908-

Date: 8/10/75, Katonah, N.Y.

Intvr: Gagne, Cole

Topic: Composers–Influences; Neo-classicism

Works: Concerto for orchestra; Double concerto; Quartets, string, nos. 1, 2; Sonata, piano; Sonata, violoncello

List: Y

Biog: Y

Source: GAGNE S, pp. 87-100

Lang: ENG

237 Carter, Elliott, 1908-

Intvr: Varga, Bálint András

Topic: Composition–Influences; Sound; Style (Individual)

List: N

Biog: N

Source: NHQ "Three questions on music: Extracts from a book of interviews in the making." 93 (Spr. 1984): 197-202

Lang: ENG

238 Carter, Elliott, 1908-

Intvr: Rosen, Charles

Topic: Composition–Technique; Harmony; Music & literature; Rhythm

Works: Concerto, piano; Double concerto for harpsichord, piano, 2 chamber orchestras; Quartets; Sonata, piano; Symphony of three orchestras

List: N

Biog: N
Source: CONTRECHAMPS "Entretien avec Elliott Carter." 6 (Apr. 1986): 112-22
Lang: FRE
Notes: Originally published as Charles Rosen, *The Musical language of Elliott Carter* (Washington, D.C.: Library of Congress, Music Division, 1984).

239 Carter, Elliott, 1908-
Date: 1986
Intvr: Matthew-Walker, Robert
Topic: Chamber music; Creative process
Works: Quartet, string, no. 4
List: N
Biog: N
Source: MM "Elliott Carter's new string quartet–an interview with the composer." Sept. 1986, pp. 10-12
Lang: ENG

240 Casken, John, 1949-
Intvr: Griffiths, Paul
Topic: Creative process; Harmony; Style (Individual)
Works: Kagura; Tableaux
List: Y
Biog: Y
Source: GRIFFITHS N, pp. 84-92
Lang: ENG

241 Catán, Daniel, 1949-
Intvr: Saavedra, Leonora
Topic: Babbitt, Milton, 1916-; Composers–Influences; Composers–Relations with performers; Composers as conductors; Concerts & recitals; Harmony; Hexachord; Music & literature; Nationalism; Orchestration; Serialism; 12-tone system
Works: Du; Ocaso de medianoche; A cure for form and other stories
List: Y
Biog: N
Source: ANGELES M, pp. 206-241
Lang: SPA

242 Celarianu, Michel
Topic: Stockhausen, Karlheinz. *Aus den sieben Tagen*
List: N
Biog: N
Source: M JEU "Dix jeunes compositeurs." 1 (Nov. 1970): 83-85
Lang: FRE
Notes: Daniel Charles, Costin Miereanu and Éliane Radique also participated in the interview.

243 Cerha, Friedrich, 1926-
Intvr: Bachmann, Claus-Henning
Topic: Berg, Alban. *Lulu*
List: N
Biog: N
Source: NZ "Interview: 'Lulu' bisher: ' ... ein Anschlag auf den Dramatiker Berg,' Herstellung des dritten Aktes–Gespräch mit Friedrich Cerha." 140/3 (May-June 1979): 264-66
Lang: GER

Charles, Daniel
See no. 242.

244 Charles, Daniel
  Intvr: Bosseur, Jean-Yves
  Topic: Community relations; Performance
  List: N
  Biog: N
  Source: M JEU "Dix jeunes compositeurs." 1 (Nov. 1970): 79-82
  Lang: FRE
  Notes: Renaud Gagneux, Pierre Mariétan, Michel Puig and Louis Roquin also participated in the interview.

245 Charpentier, Gabriel, 1925-
  Intvr: Laplante, Louise
  Topic: Incidental music
  Works: Le bourgeois gentil'homme; Electre; Galileo Galilei; L'île des chèvres; Titus Andronicus
  List: N
  Biog: Y
  Source: MUSCAN "Words about music: A series of ...." 35 (Apr. 1978): 22-23
  Lang: ENG, FRE

Cherepnin, Aleksandr Nikolaevich
    See **Tcherepnin, Alexander, 1899-1977.**

246 Chini, André, 1945-
  Topic: Composers Social conditions
  List: N
  Biog: N
  Source: NUTIDA "Samtal om musik och politik." 20/4 (1976-77): 28-33
  Lang: SWE
  Notes: Conversation with Mikael Edlund, Lars Hallnäs and Mats Persson.

247 Chou, Wên-Choung, 1923-
  Intvr: Pulido, Esperanza
  Topic: Arts & politics–Far East Asia; China; Instrumental music
  Works: Concerto, violoncello
  List: N
  Biog: N
  Source: HETEROFONIA "Con Chou Wen-Choung." 63 (Nov.-Dec. 1978): 13-15
  Lang: SPA

248 Chowning, John M., 1934-
  Topic: Center for Computer Research in Music and Acoustics (CCRMA); Computers; Electro-acoustics; Institut de Recherche et de Coordination Acoustique-Musique (IRCAM)
  Works: Stria
  List: N
  Biog: N
  Source: TW "The science of sound: IRCAM & John Chowning/ CCRMA." 2/8 (1985)
  Lang: ENG

249 Clementi, Aldo, 1925-
  Date: 4/7/82, Italy
  Intvr: Failla, Salvatore Enrico
  Topic: Collage in music; Counterpoint; Education; Electronic music; Philosophy & aesthetics; Style (Individual)
  List: N
  Biog: N
  Source: FAILLA M "Intervista ad Aldo Clementi: Beatles ed elettronica." pp. 19-27
  Lang: ITA

250 Cogan, Robert David, 1930-
Date: 5/83
Intvr: Cai, Liang-Yu
Topic: Creative process; Electronic music
Works: Utterances
List: N
Biog: N
Source: SONUS "Reporting from eternity: An interview with Robert Cogan." 6/1 (Fall 1985): 23-28
Lang: ENG
Notes: Previously published in *Renmin Yinyue* (China, Spr. 1984).

251 Cole, Bruce
Date: 1973
Intvr: Potter, Keith
Topic: Style (Individual)
Works: Caesura; Pantomimes; A spray of dead arrows
List: N
Biog: N
Source: CONTACT "Interview with Bruce Cole." 6 (Spr. 1973): 13-22
Lang: ENG

252 Colgrass, Michael, 1932-
Date: 1/29/76, Detroit, Mich.; 12/7/77, Ann Arbor, Mich.
Intvr: Harvith, John; Harvith, Susan Edwards
Topic: Sound recording & reproduction
List: N
Biog: Y
Source: HARVITH E, pp. 281-89
Lang: ENG

Colvig, William
See no. 447.

253 Connolly, Justin Riveogh, 1933-
Date: 2/5/71
Intvr: Potter, Keith; Villars, Chris
Topic: England–20th-century
List: N
Biog: N
Source: CONTACT "Interview with Justin Connolly." 1 (Spr. 1971): 16-20
Lang: ENG

254 Constant, Marius, 1925-
Intvr: Walter, Edith
Topic: Community relations; Concerts & recitals–20th-century music; Ensemble Intercontemporain; France–20th-century; Government & arts
List: N
Biog: Y
Source: HARMONIE "Être contemporain aujourd'hui." 125 (1977): 36-49
Lang: FRE
Notes: Ivo Malec, Paul Méfano and Tristan Murail also participated in the interview.

255 Cooke, Arnold, 1906-
Date: 11/4/66
Intvr: Arnell, Richard
Topic: Teaching; 20th-century music
List: N
Biog: Y
Source: COMP(LONDON) "Arnold Cooke: A birthday conversation." 24 (Sum. 1967): 18-20
Lang: ENG

256 Cooke, Arnold, 1906-
Date: 4/71, London, England
Intvr: Dawney, Michael
Topic: England; Teaching
Works: Mary Barton
List: Y
Biog: N
Source: COMP(LONDON) "Senior British composers–10: Arnold Cooke in conversation with Michael Dawney." 45 (Fall 1972): 5, 7-9
Lang: ENG

257 Copland, Aaron, 1900-1990.
Intvr: Ramey, Philip
Topic: Contests & awards; De Mille, Agnes, 1908-1974; Graham, Martha; New York Music Critics Circle Awards; Pulitzer prizes
Works: Appalachian spring; Rodeo; El salón México
List: N
Biog: N
Source: COP "A talk with Aaron Copland."
Lang: ENG
Notes: For details, see Roberta Lindsey, "A thematic annotated bibliography of the literary works and interviews of Aaron Copland" (Thesis, Butler Univ., 1986), p. 74.

258 Copland, Aaron, 1900-1990.
Intvr: Brant, LeRoy V.
Topic: Berkshire Festival; Festivals; Musicians
List: N
Biog: N
Source: ETUDE "America, involved in music, is becoming great in music." 71 (Apr. 1953): 9, 57
Lang: ENG

259 Copland, Aaron, 1900-1990.
Intvr: Freeman, John W.
Topic: Opera
List: N
Biog: N
Source: ON "The reluctant composer: A dialogue with Aaron Copland." 26 Jan. 1963, pp. 9-12
Lang: ENG

260 Copland, Aaron, 1900-1990.
Intvr: Klein, Howard
Topic: Style (Individual)
Works: Concerto, piano, no. 1
List: N
Biog: N
Source: NYT "Philharmonic takes on the avant-garde." 5 Jan. 1964, sec. 2, p. 9
Lang: ENG

261 Copland, Aaron, 1900-1990.
Date: 11/13/67
Intvr: Cone, Edward T.
Topic: Style (Individual)
List: N
Biog: N
Source: PNM "Conversation with Aaron Copland." 6/2 (Spr.-Sum. 1968): 57-72
Lang: ENG

262 Copland, Aaron, 1900-1990.
Intvr: Mayer, William Robert

Topic: Commissions; Composers–Relations with audiences; Creative process; Folk music; Nationalism
Works: Billy the Kid
List: N
Biog: N
Source: ASCAP "Composer in the US and Russia." 3/1 (June 1969): 22-25
Lang: ENG
Notes: Aram Ilich Khachaturian also participated in the interview. Reprinted in *The Composer Magazine* 2/2 (Sept. 1970): 44-47.

263 Copland, Aaron, 1900-1990.
Date: 7/70, N.Y.
Intvr: Jacobson, Robert
Topic: Composers as conductors; Style (Individual)
Works: Music for the theatre
List: N
Biog: N
Source: JACOB R, pp. 33-45
Lang: ENG

264 Copland, Aaron, 1900-1990.
Intvr: Henahan, Donal
Topic: Composers, American; 12-tone system
Works: Lincoln portrait
List: N
Biog: N
Source: NYT "He made composing respectable here." 8 Nov. 1970, sec. 2, pp. 17, 20
Lang: ENG

265 Copland, Aaron, 1900-1990.
Date: 1972, W. Va.
Intvr: Bessom, Malcom Eugene
Topic: American music; Composition–Technique; Electronic music; Jazz; Teaching
List: Y
Biog: N
Source: MEJ "Sounds of America: A bicentennial series." 59/7 (Mar. 1973): 38-49
Lang: ENG

266 Copland, Aaron, 1900-1990.
Date: 1/6/75, Peekskill, N.Y.
Intvr: Caras, Tracy; Gagne, Cole
Topic: Creative process; Philosophy & aesthetics
List: Y
Biog: Y
Source: GAGNE S, pp. 101-16
Lang: ENG

267 Copland, Aaron, 1900-1990.
Date: 1975
Intvr: Kenyon, Nicholas
Topic: United States
List: N
Biog: N
Source: MM "The scene surveyed." 279 (Nov. 1975): 22-23
Lang: ENG

268 Copland, Aaron, 1900-1990.
Date: 5/1/76, Ann Arbor, Mich.
Intvr: Harvith, John; Harvith, Susan Edwards
Topic: Sound recordings
List: N
Biog: N

Source: HARVITH E, pp. 152-57

Lang: ENG

Notes: First published in "Think of all the remote areas where you can't hear an orchestra," *Music Magazine* 1/4 (July-Aug. 1978): 28-29.

269 Copland, Aaron, 1900-1990.

Date: 10/19/76, England

Intvr: Dickinson, Peter

Topic: Careers in music; Composers as conductors; Motion picture music; Style (Individual)

List: N

Biog: N

Source: KEELE F "Interview with Aaron Copland." pp. 4-14

Lang: ENG

270 Copland, Aaron, 1900-1990.

Date: 8/75, 10/77, Lenox, Mass.

Intvr: Rosenberg, Bernard; Rosenberg, Deena

Topic: Careers in music; Composers–Social conditions; Creative process

Works: Appalachian spring; Billy the Kid; The cat and the mouse; Concerto, piano; Rodeo

List: N

Biog: N

Source: ROSEN M, pp. 31-38

Lang: ENG

271 Copland, Aaron, 1900-1990.

Intvr: Cromonic, Richard

Topic: Creative process

List: Y

Biog: N

Source: ACCENT "Meet The Composer: Aaron Copland–the vigorous old man of American music." 5/2 (Nov.-Dec. 1979): 8-9

Lang: ENG

272 Copland, Aaron, 1900-1990.

Intvr: Rothstein, Edward

List: N

Biog: N

Source: NYT "Fanfares for Aaron Copland at 80." 9 Nov. 1980, sec. 2, pp. 21, 24

Lang: ENG

273 Copland, Aaron, 1900-1990.

Intvr: Macauley, Ian T.

List: N

Biog: N

Source: NYT "Copland, at 80, looks to the future." 9 Nov. 1980, sec. 22, pp. 1, 9

Lang: ENG

274 Copland, Aaron, 1900-1990.

Intvr: Hershowitz, Alan

Topic: Electronic music; Motion picture music; Program music; Serial music; Sound recordings; Style (Individual); Teaching

Works: Appalachian spring; Connotations; Piano variations; *The new music: 1900-1960*

List: N

Biog: N

Source: MUS J "Aaron Copland: The American composer shares his mind with Alan Hershowitz." 39/2 (Mar.-Apr. 1981): 9-12

Lang: ENG

275 Cornejo, Rodolfo S., 1909-
Intvr: Samson, Helen F.
Topic: Composers as performers
List: Y
Biog: N
Source: SAMSON C, pp. 49-58
Lang: ENG

276 Corner, Philip, 1933-
Intvr: Zimmermann, Walter
Topic: Cage, John, 1912-1992; Culture;
Experimental music
List: N
Biog: N
Source: ZIMMER D, pp. 69-92
Lang: ENG

277 Coulthard, Jean, 1908-
Intvr: Callon, Christine
Topic: Composition–Technique
Works: Burlesca; Symphonic ode; Three
Shakespeare sonnets
List: N
Biog: Y
Source: MUSCAN "Words about music:
A series of ...." 36 (Aug. 1978):
26-27
Lang: ENG, FRE

278 Crumb, George, 1929-
Intvr: Henahan, Donal
Topic: Style (Individual)
Works: Echoes of time and the river
List: N
Biog: N
Source: NYT "Out of the gentle people."
13 Dec. 1970, sec. 2, pp. 15, 18
Lang: ENG

279 Crumb, George, 1929-
Intvr: Liebman, Stuart
Topic: Commissions; Composition–
Technique; Music & literature;
Orchestral music; Sound; Sound
recordings
List: N
Biog: N
Source: BP "Who is George Crumb and
why is he telling all those sto-
ries?" 12 Nov. 1974, pp. 32-33,
36
Lang: ENG

280 Crumb, George, 1929-
Date: 12/8/75, Media, Pa.
Intvr: Caras, Tracy; Gagne, Cole
Topic: Creative process; Performance
Works: Ancient voices of children; Black
angels; Echoes of time and the
river; Madrigals; Makrokosmos
I; Night music I; Night of the
four moons; Songs, drones, and
refrains of death; Variazioni;
Vox balaenae
List: Y
Biog: Y
Source: GAGNE S, pp. 117-30
Lang: ENG

281 Crumb, George, 1929-
Date: 5/27/76, Media, Pa.
Intvr: Alcaraz, José Antonio
Topic: Boulez, Pierre, 1925-; Com-
posers–Influences; Creativity;
Garcia Lorca, Federico, 1898-
1936; Music & literature; Poems;
Voice
List: N

Biog: N
Source: CRUMB D, pp. 117-27
Lang: SPA

282 Crumb, George, 1929-
Intvr: Blackburn, Robert T.; Risen-
hoover, Morris
Topic: Colleges & universities–Faculty;
Composers–Economic condi-
tions; Teaching
List: N
Biog: Y
Source: RISEN A, pp. 44-52
Lang: ENG

283 Crumb, George, 1929-
Date: 7/23/76-12/4/78
Intvr: Shuffett, Robert Vernon
Topics Composition–Technique; Crea-
tive process; Philosophy & aes-
thetics; Style (Individual)
List: N
Biog: Y
Source: SHUFFETT M, pp. 395-564
Lang: ENG
Notes: 25 interviews in Appendix E.

284 Crumb, George, 1929
Date: 7/19/77; 6/11/79
Intvr: Shuffett, Robert Vernon
Topic: Composition–Technique; Crea-
tivity; Philosophy & aesthetics
List: N
Biog: N
Source: COMP(CA) "Interview with
George Crumb." 10-11 (1978-
80): 29-42
Lang: ENG

285 Crumb, George, 1929-
Intvr: Varga, Bálint András
Topic: Composition–Influences; Sound;
Style (Individual)
List: N
Biog: N
Source: NHQ "Three questions on
music: extracts from a book of
interviews in the making." 93
(Spr. 1984): 197-202
Lang: ENG

286 Crumb, George, 1929-
Intvr: Shuffett, Robert Vernon
Topic: Careers in music; Composers–
Influences; Composers–Rela-
tions with performers; Creative
process; Style (Individual)
List: Y
Biog: Y
Source: GILLESPIE G "Interview:
George Crumb/Robert Shuffett."
pp. 34-37
Lang: ENG

287 Cutts, Peter P., 1927-
Date: 7/15/83, Wittenberg, N.Y.
Intvr: Eskew, Harry Lee
Topic: Creative process; Hymn writers
List: N
Biog: Y
Source: HYMN "Writing hymn texts
and tunes." 35/2 (Apr. 1984):
71-75
Lang: ENG
Notes: Brian Wren also participated in
the interview.

288 Da Costa, Noel G., 1930-
Intvr: Baker, David N., et al.

Topic: Black composers; Composers–
Influences; Composition–Tech-
nique; Performance; Style (Indi-
vidual)
List: Y
Biog: Y
Source: BAKER B, pp. 70-92
Lang: ENG

289 Dadap, Jeremiah, 1935-
Intvr: Samson, Helen F.
Topic: Education–Philippines
List: Y
Biog: N
Source: SAMSON C, pp. 59-67
Lang: ENG

290 Dallapiccola, Luigi, 1904-1975.
Intvr: Laderman, Ezra
Topic: Composers–Social conditions
List: N
Biog: N
Source: NYT "A twelve-tone man from
way back." 1 Nov. 1964, sec. 2,
p. 11
Lang: ENG

291 Dallapiccola, Luigi, 1904-1975.
Date: Sum/67
Intvr: Pinzauti, Leonardo
Topic: Beethoven, Ludwig van, 1770-
1827; Mozart, Wolfgang
Amadeus, 1756-1791; Opera;
Schoenberg, Arnold, 1874-1951
Works: Ulisse
List: N
Biog: N
Source: PINZAUTI M, pp. 29-41
Lang: ITA

Notes: Previously published in *Nuova
Rivista Musicale Italiana* 1
(Sept.-Oct. 1967): 568-79.

292 Dallapiccola, Luigi, 1904-1975.
Intvr: Helm, Everett Burton
Topic: Composer–Political conditions;
Europe
Works: Il prigioniero
List: N
Biog: N
Source: MELOS/NZ "Luigi Dallapicco-
la in einem unveröffentlichen
Gespräch." 2/6 (1976): 469-71
Lang: GER

293 Davidovsky, Mario, 1934-
Date: 6/9/75, New York City, N.Y.
Intvr: Caras, Tracy; Gagne, Cole
Topic: Philosophy & aesthetics
Works: Electronic study, no. 3; Inflex-
ions; Synchronisms, no. 1
List: Y
Biog: Y
Source: GAGNE S, pp. 131-40
Lang: ENG

294 Davidovsky, Mario, 1934-
Intvr: Brunson, William
List: N
Biog: N
Source: NUTIDA "Mario Davidovsky."
28/1 (1984-85): 34
Lang: SWE

295 Davies, Peter Maxwell, 1934-
Intvr: Schafer, Raymond Murray
Topic: Church music; Composition–
Technique; Creativity; Culture;
English music; 14th-century mu-
sic

List: N
Biog: Y
Source: SCHAFER B, pp. 173-82
Lang: ENG

296 Davies, Peter Maxwell, 1934-
Date: 9/71, Toronto, Italy
Intvr: Pinzauti, Leonardo
Topic: Composers–Influences; Composers–20th-century; Composers, American; Composition–Technique; 14th-century music; 16th-century music; Teaching
List: N
Biog: N
Source: PINZAUTI M, pp. 195-202
Lang: ITA
Notes: Previously published in *Nuova Rivista Musicale Italiana* 6 (Jan.-Mar. 1972): 87-92.

297 Davies, Peter Maxwell, 1934-
Intvr: Sutcliffe, Tom
Topic: Incidental music
Works: Blind man's buff; Taverner
List: N
Biog: Y
Source: MM   "A question of identity: Tom Sutcliffe talks with Peter Maxwell Davies about 'Blind man's buff' and 'Taverner.'" 238 (June 1972): 26-28
Lang: ENG

298 Davies, Peter Maxwell, 1934-
Intvr: Fletcher, Shane
Topic: Children, Opera for
Works: The two fiddlers
List: N
Biog: N

Source: MM "The two fiddlers: Peter Maxwell Davies talks about his children's opera, which can be seen at the Jeanetta Cochrane Theatre from Dec. 27 to Jan. 6, to Shane Fletcher." 316 (Dec. 1978): 19
Lang: ENG

299 Davies, Peter Maxwell, 1934-
Intvr: Lohner, Henning
Topic: Composers–Relations with audiences; Folk music–Scotland; Philosophy & aesthetics
Works: The martyrdom of St. Magnus
List: N
Biog: Y
Source: INTERFACE "Peter Maxwell Davies and his opera 'The Martyrdom of St. Magnus': An interview with the composer." 13 (1984): 225-47
Lang: ENG

300 Davies, Peter Maxwell, 1934-
Intvr: Griffiths, Paul
Topic: Creativity; Harmony
List: Y
Biog: Y
Source: GRIFFITHS N, pp. 31-38
Lang: ENG

301 Davies, Peter Maxwell, 1934-
Intvr: Lohner, Henning
Topic: Religion; Style (Individual)
List: Y
Biog: Y
Source: NZ "Komponieren heute: Komponieren wider die Indifferenz. Der englische Komponist Peter

Maxwell Davies im Gespräch."
147/2 (Feb. 1986): 21-24

Lang: GER

302 Davies, Victor, 1939-

Intvr: Timar, Andrew

Topic: Canadian League of Composers; Societies, associations, etc.–Canada

List: N

Biog: N

Source: MUSWORKS "Talk with Victor Davies." 10 (Wint. 1980): 4-6

Lang: ENG

303 Davison, John H. 1930-

Date: Sum/77, Plymouth, Mass.

Intvr: Horst, Pamela

Topic: Children as composers; Creative process; Education

List: N

Biog: N

Source: AR "Composition for people who 'can't' compose." 18 (Feb. 1978): 106-111

Lang: ENG

304 Dawson, Ted, 1951-

Date: 12/19/78, Montréal, Canada

Intvr: Bouliane, Yves

Works: Binaries

List: N

Biog: N

Source: MUSWORKS "Interview with Ted Dawson." 7 (Spr. 1979): 15

Lang: ENG

De Pablo, Luis
  See **Pablo, Luis de, 1930-**

305 Del Tredici, David, 1937-

Intvr: Rockwell, John

Topic: Tonality

Works: Scenes and arias from Alice in Wonderland

List: N

Biog: N

Source: NYT "Del Tredici–his success could be a signpost." 26 Oct. 1980, sec. 2, pp. 23, 28

Lang: ENG

306 Del Tredici, David, 1937-

Intvr: Conarroe, Joel

Topic: Concerts & recitals; Creative process; Notation; Orchestration; Symphony; United States

Works: Scenes and arias from Alice in Wonderland

List: N

Biog: N

Source: WORDS M "An interview with David Del Tredici." pp. 256-78

Lang: ENG

307 Del Tredici, David, 1937-

Intvr: Page, Tim

Topic: Tonality

Works: Scenes and arias from Alice in Wonderland

List: N

Biog: N

Source: NYT "The new romance with tonality." 29 May, 1983, sec. 6, pp. 22-23, 36

Lang: ENG

308 Dempster, Stuart, 1936-

Date: 10/22/77

Intvr: Samson, Valerie

Topic: Musicians–Economic condi-
tions; Trombone music
List: N
Biog: N
Source: COMP(CA) "An interview with
Stuart Dempster." 9 (1977-78):
28-38
Lang: ENG

309 Dessau, Paul, 1894-1979.
Intvr: Lombardi, Luca
Topic: Composers–Political conditions;
Education; Opera
List: N
Biog: N
Source: MELOS "Ich fuhr nach Zeuthen
zu Paul Dessau." 40/2 (Mar.-Apr.
1973): 74-78
Lang: GER

310 Dessau, Paul, 1894-1979.
Intvr: Lombardi, Luca
Topic: Brecht, Bertolt, 1898-1956; 20th-
century music
Works: Musica in memoria di Bertolt
Brecht
List: N
Biog: N
Source: RMI "A colloquio con Paul
Dessau." 8 (Apr.-June 1974):
227-33
Lang: ITA

311 Dessau, Paul, 1894-1979.
Intvr: Müller, Christa
Topic: Schoenberg, Arnold, 1874-1951
List: N
Biog: N
Source: HANSEN A "Ein Gespräch
über Arnold Schoenberg,

geführt von Christa Müller."
pp. 123-26
Lang: GER

312 Dessau, Paul, 1894-1979.
Date: 1978
Intvr: Stürzbecher, Ursula
Topic: Opera
List: Y
Biog: Y
Source: STURZ K, pp. 128-49
Lang: GER

313 Deutsch, Max, 1892-1982.
Date: 7/70
Intvr: Sir, Niel
Topic: Schoenberg, Arnold, 1874-1951;
Teaching
List: N
Biog: N
Source: PNM "Conversation with Max
Deutsch." 10/2 (Spr.-Sum. 1972):
52-59
Lang: ENG

314 Dittrich, Paul-Heinz, 1930-
Date: 12/76, Germany
Intvr: Stürzbecher, Ursula
Topic: Composers–Relations with audi-
ences; Electronic music; Music
publishing; Text setting; 20th-
century music
Works: Cantus II; Illuminations; Kam-
mermusik; Schlagzeilen für 2
Klaviere, 2 Percussionisten und
Tonband
List: Y
Biog: Y
Source: STURZ K, pp. 10-26
Lang: GER

315 Długoszewski, Lucia, 1931-
Intvr: Hughes, Allen
Topic: Experimental music
List: N
Biog: N
Source: NYT "And Miss Długoszewski experiments–a lot." 7 Mar. 1971, sec. 2, pp. 15, 25
Lang: ENG

316 Dodge, Charles, 1942-
Date: 8/31/75, Manhattan, N.Y.
Intvr: Caras, Tracy; Gagne, Cole
Topic: Computer music; Creative process
Works: Cascando; Earth's magnetic field; Extensions; Folia; In celebration; Speech songs; The story of our lives
List: Y
Biog: Y
Source: GAGNE S, pp. 141-52
Lang: ENG

317 Dodge, Charles, 1942-
Topic: Computer music; Computer speech synthesis; Notation
List: N
Biog: N
Source: TW "Charles Dodge's singing computer." 1/8 (1983)
Lang: ENG

318 Döhl, Friedhelm, 1936-
Intvr: Oesch, Hans
Topic: Sound; Style (Individual)
List: N
Biog: N
Source: MELOS/NZ "Interview mit Friedhelm Döhl." 1/5 (Sept.-Oct. 1975): 355-59
Lang: GER

319 Donatoni, Franco, 1927-
Date: Spr/70, Rome, Italy
Intvr: Pinzauti, Leonardo
Topic: 20th-century music
Works: Puppenspiel, no. 2
List: N
Biog: N
Source: PINZAUTI M, pp. 133-41
Lang: ITA
Notes: Previouly published in *Nuova Rivista Musicale Italiana* 4 (Mar.-Apr. 1970): 299-306.

320 Donatoni, Franco, 1927-
Date: 7/75
Intvr: Mâche, François-Bernard
Topic: Creativity
List: N
Biog: Y
Source: RM "Les mal entendus. Compositeurs des années 70." 314-15 (1978): 47-52
Lang: FRE

321 Donatoni, Franco, 1927-
Date: 6/1/82, Italy
Intvr: Failla, Salvatore Enrico
Topic: Audiences; Composers–Influences; Composers, Italian; Composers as authors; Pizzetti, Ildebrando, 1880-1968; Style (Individual); 20th-century music
List: N
Biog: N

Source: FAILLA M "Interviesta a Franco Donatoni: Un pentagramma per Salvare il Sud." pp. 61-72

Lang: ITA

322 Dresher, Paul, 1951-

Topic: Composition–Technique; Electronic music; Electronic music synthesizers; Sound, Environmental

Works: Other fire

List: N

Biog: N

Source: TW "Post-minimalism: Glenn Branca & Paul Dresher." 2/13 (1985)

Lang: ENG

323 Druckman, Jacob, 1928-

Date: 6/14/75, New York City, N.Y.

Intvr: Caras, Tracy; Gagne, Cole

Topic: Electronic music; Philosophy & aesthetics

Works: Animus I, III; Incenters; Quartet, string, no. 2; Synapse; Valentine; Windows

List: Y

Biog: Y

Source: GAGNE S, pp. 153-62

Lang: ENG

324 Duffy, John, 1928-

Date: 9/80, N.Y.

Intvr: Wetzler, Peter

Topic: Meet The Composer; Teaching

List: N

Biog: N

Source: EAR "'Meet The Composer' Interview/Peter Wetzler." 6/1 (Nov.-Dec. 1980): 4

Lang: ENG

325 Duffy, John, 1928-

Intvr: Tuynman, Carol E.

Topic: Meet The Composer

List: N

Biog: Y

Source: EAR "'Meet The Composer' John Duffy." 10/5 (June-July 1986): 22-23, 26

Lang: ENG

326 Durand, Joel-François

Intvr: Kampel, Stewart

Topic: Electronic music

List: N

Biog: N

Source: NYT "Composer's music reaches a clearing." 8 Mar. 1987, sec. 21, p. 16

Lang: ENG

327 Dutilleux, Henri, 1916-

Intvr: Bourdain, G. S.

Topic: Commissions; France

Works: Concerto, violin

List: N

Biog: N

Source: NYT "Henri Dutilleux–an elder statesman of music in France." 23 Mar. 1986, sec. 2, pp. 25, 35

Lang: ENG

328 Eckhardt-Gramatté, S. C. (Sophie-Carmen), 1899-1974.

Topic: Composers–Economic conditions

List: Y

Biog: Y

Source: MUSCAN "S. C. Eckhardt-Gramatté, a portrait." 23 (Oct. 1969): [8-9]

Lang: ENG, FRE

Edlund, Mikael, 1950-
See no. 246.

329 Edlund, Mikael, 1950-
Intvr: Tobeck, Christina
Topic: Composers as performers; Com-
position–Technique; Incidental
music
Works: The lost jugglery
List: N
Biog: N
Source: NUTIDA "Det är viktigt att
klara ut musikens funktion."
23/2 (1979-80): 28-30
Lang: SWE
Notes: Also published in *Nutida Musik*
30/1 (1986-87): 58-61.

330 Einem, Gottfried von, 1918-
Date: 12/10/54
Intvr: Mieg, Peter
Topic: Music & literature
List: N
Biog: N
Source: RUFER B "Gottfried von Einem."
pp. 327-28
Lang: GER
Notes: Previously published in *Welt-
woche* (Zürich), 10 Dec. 1954.

331 Eisler, Hanns, 1898-1962.
Date: 1/58-4/58
Intvr: Notowicz, Nathan
Topic: Analysis; Composers–Political
conditions; Composers, German–
20th-century; Philosophy & aes-
thetics; Schoenberg, Arnold,
1874-1951; Teaching
List: N
Biog: Y

Source: NOTOWICZ W, pp. 25-211
Lang: GER

332 Eisler, Hanns, 1898-1962.
Date: 11/6/61
Intvr: Bunge, Hans
Topic: Composers–Political conditions;
Creativity; Hölderlin, Friedrich,
1770-1843; Music & literature;
Music & politics; Nature; Philos-
ophy & aesthetics; Poems; Sing-
ing; Style (Individual)
List: N
Biog: N
Source: EISLER S
Lang: GER
Notes: Also published as Hans Bunge,
*Fragen Sie mehr über Brecht,
Hanns Eisler im Gespräch*
(München: Rogner & Bernhard,
1970).

333 Eisler, Hanns, 1898-1962.
Date: 4/58-8/62
Intvr: Bunge, Hans
Topic: Arts & politics; Brecht, Bertolt,
1898-1956; Motion picture mu-
sic; Philosophy & aesthetics;
Sociology; 20th-century music;
Vocal music
List: N
Biog: N
Source: EISLER H
Lang: GER
Notes: Also published in *Hanns Eisler:
Schriften und Dokumente* 6
(München: Rogner & Bernhard,
1976).

334 Eklund, Hans, 1927-
Intvr: Rying, Matts
Topic: Careers in music; Teaching
Works: Concertino, piano
List: N
Biog: N
Source: NUTIDA "Vi lever av romantik och känslor." 17/3 (1973-74): 20-24
Lang: SWE

335 Eliasson, Anders, 1947-
Intvr: Johnson, Bengt Emil
Topic: Philosophy & aesthetics
List: N
Biog: N
Source: NUTIDA "Vi måste vika oss under konsten." 16/3 (1972-73): 29-33
Lang: SWE

336 Éloy, Jean-Claude, 1938-
Date: 2/72
Intvr: Mâche, François-Bernard
Topic: Electronic music; Oriental music
List: N
Biog: Y
Source: RM "Les mal entendus. Compositeurs des années 70." 314-15 (1978): 53-62
Lang: FRE

337 Éloy, Jean-Claude, 1938-
Date: 2/18/79
Intvr: Crawford, Christopher
Topic: Electronic music; Style (Individual)
List: N
Biog: N
Source: MUSWORKS "Interview with Jean Claude Éloy." 8 (Sum. 1979): 8-9
Lang: ENG, FRE

338 Éloy, Jean-Claude, 1938-
Intvr: Deloche, Aimée-Catherine
Topic: Oriental music; Style (Individual)
List: N
Biog: N
Source: SILENCES "Éloy, le temps revisité." 1 (1985): 159-67
Lang: FRE

339 Engelmann, Hans Ulrich, 1921-
Intvr: Bastian, Hans Günther
Topic: Composition–Technique; Education; Form; Notation, Graphic
Works: Mini-music to Siegfried Palm, op. 38
List: N
Biog: N
Source: MB "Avantgarde-Komposition und die Frage der Umsetzung in der Musikpädagogik, dargestellt am Beispiel von H. U. Engelmann's 'Mini-music to Siegfried Palm, op. 38.'" 10/7-8 (1978): 463-67
Lang: GER

340 Enríquez, Manuel, 1926-
Intvr: Cano, Isabel Farfán
Topic: Schools of music; Teaching
List: N
Biog: N
Source: HETEROFONIA "Entrevista con Manuel Enriquez, director del conservatorio." 28 (Jan.-Feb. 1973): 18-19
Lang: SPA

341 Enríquez, Manuel, 1926-
Intvr: Angeles González, María
Topic: Composers–Relations with performers; Composition–Influences; Composition–Technique; Creative process; Electronic music; Fellowships & scholarships; Multi-media compositions; Societies, associations, etc.–Mexico
Works: Ambivalencia; Quartet, strings, no. 2; Symphony, no. 2
List: Y
Biog: N
Source: ANGELES M, pp. 36-53
Lang: SPA

342 Erb, Donald, 1927-
Intvr: Felder, David
Topic: Musicians–United States; Style (Individual)
List: N
Biog: N
Source: COMP(CA) "An interview with Donald Erb." 10-11 (1978-80): 43-52
Lang: ENG

343 Erickson, Kim
Date: 2/85, Northwestern Ontario, Canada
Intvr: Pearson, Tina
Works: Alone
List: N
Biog: Y
Source: MUSWORKS "An interview with Kim Erickson." 31 (Spr. 1985): 12-13
Lang: ENG

344 Erickson, Robert, 1917-
Intvr: Dunbar, Daniel C.
Topic: Experimental music; Improvisation; Instrument making; Percussion instruments; Tone color
List: Y
Biog: N
Source: PN "An interview with Robert Erickson." 25/3 (Mar. 1987): 4-22
Lang: ENG

345 Escher, Rudolf, 1912-1980.
Intvr: Schönberger, Elmer
Topic: Debussy, Claude, 1862-1918; Serial music; Theory
Works: Quintet, wind; Sinfonia
List: Y
Biog: Y
Source: KN "Rudolf Escher: Thinking in and about music." 5 (June 1977): 3-17
Lang: ENG
Notes: Previously published in a summarized form in the weekly *Vrij Nederland.*

346 Febel, Reinhard, 1952-
Intvr: Hinz, Klaus-Michael
Topic: Composition–Technique; Philosophy & aesthetics; Serialism; Tonality
List: N
Biog: N
Source: JUNG L "Tonalität nach ihrer Katastrophe," pp. 48-53
Lang: GER

347 Felciano, Richard, 1930-
Intvr: Wyton, Alec
Topic: Church music; Electronic music

Works: Sic transit
List: N
Biog: N
Source: M AGO "An interview with Richard Felciano." 4/11 (Nov. 1970): 44-47
Lang: ENG

348 Feldman, Morton, 1926-1987.
Date: 8/64
Intvr: Ashley, Robert
Topic: Philosophy & aesthetics; 20th-century music
List: N
Biog: N
Source: SCHWARTZ C "An interview with Robert Ashley, August 1964." pp. 362-66
Lang: ENG
Notes: Also published in *Kulchur* 18 (Sum. 1965): 20-24, in part in *Verbal Anthology* (London: Experimental Music Catalogue, 1972): 7-9.

349 Feldman, Morton, 1926-1987.
Date: 5/1/66, London, England
Topic: Composition–Technique
List: N
Biog: N
Source: COMP(LONDON) "Pre-determinate/indeterminate." 19 (Spr. 1966): 3-4
Lang: ENG

350 Feldman, Morton, 1926-1987.
Topic: Composers–Relations with audiences; Composers, German; 12-tone system
List: N

Biog: N
Source: NUTIDA "Konversation utan Stravinsky." 11/3-4 (1967-68): 46-51
Lang: SWE
Notes: Originally published in *Source* 2 (1967).

351 Feldman, Morton, 1926-1987.
Intvr: Bosseur, Jean-Yves
Topic: Community relations; Composers–Influences; Composition–Technique; Music & politics; Philosophy & aesthetics; Style (Individual)
Works: Momentform
List: N
Biog: N
Source: RE "À l'écart des grandes villes: Entretien avec Jean-Yves Bosseur." 21 (1968): 3-8
Lang: FRE

352 Feldman, Morton, 1926-1987.
Date: 5/27/76, London, England
Intvr: Bryars, Gavin; Orton, Fred
Topic: Cage, John, 1912-1992; Music & art
Works: De Kooning; Rothko chapel; Summer space
List: N
Biog: N
Source: SI "Morton Feldman, interview by Fred Orton and Gavin Bryars." 984 (Nov.-Dec. 1976): 244-48
Lang: ENG

353 Feldman, Morton, 1926-1987.
Intvr: Zimmermann, Walter
Topic: Composers–20th-century; Creative process; Music & art

List: N
Biog: N
Source: ZIMMER D, pp. 1-20
Lang: ENG
Notes: Also published in French in *Contrechamps* 6 (Apr. 1986): 11-23.

354 Feldman, Morton, 1926-1987.
Date: 8/17/80, Buffalo, N.Y.
Intvr: Caras, Tracy; Gagne, Cole
Topic: Creative process
Works: Extensions; Intersection; Quartet, string; Rothko chapel; The viola in my life
List: Y
Biog: Y
Source: GAGNE S, pp. 163-77
Lang: ENG

355 Feldman, Morton, 1926-1987.
Intvr: Gena, Peter
Topic: Audiences; Cage, John, 1912-1992; Composers–Relations with performers; Europe; Harmony; Philosophy & aesthetics; United States
List: N
Biog: N
Source: GENA J "H. C. E. (Here Comes Everybody). Morton Feldman in conversation with Peter Gena." pp. 51-73
Lang: ENG

356 Feldman, Morton, 1926-1987.
Date: 11/9/83, Washington, D.C.
Intvr: Moore, Thomas
Topic: Interpretation; Music & art
List: N
Biog: N

Source: SONUS "We must pursue anxiety: An interview with Morton Feldman." 4/2 (Spr. 1984): 14-19
Lang: ENG

357 Feldman, Morton, 1926-1987.
Intvr: Williams, Jan
Topic: Creativity; Notation, Graphic; Orchestration; Percussion music
Works: Flute and orchestra; Instruments III; The King of Denmark; Why patterns?
List: N
Biog: N
Source: PN "An interview with Morton Feldman." 21/6 (Sept. 1983): 4-14
Lang: ENG

Feldman, Morton, 1926-1987.
See nos. 219–220.

358 Feldman, Morton, 1926-1987.
Date: 3/18/85, Buffalo, N.Y.
Intvr: Borradori, Giovanna
Topic: Cage, John, 1912-1992.; Modernism; Philosophy & aesthetics; Webern, Anton von, 1883-1945
List: N
Biog: N
Source: MR "Una liaison tra Webern e Cage." 19 (Apr. 1986): 53-66
Lang: ITA

359 Feliciano, Francisco F., 1942-
Intvr: Samson, Helen F.
List: Y
Biog: N
Source: SAMSON C, pp. 68-74
Lang: ENG

360 Ferneyhough, Brian, 1943-
Intvr: Gulli, Donatello
Topic: Notation; 20th-century music
Works: Cassandra's dream song; Epicycle; Missa brevis; Time and motion study II, III
List: N
Biog: N
Source: MR "Una ricerca in corso. Intervista con Brian Ferneyhough." 4 (Apr. 1981): 137-48
Lang: ITA
Notes: Originally published in *Information Booklet, B. Ferneyhough* (London: Peters, 1979).

361 Ferneyhough, Brian, 1943-
Date: 11/81, Stockholm, Sweden
Intvr: Zivkovic, Zagorka
Topic: Audiences; Boulez, Pierre, 1925-; Education; Form; Philosophy & aesthetics; Rhythm; Stockhausen, Karlheinz–Influences; Style (Individual); 20th-century music
List: N
Biog: Y
Source: ARTES "Musik ska fläka upp sitt innanmäte. Om tonsättaren Brian Ferneyhough." June 1982, pp. 63-80
Lang: SWE

362 Ferneyhough, Brian, 1943-
Date: 1982
Intvr: Bons, Joël
Topic: Composers–Netherlands; Contests & awards; Gaudeamus Music Week; Teaching
List: N
Biog: Y

Source: KN "Ear mail: Brian Ferneyhough in conversation with Joël Bons." 20 (Dec. 1984): 11-15
Lang: ENG
Notes: An edited version of a conversation held in 1982. Also published in French in *Contrechamps* 3 (Sept. 1984): 57-61.

363 Ferneyhough, Brian, 1943-
Date: 10/83, Freiburg, Germany; Bruxelles, Belgium
Intvr: Toop, Richard
Topic: Arts–Roman era; Composition–Technique; Style (Individual); Theory
Works: Carceri d'invenzione; Lemma-icon-epigram; Superscriptio
List: N
Biog: N
Source: ENTRETEMPS "À propos de superscriptio–Entretien avec Brian Ferneyhough." 3 (1987): 89-93
Lang: FRE
Notes: Translated from the English by Jean-Philippe Guye.

364 Ferneyhough, Brian, 1943-
Intvr: Griffiths, Paul
Topic: Audiences; Composition–Influences; Creativity; Music & art; Neo-romanticism; Style (Individual)
List: Y
Biog: Y
Source: GRIFFITHS N, pp. 65-83
Lang: ENG

365 Ferrari, Luc, 1928-
Date: 10/12/68-10/14/68, Amiens,
France; 8/13/69, Bergamo,
Italy ; 3/17/70, Paris, France
Intvr: Pauli, Hansjörg
Topic: Communications industries;
Community relations; Compos-
ers–Relations with audiences;
Composition–Technique; Music
& politics; Philosophy & aesthet-
ics; Style (Individual)
List: N
Biog: Y
Source: PAULI F, pp. 37-59
Lang: GER
Notes: Originally done for a series of
radio programs on Hessischer
Rundfunk Frankfurt.

366 Ferrari, Luc, 1928-
Date: 1/72
Intvr: Mâche, François-Bernard
Topic: Philosophy & aesthetics
List: N
Biog: Y
Source: RM "Les mal entendus. Com-
positeurs des années 70." 314-15
(1978): 63-69
Lang: FRE

367 Ferrero, Lorenzo, 1951-
Intvr: Gerhartz, Leo Karl
Topic: Opera
Works: Marilyn
List: N
Biog: N
Source: NZ "'Auch die Avantgarde steht
in Entwicklungsprozessen ....'
Gespräch mit dem italienischen

Komponisten Lorenzo Ferrero."
143/9 (Sept. 1982): 4-7
Lang: GER

368 Ferrero, Lorenzo, 1951-
Date: 1/4/83, Italy
Intvr: Failla, Salvatore Enrico
Topic: Cage, John, 1912-1992; Neo-
romanticism; Psychology;
Rameau, Jean Philippe, 1683-
1764
Works: Adagio cantabile; Marilyn
List: N
Biog: N
Source: FAILLA M "Intervista a Loren-
zo Ferrero: Sul lettino dello psi-
canalista d'è sdraiata una nota
in crisi." pp. 103-113
Lang: ITA

369 Finckel, Edwin A., 1917-
Intvr: Fruchter, Rena
Topic: Careers in music
List: N
Biog: N
Source: NYT "Concert to honor Essex
composer." 12 May 1985, sec.
11, p. 11
Lang: ENG

370 Finney, Ross Lee, 1906-
Date: 10/26/75, New York City, N.Y.
Intvr: Caras, Tracy; Gagne, Cole
Topic: Chamber music; Composition–
Technique; Creative process
Works: Landscapes remembered;
Spaces; Summer in Valley
City; Variations on a memory
List: Y
Biog: Y

Source: GAGNE S, pp. 179-91
Lang: ENG

371 Firkusny, Rudolf, 1912-
Intvr: Hertelendy, Paul
Topic: Performance
List: N
Biog: Y
Source: CK "A noted classical performer talks about tempo, Czech composers, and classical repertoire." 3/7 (July 1977): 30
Lang: ENG

372 Firsova, Elena, 1950-
Intvr: Polin, Claire C. J.
Topic: Composers–Union of Soviet Socialist Republics (former); Women composers
List: N
Biog: N
Source: TEMPO "Interviews with Soviet composers. II: Firsova, Gubaidulina, Loudova, Smirnov." 151 (Dec. 1984): 13-16
Lang: ENG
Notes: Sofia Asgatovna Gubaidulina, Ivana Loudová and Dmitri Smirnov also participated in the interview.

373 Fleischmann, Aloys, 1910-
Intvr: Dawney, Michael
Topic: Irish music
List: N
Biog: N
Source: COMP(LONDON) "Aloys Fleischmann." 57 (Spr. 1976): 37-38
Lang: ENG

374 Flothuis, Marius, 1914-
Intvr: Jurres, André; Wouters, Jos
Topic: Audiences; Pijper, Willem, 1894-1947; 12-tone system
List: N
Biog: Y
Source: WOUTERS F, pp. 22-39
Lang: ENG, GER
Notes: Guillaume Landré also participated in the interview.

375 Floyd, Carlisle, 1926-
Intvr: Goldovsky, Boris
Topic: Audiences; Bernstein, Leonard, 1918-1990; Composers–Relations with performers; Menotti, Gian Carlo, 1911-; Opera–20th-century
Works: Susannah; Wuthering Heights
List: N
Biog: N
Source: OF "The state of opera: A dialogue." 4/3 (Sum. 1971): 19-31
Lang: ENG
Notes: Edited by Leland Fox.

376 Fortier, Marc, 1940-
Intvr: Champagne, Jane
Topic: Canada–Québec; Composers, Authors & Publishers Association of Canada (CAPAC); Television music
Works: Pirouettes; Un doigt de la lune
List: N
Biog: Y
Source: CC "Interview! Marc Fortier." 99 (Mar. 1975): 22-29
Lang: ENG, FRE

377 Foss, Lukas, 1922-
Intvr: Ericson, Raymond
Topic: Composers–Relations with per-
formers; Serial music
List: N
Biog: N
Source: NYT "Buffalo takes a flyer on
Foss." 24 Nov. 1963, sec. 2, p.
13
Lang: ENG

378 Foss, Lukas, 1922-
Date: 4/3/70, Pittsburgh, Pa.
Topic: Performance
Works: Phorion
List: N
Biog: N
Source: M ART "Foss talks about 'stolen
goods' and the mystique of the
new." 3/4 (Sept.-Oct. 1970): 34-
35
Lang: ENG

379 Foss, Lukas, 1922-
Date: 1/3/75, New York City, N.Y.
Intvr: Caras, Tracy; Gagne, Cole
Topic: Creative process
List: Y
Biog: Y
Source: GAGNE S, pp. 193-208
Lang: ENG

380 Foss, Lukas, 1922-
Intvr: Horowitz, Joseph
Topic: Composers as conductors; Sym-
phony
List: N
Biog: N
Source: NYT "His orchestra grows in

Brooklyn." 21 Oct. 1979, sec.
2, p. 25
Lang: ENG

381 Foss, Lukas, 1922-
Intvr: Varga, Bálint András
Topic: Composition–Influences; Sound;
Style (Individual)
List: N
Biog: N
Source: NHQ "Three questions on
music: Extracts from a book of
interviews in the making." 93
(Spr. 1984): 197-202
Lang: ENG

382 Fox, Jim, 1953-
Intvr: Childs, Barney
Topic: Improvisation
List: N
Biog: N
Source: PNM "Interview with Jim Fox."
24/2 (Spr.-Sum. 1986): 236-41
Lang: ENG

383 Françaix, Jean, 1912-
Intvr: Strobel, Heinrich
Topic: Opera
Works: Apokalypse
List: N
Biog: N
Source: MELOS "Gespräch mit Jean
Françaix." 17/1 (Jan. 1950): 7-9
Lang: GER

384 Françaix, Jean, 1912-
Intvr: Karp, Judith
Topic: France
List: N
Biog: N

Source: NYT "Music in France and Jean Françaix." 21 June 1981, sec. 2, p. 19

Lang: ENG

385 Francis, Bruce

Intvr: Marshall, Jon

Topic: Black composers; Composers–Social conditions

List: N

Biog: N

Source: COMP(CA) "Interview with Bruce Francis." 2/1 (June 1970): 9-11

Lang: ENG

386 Franzén, Olov Alfred, 1946-

Intvr: Johnson, Bengt Emil

Topic: Style (Individual)

Works: Beyond; Tri

List: N

Biog: N

Source: NUTIDA "Kulturkretsens tryck och fjällviddens gemenskap." 17/3 (1973-74): 25-27

Lang: SWE

387 Freedman, Harry, 1922-

Topic: Composers–Economic conditions; Vocal music

List: Y

Biog: Y

Source: MUSCAN "Harry Freedman, a portrait." 8 (Jan. 1968): [8-9]

Lang: ENG, FRE

388 Freedman, Harry, 1922-

Date: Sum/68, Ontario, Canada

Intvr: MacMillan, Keith (Campbell)

Topic: Camps, Music; Interprovincial Music Camp; Teaching

List: N

Biog: N

Source: MUSCAN "Composer at camp." 14 (Oct. 1968): 5-7, 10-12

Lang: ENG, FRE

Notes: William Alexander McCauley also participated in the conversation.

389 Freedman, Harry, 1922-

Intvr: Schulman, Michael

Topic: Composers–Economic conditions; Creative process; Jazz

List: N

Biog: Y

Source: CC "Interview! Harry Freedman." 96 (Dec. 1974): 4-11

Lang: ENG, FRE

390 Freedman, Harry, 1922-

Intvr: Jones, Gaynor

Topic: Ballet music; Canada; Motion picture music

List: N

Biog: Y

Source: M MAG "Speaking freely with Harry Freedman." 10/2 (June-July 1987): 18-21

Lang: ENG

391 Fricker, Peter Racine, 1920-1990.

Intvr: Schafer, Raymond Murray

Topic: Philosophy & aesthetics; Style (Individual)

List: N

Biog: N

Source: SCHAFER B, pp. 137-46

Lang: ENG

392 Fritsch, Johannes Georg, 1941-
Intvr: Schürmann, Hans G.
Topic: Electronic music; *Feedback*
papers
List: N
Biog: Y
Source: MUSICA "Lockerung von Phantasie oder Energieverläufe in der Zeit. Ein Gespräch mit Johannes Fritsch und Rolf Gehlhaar." 30 (1976): 20-25
Lang: GER
Notes: Rolf Gehlhaar also participated in the interview.

393 Frize, Nicolas, 1950-
Intvr: Caplan, Hedy; Donze, Gilles
Topic: Community relations
List: N
Biog: Y
Source: EAR "Meet The Composer: Nicolas Frize." 12/4 (June 1987): 22-23
Lang: ENG

Gagneux, Renaud
See no. 244.

394 Gál, Hans, 1890-1987.
Intvr: Anderson, Martin J.
Topic: Composers–Social conditions
List: Y
Biog: Y
Source: BMSJ "Hans Gál: A conversation with Martin J. Anderson." 9 (1987): 32-44
Lang: ENG

395 Galindo, Blas, 1910-
Intvr: Pulido, Esperanza

Topic: Composition–Technique; Electronic music
List: N
Biog: N
Source: HETEROFONIA "Conversación con el compositor Blas Galindo." 20 (Sept.-Oct. 1971): 17-19
Lang: SPA

396 Gamilla, Alice Doria, 1931-
Intvr: Samson, Helen F.
Topic: Television music
Works: A million thanks to you
List: Y
Biog: N
Source: SAMSON C, pp. 75-85
Lang: ENG

397 Garant, Serge, 1929-1986.
Topic: Canada
Works: Anerca; Phrases II
List: N
Biog: N
Source: MUSCAN "Serge Garant, a portrait." 10 (Apr. 1968): [8-9]
Lang: ENG, FRE

398 Gardner, Samuel, 1891-1984.
Date: 12/7/74, N.Y.
Intvr: Harvith, John; Harvith, Susan Edwards
Topic: Sound recording & reproduction
List: N
Biog: N
Source: HARVITH E, pp. 45-51
Lang: ENG

399 Gavazzeni, Gianandrea, 1909-
Intvr: Nicastro, Aldo
Topic: Criticism; Opera; Orchestration

Works: Parisina
List: N
Biog: N
Source: RASS MC "'Parisina o della
liaisons dangereuses'–intervista
con Gianandrea Gavazzeni."
32/1 (Jan. 1979): 15-18
Lang: ITA

Gehlhaar, Rolf, 1943-
See no. 392.

400 Genzmer, Harald, 1909-
Date: 11/82
Intvr: Weis, Günther
Topic: Educational materials; Hin-
demith, Paul, 1895-1963; Teach-
ing
List: Y
Biog: N
Source: VALENTIN H "Gespräch mit
Harald Genzmer." pp. 27-40
Lang: GER

401 Ghatham, Rhys
Intvr: Anderson, Beth
Topic: Style (Individual)
List: N
Biog: N
Source: EAR "Interview with Rhys
Ghatham." 2/7 (Nov. 1976): [4-5]
Lang: ENG

402 Gideon, Miriam, 1906-
Date: 4/76, N.Y.
Intvr: Rosenberg, Bernard; Rosenberg,
Deena
Topic: Careers in music; Composers–
Social conditions

Works: Fantasy on Irish folk motives;
The hound of heaven; Of shad-
ows numberless; Sinfonia brevis;
Songs of youth and madness
List: N
Biog: N
Source: ROSEN M, pp. 61-69
Lang: ENG

403 Gifford, Helen Margaret, 1935-
Date: 6/10/81
Intvr: Stevens, Lynne
Topic: Creative process; Style (Indi-
vidual)
List: N
Biog: N
Source: NMA "Helen Gifford: An inter-
view." 4 (1985): 35-37
Lang: ENG

404 Glass, Philip, 1937-
Date: 11/23/75, London, England
Intvr: Potter, Keith; Smith, Dave
Topic: Concerts & recitals–20th-century
music; Creative process
Works: Einstein on the beach; Music in
eight parts; Music in twelve parts;
Piece in the shape of a square
List: N
Biog: N
Source: CONTACT "Interview with
Philip Glass." 13 (Spr. 1976):
25-30
Lang: ENG

405 Glass, Philip, 1937-
Intvr: Zimmermann, Walter
Topic: Composers–Relations with performers; Form; Harmony; Performance practice

Works: Music in twelve parts; Music with changing parts
List: N
Biog: N
Source: ZIMMER D, pp. 103-16
Lang: ENG

406 Glass, Philip, 1937-
Intvr: Palmer, Robert
Topic: Popular music; Style (Individual)
List: N
Biog: N
Source: NYT "Philip Glass comes to Carnegie Hall–at last." 28 May 1978, sec. 2, pp. 13, 15
Lang: ENG

407 Glass, Philip, 1937-
Intvr: Cooper, Michael
Works: Satyagraha
List: N
Biog: N
Source: EAR "An exclusive interview with Philip Glass and Constance de Jong. Concerning their new opera: Satyagraha." 5/3 (Nov.-Dec. 1979): 3-5
Lang: ENG
Notes: Reprinted in *Feedback Papers* 19 (Feb. 1980): 2-5.

408 Glass, Philip, 1937-
Date: 3/30/80, Toronto, Canada
Intvr: Gibson, Jon, et al.
Topic: Composition–Technique; Popular music; 20th-century music; Vocal music
Works: North star; Satyagraha
List: N
Biog: N

Source: MUSWORKS "A talk with Philip Glass, edited by Andrew Timar, transcribed by Miguel Frasconi." 13 (Fall 1980): 10-12, 20-28
Lang: ENG

409 Glass, Philip, 1937-
Date: 11/13/80, New York City, N.Y.
Intvr: Caras, Tracy; Gagne, Cole
Topic: Composition–Technique; Creative process
Works: Akhnaten; Dance music; Einstein on the beach; Music in fifths; Music in twelve parts; 1 + 1
List: Y
Biog: Y
Source: GAGNE S, pp. 209-29
Lang: ENG

410 Glass, Philip, 1937-
Topic: Computer music; Electronic music; Minimal music; Sound; Style (Individual)
List: N
Biog: N
Source: TW "The new polyphony: Philip Glass & David Borden." 1/16 (1983)
Lang: ENG

411 Glass, Philip, 1937-
Intvr: Diliberto, John
Topic: Composition–Technique; Electronic musical instruments
List: N
Biog: Y
Source: EM "The electro-acoustic world of Philip Glass." 2/10 (Oct. 1986): 35-40
Lang: ENG

412 Glass, Philip, 1937-
Date: 11/86
Intvr: McDonagh, Michael
Topic: Style (Individual)
Works: Akhnaten; Satyagraha
List: N
Biog: Y
Source: OPTION "Philip Glass." N2
(May-June 1987): 62-64, 66
Lang: ENG

413 Glick, Srul Irving, 1934-
Topic: Canada; 20th-century music
Works: Heritage; Symphony, no. 2
List: Y
Biog: Y
Source: MUSCAN "Srul Irving Glick, a
portrait." 5 (Oct. 1967): [8-9]
Lang: ENG, FRE

414 Goebel, Johannes, 1949-
Date: 5/31/84, Cologne, Germany
Intvr: Barlow, Klarenz
Topic: Electronic music studios
List: N
Biog: N
Source: MUSTEXTE "Willkommen
in BYTEschland! ...." 6 (Oct.
1984): 36-37
Lang: GER

415 Goehr, Alexander, 1932-
Intvr: Schafer, Raymond Murray
Topic: Composition–Technique; Philos-
ophy & aesthetics; Serialism
List: N
Biog: Y
Source: SCHAFER B, pp. 162-72
Lang: ENG

416 Goehr, Alexander, 1932-
Intvr: Dawney, Michael
Topic: Teaching
List: N
Biog: N
Source: COMP(LONDON) "The com-
poser speaks–3. Alexander
Goehr." 46 (Wint. 1972-73):
11-13
Lang: ENG

417 Goehr, Alexander, 1932-
Intvr: Northcott, Bayan
Topic: Composers–Influences; Eisler,
Hanns, 1898-1962; Indian music
Works: The deluge
List: Y
Biog: Y
Source: NORTH M "Interview I: To-
wards the little symphony." pp.
9-16
Lang: ENG

418 Goehr, Alexander, 1932-
Intvr: Northcott, Bayan
Topic: Choral music; Composers–Influ-
ences; Serialism
Works: Sutter's gold
List: Y
Biog: Y
Source: NORTH M "Interview II: To-
wards Babylon." pp. 104-7
Lang: ENG

419 Goehr, Alexander, 1932-
Intvr: Schiffer, Brigitte
Topic: Education–China
List: N
Biog: Y

Source: NZ "Auslandsjournal: ... Die Folgen der Kulturrevolution. Interview mit Alexander Goehr über seine Lehrtätigkeit in China." 142/2 (Mar.-Apr. 1981): 155-57
Lang: GER

420 Goehr, Alexander, 1932-
Intvr: Griffiths, Paul
Topic: Composition–Technique; Creative process
Works: Little symphony
List: Y
Biog: Y
Source: GRIFFITHS N, pp. 13-21
Lang: ENG

421 Goeyvaerts, Karel, 1923-
Intvr: Gronemeyer, Gisela; Oehlschlägel, Reinhard
Topic: Creative process; Style (Individual)
Works: Litanie I-V
List: Y
Biog: N
Source: MUSTEXTE "Auf der Suche nach dem Ritus des Menschen: Karel Goeyvaerts im Gespräch über 'Litanie I-V.'" 6 (Oct. 1984): 19-25
Lang: GER

422 Gold, Ernest, 1921-
Intvr: Ulrich, Allan
Topic: Motion picture music; Philosophy & aesthetics
Works: Exodus; It's a mad, mad, mad, mad world; On the beach; Pressure point; The secret of Santa Vittoria

List: N
Biog: N
Source: ULRICH A, pp. 12-18
Lang: ENG

423 Goldmann, Friedrich, 1941-
Date: 5/77
Intvr: Stürzbecher, Ursula
Topic: Composers–Influences; Germany, East (former); Incidental music; Sociology
Works: Symphonies, nos. 1, 2
List: Y
Biog: Y
Source: STURZ K, pp. 28-42
Lang: GER

424 Gould, Morton, 1913-
Topic: Concerts & recitals–20th-century music; Criticism; Electronic music
List: N
Biog: N
Source: M ART "Composers' forum." 1/2 (Apr.-May 1968): 49-56
Lang: ENG
Notes: Conversation with Otto Luening and Ned Rorem.

425 Gould, Morton, 1913-
Intvr: James, Jeff
Topic: American Society of Composers, Authors, and Publishers (ASCAP); Sound recording & reproduction;
List: N
Biog: N
Source: FANFARE "Morton Gould: On the barricades." 10/2 (Nov.-Dec. 1986): 386-94
Lang: ENG

426 Graaff, Huba de, 1959-
Intvr: Baartman, Nicoline
Topic: Composition–Technique; Electronic musical instruments
Works: De slager
List: N
Biog: Y
Source: KN "There is nothing as boring as a modern concert." 24 (1987): 38-40
Lang: ENG

427 Grewin, Christer
Intvr: Johnson, Bengt Emil
Topic: Music & literature; Sound
List: N
Biog: N
Source: NUTIDA "Lyrisk protest och ljudteknik interpretation. Samtal med Christer Grewin." 16/4 (1972-73): 33-35
Lang: SWE

428 Grundman, Clare Ewing, 1913-
List: N
Biog: Y
Source: ACCENT "Meet The Composer: An interview with Clare Grundman." 1/3 (May-June 1976): 25-26
Lang: ENG

429 Gruner, Joachim, 1933-
Date: 1978
Intvr: Stürzbecher, Ursula
Topic: Children, Opera for; Incidental music
Works: Concerto, tuba
List: Y
Biog: Y

Source: STURZ K, pp. 318-30
Lang: GER

430 Guaccero, Domenico, 1927-
Date: 10/17/82, Italy
Intvr: Failla, Salvatore Enrico
Topic: Collage in music; Electronic music; Style (Individual)
List: N
Biog: N
Source: FAILLA M "Intervista a Domenico Guaccero: Le note in teatro diventano Poesia." pp. 95-102
Lang: ITA

Gubaidulina, Sofia Asgatovna, 1931-
See no. 372.

431 Gubaidulina, Sofia Asgatovna, 1931-
Date: 9/4/86, Moscow, USSR (former)
Intvr: Dümling, Albrecht
Topic: Style (Individual); Women composers
List: Y
Biog: N
Source: MUSTEXTE "Auf dem Weg nach innen: Die sowjetische Komponistin Sofia Gubaidulina im Gespräch." 21 (Oct. 1987): 8-11
Lang: GER

432 Gutiérrez Heras, Joaquín, 1927-
Intvr: Saavedra, Leonora
Topic: Cage, John, 1912-1992; Genre; Mexico; Motion picture music; Neoclassicism; Poetry; Polyphony; Serialism; Style (Individual); Tonality; 12-tone system

Works: Remedios varo
List: Y
Biog: Y
Source: ANGELES M, pp. 54-87
Lang: SPA

433 Hakim, Talib Rasul, 1940-1988.
Intvr: Baker, David N., et al.
Topic: Black composers; Composers–
Influences; Composition–Tech-
nique; Performance; Style (Indi-
vidual)
List: Y
Biog: Y
Source: BAKER B, pp. 93-107
Lang: ENG

434 Halffter, Rodolfo, 1900-
Intvr: Angeles González, María
Topic: Composers–Political conditions;
Gruppo de los Ocho; Mexico;
Neo-classicism; Spain; Tonality;
12-tone system
Works: Tientos
List: Y
Biog: N
Source: ANGELES M, pp. 11-35
Lang: SPA

435 Halffter Jiménez, Cristóbal, 1930-
Date: 4/75
Intvr: Mâche, François-Bernard
Topic: Spain
Works: Concerto, violoncello
List: N
Biog: Y
Source: RM "Les mal entendus. Com-
positeurs des années 70." 314-
15 (1978): 71-78
Lang: FRE

436 Halffter Jiménez, Cristóbal, 1930-
Intvr: Acebes, Maria
Topic: Community relations; Educa-
tion; Style (Individual); Tone
color
List: N
Biog: Y
Source: HETEROFONIA "Cristóbal
Halffter un musico de nuestro
tiempo." 24 (May-June 1972):
11-15
Lang: SPA

437 Hall, Ian, 1940-
Intvr: Ofori, Agyare Twumasi-Ankra
Topic: African music
Works: Bloomsbury mass
List: N
Biog: N
Source: BPM "Conversation with .... Ian
Hall: The proud 'African.'" 4
(Fall 1976): 313-19
Lang: ENG

438 Haller, Hans Peter, 1929-
Date: 5/3/84, Freiburg, Switzerland
Intvr: Barlow, Klarenz
Topic: Computers; Electronic music
studios
List: N
Biog: N
Source: MUSTEXTE "Willkommen in
BYTEschland! ...." 6 (Oct. 1984):
35
Lang: GER

439 Hallnäs, Lars
Intvr: Johnson, Bengt Emil
Topic: Composers–20th-century; Nature
List: N

Biog: N
Source: NUTIDA "Musik med ett stort
        streck över .... " 17/3 (1973-
        74): 27-30
Lang: SWE

Hallnäs, Lars
    See no. 246.

440 Hambraeus, Bengt, 1928-
    Intvr: Stout, Alan
    Topic: Composition–Modern organ
    List: N
    Biog: N
    Source: CM "A conversation between
            Bengt Hambraeus and Alan
            Stout." 7/1 (1972): 40-42
    Lang: ENG

441 Hamel, Peter Michael, 1947-
    Intvr: Timmermann, Tonius
    Topic: Music therapy; Style (Individu-
            al); 20th-century music
    Works: Dharana
    List: N
    Biog: Y
    Source: MUSTEXTE   "Musik durch
            Selbsterfahrung: Gedanken von
            und über den Komponisten Peter
            Michael Hamel." 4 (Apr. 1984):
            14-18
    Lang: GER

442 Hamilton, Iain Ellis, 1922-
    Intvr: Schafer, Raymond Murray
    Topic: Creativity; Form; Style (Indi-
            vidual)
    List: N
    Biog: N
    Source: SCHAFER B, pp. 155-61
    Lang: ENG

443 Hanson, Howard, 1896-1981.
    Intvr: Williams, David Russell
    List: N
    Biog: N
    Source: PNM   "Howard Hanson." 20
            (Fall 1981-Sum. 1982): 12-25
    Lang: ENG

444 Hanson, Sten, 1936-
    Date: 2/18/81
    Intvr: Zapf, Donna
    Topic: Music & art; Poetry
    List: N
    Biog: N
    Source: MUSWORKS   "Sten Hansen's
            [sic] meta music." 15 (1981):
            14-16
    Lang: ENG

445 Harris, Roy, 1898-1979.
    Intvr: Bernheimer, Martin
    Topic: Experimental music
    Works: Symphony, no. 11
    List: N
    Biog: N
    Source: NYT "Harris has no patience
            with fashionable phoniness." 4
            Feb. 1968, sec. 3, p. 21
    Lang: ENG

446 Harris, Theodore, 1912-
    Date: N.Y.
    Intvr: Grobel, Lawrence
    Topic: Opera
    Works: The first President
    List: N
    Biog: N
    Source: NYT "Composer with patience."
            23 Sept. 1973, sec. 1, p. 110
    Lang: ENG

447 Harrison, Lou, 1917-
Date: Sum/73, Calif.
Intvr: Leyland, Winston
Topic: Composers–Influences; Creativity; Homosexuality; Language
Works: Peace pieces; Young Caesar
List: N
Biog: N
Source: GARLAND L "Winston Leyland interviews Lou Harrison." pp. 70-84
Lang: ENG
Notes: William Colvig also participated in the interview. Originally published in *Gay Sunshine Journal* 23 (Nov. 1974).

448 Harrison, Lou, 1917-
Date: 4/28/79, Toronto, Canada
Intvr: Crawford, Christopher, et al.
Topic: Culture; Temperament
List: N
Biog: N
Source: MUSWORKS "Interview with Lou Harrison." 9 (Fall 1979): 3-6
Lang: ENG

449 Harrison, Lou, 1917-
Date: Fall/84, Paris, France
Intvr: Simon, Larry
Topic: Motion picture music
List: N
Biog: N
Source: EAR "Interview with Lou Harrison." 9/5-10/1 (Fall 1985): 18, 36
Lang: ENG

450 Harrison, Lou, 1917-
Intvr: Doty, David B.
Topic: Composition–Technique; Gamelan; Just intonation; Tuning
List: N
Biog: N
Source: ONE "The Lou Harrison interview with David B. Doty." 3/2 (Spr. 1987): 1-2, 4-15
Lang: ENG

451 Hartmann, Karl Amadeus, 1905-1963.
Intvr: Lewinski, Wolf-Eberhard von
Topic: Creative process; Genre
List: N
Biog: N
Source: MELOS "Das letzte Gespräch mit Karl Amadeus Hartmann." 31/1 (Jan. 1964): 12-15
Lang: GER

452 Harvey, Jonathan Dean, 1939-
Topic: Center for Computer Research in Music and Acoustics (CCRMA); Computers; Electro-acoustics; Institut de Recherche et de Coordination Acoustique-Musique (IRCAM)
List: N
Biog: N
Source: TW "The science of sound: IRCAM & John Chowning/ CCRMA." 2/8 (1985)
Lang: ENG

453 Harvey, Jonathan Dean, 1939-
Intvr: Griffiths, Paul
Topic: Composers–Influences; Creativity
List: Y

Biog: Y
Source: GRIFFITHS N, pp. 46-53
Lang: ENG

454 Hassell, John Marshall, 1937-
Topic: Electronic music; Gamelan
List: N
Biog: N
Source: TW "Trans-world synthesis. Part 1: John Hassell & Eberhard Schoener." 2/5 (1985)
Lang: ENG

455 Hauk, Günter, 1932-
Date: 5/31/67
Intvr: Grabs, Manfred
Topic: Composition–Technique; Eisler, Hanns, 1898-1962; Teaching
Works: Verwandlungen
List: Y
Biog: N
Source: GRABS H "Interviews mit Eisler-Schülern." pp. 203-7
Lang: GER

456 Haupt, Walter
Intvr: Lohmüller, Helmut
Topic: Experimental music; Incidental music
List: N
Biog: N
Source: MELOS "Ich traf Walter Haupt." 41/4 (1974): 204-7
Lang: GER

457 Hayman, Richard Perry, 1951-
Intvr: Monahan, Gordon
Topic: Experimental music; Performance practice
Works: Dreamsound

List: N
Biog: N
Source: MUSWORKS "Sound asleep: Dreaming of music." 38 (Spr. 1987): 24-26
Lang: ENG

458 Headington, Christopher, 1930-
Intvr: Barfoot, Terry
Topic: Composers–Social conditions
List: N
Biog: Y
Source: BMSJ "Christopher Headington–interview." 4 (1982): 12-18
Lang: ENG

459 Hein, Folkmar
Date: 5/10/84, Berlin, Germany
Intvr: Barlow, Klarenz
Topic: Computer music
List: N
Biog: N
Source: MUSTEXTE "Willkommen in BYTEschland! ...." 6 (Oct. 1984): 36
Lang: GER

Heller, Barbara
  See **Heller-Reichenbach, Barbara, 1936-**.

460 Heller-Reichenbach, Barbara, 1936-
Date: 7/3/86, Cologne, Germany
Intvr: Barlow, Klarenz
Topic: Careers in music; Women composers
Works: Tagebuchblätter
List: N
Biog: Y
Source: SONNTAG A, v. 1, pp. 7-16
Lang: GER

Henkemans, Hans, 1913-
See no. 38.

461 Henry, Pierre, 1927-
Topic: Composition–Technique; Electro-
acoustics; France–20th-century;
Musique concrète; Philosophy
& aesthetics
Works: Futurestique ('For the inaugura-
tion of the main room'); Les
voyages
List: N
Biog: N
Source: TW "French musique concrète:
Pierre Schaeffer & Pierre Henry."
2/3 (1985)
Lang: ENG

462 Henry, Pierre, 1927-
Intvr: Diliberto, John
Topic: Electronic music; Sound
List: N
Biog: N
Source: EM "Pierre Schaeffer & Pierre
Henry: Pioneers in sampling."
2/12 (Dec. 1986): 54-59, 72
Lang: ENG
Notes: Pierre Schaeffer also participat-
ed in the interview.

463 Henze, Hans Werner, 1926-
Date: 1965
Intvr: Geitel, Klaus
Topic: Opera buffa
Works: Der junge Lord
List: Y
Biog: Y
Source: BROCK H "Der Einzelgänger
(1965)." pp. 111-14
Lang: GER

Notes: Previously published in "Mit-
telpunkt des Werks: Der Einzelgänger," *Die Welt* 78 (2 Apr.
1965).

464 Henze, Hans Werner, 1926-
Date: 1966, Salzburg, Austria
Intvr: Geitel, Klaus
Topic: Composition–Technique
Works: Bassariden
List: Y
Biog: Y
Source: BROCK H "Tradition und Kul-
turerbe (1966)." pp. 114-17
Lang: GER
Notes: Previously published in "Henzes
Bekenntnis zur Tradition," *Die
Welt* (13 July 1966).

465 Henze, Hans Werner, 1926-
Date: 1966
Intvr: Georges, Horst
Topic: Music & psychology; Opera
Works: Bassariden
List: N
Biog: N
Source: BROCK H "Tiefenpsychologie
in der Musik." pp. 118-22
Lang: GER
Notes: Previously published in "In
jedem Menschen Leben ein
Pentheus und ein Dionysos,"
*Opern-Journal der Deutschen
Oper Berlin* (Sept. 1966).

466 Henze, Hans Werner, 1926-
Date: 8/67
Intvr: Pinzauti, Leonardo
Topic: Music & politics; 20th-century
music

List: N
Biog: N
Source: PINZAUTI M, pp. 19-28
Lang: ITA
Notes: Previouly published in *Nuova Rivista Musicale Italiana* 1/2 (July-Aug. 1967): 359-66.

467 Henze, Hans Werner, 1926-
Date: 1967
Intvr: Lewinski, Wolf-Eberhard von
Topic: Opera; Style (Individual)
List: N
Biog: N
Source: MELOS "Zwanzig Fragen an Hans Werner Henze." 34/11 (Nov. 1967): 395-99
Lang: GER
Notes: Also published in *Hans Werner Henze: Musik und Politik* (München: Deutscher Taschenbuch Verlag, 1984), pp. 122-26.

468 Henze, Hans Werner, 1926-
Date: 1969
Intvr: Makowsky, J. A.
Topic: Community relations; Composers–Political conditions; Composers–Social conditions; Philosophy & aesthetics; Socialism; Symphony–Orchestration
Works: Floss der Medusa
List: N
Biog: N
Source: BROCK H "Musik ist nolens volens politisch." pp. 136-43
Lang: GER
Notes: Also published in *Züricher Student* (June 1969); Italian translation in *Musica e Politica* (Venezia:

La Biennale di Venezia, 1977), pp. 485-89.

469 Henze, Hans Werner, 1926-
Date: 9/28/70; 9/30/70, Berlin, Germany; 10/10/70, Marino, Italy
Intvr: Pauli, Hansjörg
Topic: Collaborators in music; Composers–Political conditions; Music & politics; Philosophy & aesthetics; Socialism; Style (Individual)
Works: El Cimarrón
List: N
Biog: N
Source: BROCK H "Die Krise des bürgerlichen Künstlers ...." pp. 149-55
Lang: GER
Notes: Previously published in *Für Wen Komponieren Sie Eigentlich?* (Frankfurt am Main: S. Fischer, 1971), pp. 60-82. Originally done for a series of radio programs on Hessischer Rundfunk Frankfurt.

470 Henze, Hans Werner, 1926-
Date: 1971
Intvr: Lück, Hartmut
Topic: Music & politics
Works: El Cimarrón; Symphony, no. 6
List: N
Biog: N
Source: BROCK H "Aufgaben und Möglichkeiten revolutionärer Musik." pp. 165-72
Lang: GER
Notes: Previously published in *Neue Musikzeitung* 20/1 (Feb.-Mar. 1971).

471 Henze, Hans Werner, 1926-
Date: 1971
Intvr: Lück, Hartmut
Topic: Cuba
List: N
Biog: N
Source: BROCK H "Musikleben in Kuba." pp. 172-75
Lang: GER
Notes: Previously published in *Neue Musikzeitung* 20/1 (Feb.-Mar. 1971).

472 Henze, Hans Werner, 1926-
Date: 1971
Intvr: Stürzbecher, Ursula
Topic: Composition–Technique; Cuba; Music & politics
Works: Symphony, no. 6
List: N
Biog: N
Source: BROCK H "Werkstattgespräch." pp. 175-81
Lang: GER
Notes: First published in *Werkstattgespräche mit Komponisten* (Köln: Musikverlag Hans Gerig, 1971).

473 Henze, Hans Werner, 1926-
Intvr: Peyser, Joan
Topic: Germany, West (former)–20th-century; Socialism
Works: The tedious journey to the flat of Natasha Ungeheuer
List: N
Biog: N
Source: NYT "Henze: Where the 'action' music is." 16 July 1972, sec. 2, p. 11
Lang: ENG

474 Henze, Hans Werner, 1926-
Date: 1972
Intvr: Jungheinrich, Hans-Klaus
Topic: Opera; Socialism
Works: El Cimarrón; Show
List: N
Biog: N
Source: BROCK H "Musica impura–Musik als Sprache." pp. 190-99
Lang: GER
Notes: Previously published in *Melos* 39/4 (1972).

475 Henze, Hans Werner, 1926-
Date: 1973
Topic: Music & politics
List: N
Biog: N
Source: BROCK H "Die DKP–die Hauptaufgaben fortschrittlicher Musiker." pp. 205-7
Lang: GER
Notes: Previously published in *Rhythmus* 1 (1973).

476 Henze, Hans Werner, 1926-
Date: 1975
Intvr: Schultz, Klaus
Topic: Music & literature
Works: Bassariden
List: N
Biog: N
Source: BROCK H "Komponist als Interpret–gegen die 'Material-Disziplin.'" pp. 244-52
Lang: GER
Notes: Previously published in *Frankfurter Opernhefte* (10 May 1975).

477 Henze, Hans Werner, 1926-
Date: 1980
Intvr: Kolland, Hubert
Topic: Composers–Political conditions;
         Opera; 20th-century music–Style
List: N
Biog: N
Source: BROCK H "Die Schwierigkeit,
         ein bundesdeutscher Komponist
         zu sein: Neue Musik zwischen
         Isolierung und Engagement."
         pp. 300-31
Lang: GER
Notes: Previously published in *Das
         Argument,* Sonderband 42
         (1980).

478 Henze, Hans Werner, 1926-
Intvr: Bachmann, Claus-Henning
Topic: Philosophy & aesthetics; Sound
Works: Symphony, no. 7
List: N
Biog: N
Source: NZ "Komponieren heute: 'Ich
         wollte gern, das es mir einmal
         glückt ....' Notizen über und
         ein Gespräch mit Hans Werner
         Henze anlässlich der Urauf-
         führung seiner siebten Sin-
         fonie ...." 146/3 (Mar. 1985).
         24-27
Lang: GER

479 Henze, Hans Werner, 1926-
Date: 4/86; 9/86
Intvr: Rexroth, Dieter
Topic: Arts & politics; Death; Sociology
Works: Orpheus
List: N
Biog: N

Source: REX K "Ich kann mich in Zusam-
         menhängen sehen. Aus einem
         Gespräch." pp. 315-21
Lang: GER

480 Henze, Hans Werner, 1926-
Intvr: Hübner, Ursula
Topic: Composers as conductors; Phi-
         losophy & aesthetics; Program
         music
List: N
Biog: N
Source: MUSICA "Das Interview: Hans
         Werner Henze im Gespräch mit
         Ursula Hübner." 40 (July-Aug.
         1986): 339-42
Lang: GER

481 Henze, Hans Werner, 1926-
Intvr: Strasfogel, Ian
Topic: Opera; Style (Individual)
Works: English cat
List: Y
Biog: Y
Source: REX K "All knowing music: A
         dialogue on opera. Hans Werner
         Henze and Ian Strasfogel." pp.
         137-42
Lang: ENG

482 Henze, Hans Werner, 1926-
Date: 1986
Intvr: Rexroth, Dieter
Topic: Composers–Social conditions;
         Serial music
List: N
Biog: Y
Source: NZ "Komponieren heute: 'Ich
         begreife mich in der Schönberg-
         Tradition'–Hans Werner Henze

im Gespräch." 147/11 (Nov. 1986): 23-28

Lang: GER

483 Hespos, Hans-Joachim, 1938-
Intvr: Krellmann, Hanspeter
Topic: Composition–Technique
Works: Interactions
List: N
Biog: N
Source: MELOS "Ich sprach mit Hans-Joachim Hespos." 41/3 (May-June 1974): 140-43
Lang: GER

484 Hespos, Hans-Joachim, 1938-
Intvr: Krellmann, Hanspeter
Topic: Notation; Philosophy & aesthetics
List: N
Biog: N
Source: MUSICA "Stolperdrähte zum Neu-anderen. Gespräch mit dem Komponisten Hans-Joachim Hespos." 30 (May-June 1976): 212-15
Lang: GER

485 Hespos, Hans-Joachim, 1938-
Date: 6/20/77, Delmenhorst, Germany
Intvr: Oehlschlägel, Reinhard
Topic: Creative process; Form
List: N
Biog: N
Source: MUSTEXTE "Ich komponiere mit der eigenen Überraschung." 8 (Feb. 1985): 27-34
Lang: GER

486 Hétu, Jacques, 1938-
Topic: Canada
List: Y
Biog: Y
Source: MUSCAN "Jacques Hétu, a portrait." 27 (Mar. 1970): [8-9]
Lang: ENG, FRE

487 Hiller, Lejaren Arthur, 1924-
Date: 6/20/68, Urbana, Ill.
Intvr: Austin, Larry
Topic: Computer music; Computers
Works: HPSCHD
List: N
Biog: N
Source: SOURCE "John Cage, Lejaren Hiller: HPSCHD." 2/2 (July 1968): 14-19
Lang: ENG

488 Hiller, Lejaren Arthur, 1924-
Date: 5/25/80, Buffalo, N.Y.
Intvr: Caras, Tracy; Gagne, Cole
Topic: Composition–Technique
List: Y
Biog: Y
Source: GAGNE S, pp. 231-48
Lang: ENG

489 Hindemith, Paul, 1895-1963.
Date: 3/30/49, N.Y.
Topic: Germany
List: N
Biog: N
Source: NYT "P. Hindemith views on musical decline." 31 Mar. 1949, sec. 1, p. 31
Lang: ENG

490 Hobbs, Christopher, 1950-
Date: 1971
Intvr: Evans, Peter; West, Poter
Topic: Experimental music; Scratch Orchestras
List: N
Biog: N
Source: CONTACT "Interview with Christopher Hobbs." 3 (Fall 1971): 17-23
Lang: ENG

491 Höller, York, 1944-
Intvr: Conen, Hermann
Topic: Electronic music; Theory
Works: Gestaltkomposition
List: N
Biog: N
Source: CONTRECHAMPS "Entretien avec York Höller." 3 (Sept. 1984): 50-56
Lang: FRE
Notes: English translation published in *Tempo* 152 (Mar. 1985): 2-6.

492 Hoffmann, Niels Frédéric, 1943-
Intvr: Krellmann, Hanspeter
Topic: Composers–Social conditions; Philosophy & aesthetics
List: N
Biog: N
Source: MUSICA "Auf der Suche nach einem neuen Verständnis von Musik. Gespräch mit dem Komponisten Niels Frédéric Hoffmann." 30 (July-Aug. 1976): 295-300
Lang: GER

493 Hoffmann, Niels Frédéric, 1943-
Intvr: Wolff, Jochem
Topic: Collaborators in music; Composers–Political conditions; Composers–20th-century; Creative process; Operas; Philosophy & aesthetics; Style (Individual)
Works: Das grosse Schlachten; Die Piratinnen; Der Wert des Scheins
List: N
Biog: N
Source: JUNG L "Ich denke sehr an ein Publikum," pp. 84-95
Lang: GER

494 Holewa, Hans, 1905-
Intvr: Rying, Matts
Topic: Legends & myths; 12-tone system
Works: Apollos förvandling
List: N
Biog: N
Source: NUTIDA "Fäst Orfeus lyra uppå himmelen." 18/2 (1974-75): 26-29
Lang: SWE

495 Hollingsworth, Stanley, 1924-
Date: 2/57
Intvr: Land, Barbara
Topic: Television opera
Works: La grande bretèche
List: N
Biog: N
Source: NYT "Composer serious about TV music." 10 Feb. 1957, sec. 2, p. 11
Lang: ENG

496 Holloway, Robin, 1943-
Intvr: Griffiths, Paul
Topic: Creative process
Works: Clarissa; Concerto for orchestra, no. 1; Scenes from Schumann
List: Y
Biog: Y
Source: GRIFFITHS N, pp. 113-24
Lang: ENG

497 Honegger, Arthur, 1892-1955.
Intvr: Gavoty, Bernard
Topic: Composers, French; Creativity
List: N
Biog: N
Source: RUFER B "Arthur Honegger." pp. 271-77
Lang: GER

498 Hoover, Katherine, 1937-
Intvr: Grimes, Ev
Topic: Performance practice; Philosophy & aesthetics; Teaching
List: N
Biog: Y
Source: EAR "Meet The Composer: Katherine Hoover." 11/4 (Dec.-Jan. 1986-87): 20-22
Lang: ENG

499 Hopkins, Kenyon
Intvr: Bachmann, Gideon
Topic: Motion picture music
Works: Baby doll; The strange one; Twelve angry men
List: N
Biog: N
Source: FTM "Composing for films: Kenyon Hopkins interviewed by Gideon Bachmann." 16 (Sum. 1957): 15-16
Lang: ENG

500 Horovitz, Joseph, 1926-
Intvr: Gregson, Edward
Topic: Analysis; Brass band music
Works: Concerto, euphonium; Sinfonietta
List: N
Biog: N
Source: SBC "The composer speaks." 1/3 (1972): 73-75
Lang: ENG

501 Hovhaness, Alan Scott, 1911-
Intvr: Westbrook, Peter
Topic: Composition–Influences; Composition–Technique; Oriental music
Works: Symphonies, no. 3, no. 8 ("Arjuna"), no. 9 ("St. Vartan")
List: N
Biog: Y
Source: DB "Angelic cycles." 49/3 (Mar. 1982): 27-29
Lang: ENG

502 Hovhaness, Alan Scott, 1911-
Date: 1984
Intvr: Gillespie, Don Chance; Morrow, Charlie
Topic: Performance; Style (Individual)
List: N
Biog: N
Source: EAR "Interview with Alan Hovhaness." 9/2 (July-Aug. 1984): 6-7
Lang: ENG

503 Hovhaness, Alan Scott, 1911-
Intvr: Page, Tim
Topic: Philosophy & aesthetics
Works: Symphony, no. 61 ("Mount St. Helens")
List: N
Biog: N
Source: NYT "Alan Hovhaness offers his 61st symphony." 3 Aug. 1986, sec. 1, p. 52
Lang: ENG
Notes: The interview was conducted by telephone.

504 Howells, Herbert, 1892-1983.
Intvr: Palmer, Christopher
Topic: Composers–Influences
List: Y
Biog: N
Source: PALMER H "1. Autobiographical notes." pp. 11-17
Lang: ENG

505 Hübler, Klaus, 1924-
Intvr: Nyffeler, Max
Topic: Instrumental music; Philosophy & aesthetics
List: N
Biog: N
Source: MUSTEXTE "Bis das Instrument seinen Geist offenbart: Klaus K. Hübler im Gespräch." 20 (July Aug. 1987): 4-7
Lang: GER

506 Hummel, Franz, 1939-
Intvr: Schneider, Norbert Jürgen
Topic: Style (Individual)
List: Y
Biog: N

Source: MUSTEXTE "Zeige deine Wunde: Franz Hummel im Gespräch." 19 (Apr. 1987): 23-24
Lang: GER

507 Hykes, David Bond, 1953-
Intvr: Reinhard, Johnny
Topic: Harmonic choir; Philosophy & aesthetics; Singing
List: N
Biog: N
Source: EAR "An interview with David Hykes." 7/5 (Nov.-Jan. 1982-83): 22
Lang: ENG

508 Ibarra Groth, Federico, 1946-
Date: Fall/80
Intvr: Angeles González, María
Topic: Art–Influences; Careers in music; Composers–Relations with audiences; Incidental music; Legends & myths; Mexico; Music & literature; Nationalism; Painting; Poetry; Style (Individual); Tonality; 20th-century music–Influences
Works: Cantatas, nos. 1-6; Cinco misterios Eleúicos; Concerto, piano
List: Y
Biog: N
Source: ANGELES M, pp. 175-205
Lang: SPA

509 Ireland, John, 1879-1962.
Intvr: Schafer, Raymond Murray
Topic: Composers, English–20th-century
List: N

Biog: Y
Source: SCHAFER B, pp. 24-35
Lang: ENG

510 Jacob, Gordon, 1895-1984.
Intvr: Gregson, Edward
Topic: Brass band music; Performance; Symphony
Works: Rhapsody for piano
List: N
Biog: N
Source: SBC "The composer speaks." 1/2 (1972): 41-42, 63
Lang: ENG

511 Jacob, Gordon, 1895-1984.
Date: 7/82, Essex, England
Intvr: Foreman, Lewis
Topic: Community relations
List: N
Biog: Y
Source: BMSJ "Gordon Jacob in interview." 7 (Oct. 1985): 59-67
Lang: ENG

512 Joachim, Otto, 1910-
Topic: Composers–Economic conditions; 20th-century music
List: Y
Biog: Y
Source: MUSCAN "Otto Joachim, a portrait." 20 (June 1969): [10-11]
Lang: ENG, FRE

513 Johanson, Sven-Eric, 1919-
Intvr: Nordwall, Ove
Topic: Composers–Relations with audiences; Opera
Works: Kunskapens vin
List: N

Biog: N
Source: NUTIDA "Åtta svar på nio fragor." 8/3-4 (1964-65): 116-20
Lang: SWE

Johnson, Bengt Emil, 1936-
See no.106

514 Johnson, Bengt Emil, 1936-
Date: 4/84
Intvr: Morrow, Charlie
Topic: Radio broadcasting–Sweden
List: N
Biog: N
Source: EAR "Interviews by Charlie Morrow." 9/1 (May-June 1984): 34, 36
Lang: ENG

515 Johnson, Robert Sherlaw, 1932-
Date: 5/72, Oxford, England
Intvr: Dawney, Michael
Topic: Electronic music; Mass; Messiaen, Olivier, 1908-1992
Works: Asterogenesis; Carmina vernalia; Christus resurgens; Festival mass for Easter; Green whispers of gold; Sonata, piano, no. 2
List: Y
Biog: N
Source: COMP(LONDON) "The composer speaks–4. Robert Sherlaw Johnson: In conversation with Michael Dawney." 49 (Fall 1973): 7-10
Lang: ENG

516 Johnston, Benjamin Burwell, 1926-
Intvr: Zimmermann, Walter
Topic: Just intonation; Partch, Harry, 1901-1974

List: N
Biog: N
Source: ZIMMER D "Ben Johnston about Harry Partch." pp. 347-71
Lang: ENG

517 Johnston, Benjamin Burwell, 1926-
Date: 2/3/80, New York City, N.Y.
Intvr: Caras, Tracy; Gagne, Cole
Topic: Performance practice
Works: Carmilla; Nine variations; Quintet for groups; Sonata for microtonal piano; Two sonnets of Shakespeare; Visions and spells; The wooden bird
List: Y
Biog: Y
Source: GAGNE S, pp. 249-67
Lang: ENG

518 Jolas, Betsy, 1926-
Intvr: Peyser, Joan
Topic: Sexism; Women composers
List: N
Biog: N
Source: NYT "Why can't a woman compose like a man?" 17 June 1973, sec. 2, pp. 17, 34
Lang: ENG
Notes: Barbara Kolb also participated in the interview.

519 Jolas, Betsy, 1926-
Intvr: Henahan, Donal
List: N
Biog: N
Source: NYT "Betsy Jolas winning recognition in U. S." 30 Aug. 1976, sec. 1, p. 15
Lang: ENG

520 Jolas, Betsy, 1926-
Intvr: Pulido, Esperanza
Topic: France; Teaching; Women composers
List: N
Biog: N
Source: HETEROFONIA "Con Betsy Jolas en Paris." 63 (Nov.-Dec. 1978): 7-10
Lang: SPA

521 Jolivet, André, 1905-1974.
Intvr: Cadieu, Martine
List: N
Biog: N
Source: TEMPO "A conversation with André Jolivet." 59 (Fall 1961): 2-4
Lang: ENG
Notes: Previously published in *Les Nouvelles Littéraires* (1961).

522 Kaan, Fred
Date: 6/10/80, Princeton, N.J.
Intvr: Eskew, Harry Lee
Topic: Hymns
List: N
Biog: Y
Source: HYMN "An interview with Fred Kaan." 31 (Oct. 1980): 226-30
Lang: ENG

523 Kabalevsky, Dmitry Borisovich, 1904-1987.
Intvr: Frankel, Max
Works: Symphony, no. 4
List: N
Biog: N
Source: NYT "Optimistic Russian: Kabalevsky, in speaking of his

fourth symphony, reveals attitude to life." 27 Oct. 1957, sec. 2, p. 9

Lang: ENG

524 Kagel, Mauricio, 1931-
Date: 8/68
Intvr: Schmidt, Felix
Topic: Beethoven, Ludwig van, 1770-1827; Chamber music; Interpretation
Works: Ludwig van
List: N
Biog: N
Source: SCHMIDT T "Beethovens Erbe ist die moralische Aufrüstung." pp. 77-86
Lang: GER
Notes: Previously published in *Der Spiegel* 7 (Sept. 1970).

525 Kagel, Mauricio, 1931-
Date: 10/29/68-10/30/68; 11/1/68, Hamburg, Germany
Intvr: Pauli, Hansjörg
Topic: Community relations; Composers–Relations with audiences; Composers–Relations with performers; Creative process; Motion picture music; Music & politics; Philosophy & aesthetics
Works: Solo; Sur scène
List: N
Biog: Y
Source: PAULI F, pp. 83-105
Lang: GER
Notes: Originally done for a series of radio programs on Hessischer Rundfunk Frankfurt.

526 Kagel, Mauricio, 1931-
Date: 4/14/69, Rome, Italy
Intvr: Pinzauti, Leonardo
Topic: Mozart, Wolfgang Amadeus, 1756-1791; Music & politics; Sociology; Sound; Webern, Anton von, 1883-1945
Works: Der Schall
List: N
Biog: N
Source: PINZAUTI M, pp. 107-18
Lang: ITA
Notes: Previously published in *Nuova Rivista Musicale Italiana* 3 (Mar.-June 1969): 486-95.

527 Kagel, Mauricio, 1931-
Date: 5/71
Intvr: Spingel, Otto
Topic: Opera; Satire in music; Style (Individual)
Works: Staatstheater
List: N
Biog: N
Source: SCHMIDT T "Zu Staatstheater." pp. 89-103
Lang: GER
Notes: Previously published in *Oper* (Sept. 1971).

528 Kagel, Mauricio, 1931-
Intvr: Bosseur, Jean-Yves
Topic: Collaborators in music; Incidental music
List: N
Biog: N
Source: M JEU "Entretien avec Mauricio Kagel: Une introduction au prochain dossier de 'Musique en jeu.'" 5 (1971): 99-106
Lang: FRE

529 Kagel, Mauricio, 1931-
Date: 6/19/72
Topic: Amateur musicians; Composi-
tion–Technique
Works: Programm
List: N
Biog: N
Source: FP "Über Programm: Gespräch
mit Mauricio Kagel." 5 (Jan.
1973): 17-21
Lang: GER
Notes: Also published in *Melos* 40/3
(May-June 1973): 138-42.

530 Kagel, Mauricio, 1931-
Date: 1/73-2/73, East Asia; Greece
Intvr: Vetter, Klaus
Topic: Arts & politics; Audiences–Asia;
Cultural affairs; Culture–Asia;
Culture–Germany, West (former);
India; Iran; Japan; Music & archi-
tecture; Performance; Primitive-
ness
Works: Tactil für drei
List: N
Biog: N
Source: SCHMIDT T "Asien-Report."
pp. 125-93
Lang: GER
Notes: Originally published as the first
article of a discussion series at
the Goethe-Institut, München.

531 Kagel, Mauricio, 1931-
Intvr: Burde, Wolfgang
Topic: Opera; Romanticism
Works: Aus Deutschland
List: N
Biog: N
Source: NZ "'Aus Deutschland'–ein
Gespräch mit Mauricio Kagel

über seine Lieder-Oper." 142/4
(July-Aug. 1981): 366-69
Lang: GER

532 Kagel, Mauricio, 1931-
Intvr: Schöning, Klaus
Topic: Philosophy & aesthetics; Radio
play
List: Y
Biog: Y
Source: SCHONING B, pp. 321-25
Lang: GER

533 Kagel, Mauricio, 1931-
Intvr: Stegemann, Michael
Topic: Style (Individual)
List: N
Biog: N
Source: NZ "NZ-Serie: Komponieren
heute. 'Aus Deutschland' ...?!
Ein Gespräch mit Mauricio
Kagel." 144/9 (Sept. 1983): 18-21
Lang: GER

534 Kagel, Mauricio, 1931-
Intvr: Klüppelholz, Werner
Topic: Audiences–20th century music;
Philosophy & aesthetics; Schools
of music–Germany; Teaching
List: N
Biog: N
Source: KLUP W, pp. 58-65
Lang: GER

535 Kagel, Mauricio, 1931-
Intvr: Schmidt, Felix
Topic: Composers–Influences; Composers–Relations with performers; Criticism; 19th-century
music–Influences; Philosophy
& aesthetics; Style (Individual)

List: N
Biog: N
Source: SCHMIDT M, pp. 189-204
Lang: GER

536 Kagel, Mauricio, 1931-
Intvr: Varga, Bálint András
Topic: Style (Individual)
List: N
Biog: N
Source: NZ "Komponieren heute: Musik
         hören ist Geschichte hören. Ein
         Gespräch mit Mauricio Kagel."
         146/6 (June 1985): 20-24
Lang: GER

537 Karkoschka, Erhard, 1923-
Date: 4/26/84, Stuttgart, Germany
Intvr: Barlow, Klarenz
Topic: Computers
List: N
Biog: N
Source: MUSTEXTE "Willkommen in
         BYTEschland! ...." 6 (Oct. 1984):
         31-32
Lang: GER

538 Kasemets, Udo, 1919-
List: Y
Biog: Y
Source: MUSCAN "Udo Kasemets, a
         portrait." 22 (Sept. 1969): [8-9]
Lang: ENG, FRE

539 Kasilag, Lucrecia R., 1918-
Intvr: Samson, Helen F.
List: Y
Biog: N
Source: SAMSON C, pp. 86-99
Lang: ENG

540 Katzer, Georg, 1935-
Date: 7/77
Intvr: Stürzbecher, Ursula
Topic: Children, Opera for; Composi-
         tion–Technique; Eisler, Hanns,
         1898-1962; Electronic music
Works: Baukasten; Bum-Bum; Szene
         für Kammerensemble
List: Y
Biog: Y
Source: STURZ K, pp. 173-93
Lang: GER

541 Kay, Ulysses Simpson, 1917-
Intvr: Baker, David N., et al.
Topic: Black composers; Composers–
         Influences; Composition–Tech-
         nique; Performance; Style (Indi-
         vidual)
List: Y
Biog: Y
Source: BAKER B, pp. 139-71
Lang: ENG

542 Kelemen, Milko, 1924-
Intvr: Prieberg, Fred K.
Topic: Composers–Social conditions;
         Opera
Works: Belagerungszustand
List: N
Biog: N
Source: MELOS "Zwanzig Fragen an
         Milko Keleman." 4/2 (Mar.-
         Apr. 1974): 65-71
Lang: GER

543 Kelemen, Milko, 1924-
Intvr: Kaiser, Joachim
Topic: Careers in music; Composition–
         Technique; Music & psychol-
         ogy; Opera

Works: Apocalyptica; L'état
List: N
Biog: N
Source: KELEMEN L "Entretien de Joachim Kaiser avec Milko Kelemen." pp. 9-26
Lang: FRE

544 Keller, Alfred, 1907-
Date: 11/73
Intvr: Smith, Joan Allen
Topic: Schoenberg, Arnold, 1874-1951; 12-tone system
List: N
Biog: N
Source: SMITH S, pp. 227-33
Lang: ENG
Notes: Hans Curjel, administrator, and Erich Schmid also participated in the interview.

545 Kenins, Talivaldis, 1919-
Topic: Composers–Economic conditions; 20th-century music
List: Y
Biog: Y
Source: MUSCAN "Talivaldis Kenins, a portrait." 18 (Apr. 1969): [8-9]
Lang: ENG, FRE

546 Kessler, Thomas, 1937-
Date: 5/1/84, Basel, Switzerland
Intvr: Barlow, Klarenz
Topic: Computer music
List: N
Biog: N
Source: MUSTEXTE "Willkommen in BYTEschland! ...." 6 (Oct. 1984): 34
Lang: GER

547 Ketting, Otto, 1935-
Intvr: Jurres, André; Wouters, Jos
Topic: Audiences; Pijper, Willem, 1894-1947; 12-tone system
List: N
Biog: Y
Source: WOUTERS F, pp. 78-91
Lang: ENG, GER
Notes: Peter Schat also participated in the interview.

548 Ketting, Otto, 1935-
Topic: Motion picture music
List: N
Biog: N
Source: KN "Composers' voice: A supplementary interview." 3 (June 1976): 62-63
Lang: ENG

549 Ketting, Otto, 1935-
Intvr: Schönberger, Elmer
Topic: Creative process; Motion picture music; Orchestral music
List: N
Biog: N
Source: KN "Otto Ketting, his symphonies, his film music and Dutch musical life." 10 (Dec. 1979): 10-14
Lang: ENG
Notes: Slightly altered version of the interview previously published in the weekly *Vrij Nederland* (31 Mar. 1979).

550 Keuris, Tristan, 1946-
Intvr: Schönberger, Elmer
Topic: Composition–Technique
Works: Serenade for oboe and orchestra; Sinfonia

List: Y
Biog: Y
Source: KN "Tonality reconsidered. Tristan Keuris: 'Strive as you will, after greater diversification it all ends up sounding the same.'" 5 (June 1977): 18-25
Lang: ENG
Notes: Previously published in a summarized form in the weekly *Vrij Nederland.*

551 Keuris, Tristan, 1946-
Intvr: Beer, Roland de
Topic: Composition–Technique; Creative process
Works: Movements
List: Y
Biog: N
Source: KN "Movements by Tristan Keuris–'I must always feel: How the hell did you do that?'" 15 (June 1982): 1-13
Lang: ENG

552 Khachaturian, Aram Ilich, 1903-1978.
Intvr: Henahan, Donal
Topic: Composers as conductors
Works: Symphony, no. 3
List: N
Biog: N
Source: NYT "Khachaturian here to begin tour as a conductor." 17 Jan. 1968, sec. 1, p. 38
Lang: ENG

Khachaturian, Aram Ilich, 1903-1978.
See no. 262.

553 Kim, Earl, 1920-
Date: 5/86
Intvr: Jeon, Mee-Eun
Topic: Composers–Influences; Musicians; Style (Individual); Voice
List: N
Biog: N
Source: SONUS "I am concerned with what is good: An interview with Earl Kim." 7/2 (Spr. 1987): 1-9
Lang: ENG
Notes: Previously published in Korean in *Auditorium* (Seoul, Korea), Nov. 1986.

554 Kirchner, Leon, 1919-
Intvr: Peyser, Joan
Works: Lily
List: N
Biog: N
Source: NYT "For him, music is its own compensation." 1 Jan. 1984, sec. 2, pp. 13, 17
Lang: ENG

555 Knussen, Oliver, 1952-
Intvr: Griffiths, Paul
Topic: Children, Music for; Creativity; Sociology
Works: Wild things
List: Y
Biog: Y
Source: GRIFFITHS N, pp. 54-64
Lang: ENG

556 Knussen, Oliver, 1952-
Intvr: Page, Tim
Topic: Berkshire Festival; Festivals
List: N
Biog: N

Source: NYT "A composer at home in Tanglewood." 1 Aug. 1986, sec. 3, p. 3

Lang: ENG

557 Kochan, Günter, 1930-

Date: 2/78

Intvr: Stürzbecher, Ursula

Topic: Audiences; Culture–Germany, East (former); Eisler, Hanns, 1898-1962; Symphony

Works: Symphonies, nos. 1-3

List: Y

Biog: Y

Source: STURZ K, pp. 194-217

Lang: GER

558 Kodály, Zoltán, 1882-1967.

Intvr: Klein, Howard

Topic: Education; 20th-century music

List: N

Biog: N

Source: NYT "Kodály, 82, goes to Dartmouth." 1 Aug. 1965, sec. 2, p. 11

Lang: ENG

559 Koenig, Gottfried Michael, 1926-

Date: 8/25/78, Utrecht, Netherlands

Intvr: Roads, Curtis B.

Topic: Computer music; Computers–Programs

List: N

Biog: Y

Source: CMJ "An interview with Gottfried Michael Koenig." 2/3 (Dec. 1978): 11-15, 29

Lang: ENG

560 Kokkonen, Joonas, 1921-

Date: 1/25/76-10/28/77, Järvenpää, Finland

Intvr: Mäkinen, Timo

Topic: Composition–Technique; Education; Ethnic music; Musicians–Social conditions; Opera; Philosophy & aesthetics; Savonlinnan Oopperajuhlat

List: Y

Biog: N

Source: KOK J

Lang: FIN

Kolb, Barbara, 1939-
See no. 518.

561 Kolb, Barbara, 1939-

Date: 7/27/75, New York City, N.Y.

Intvr: Caras, Tracy; Gagne, Cole

Topic: Creativity

Works: Chansons bas; Solitaire; Soundings; Three place settings; Trobar clus

List: Y

Biog: Y

Source: GAGNE S, pp. 269-79

Lang: ENG

562 Komorous, Rudolf, 1931-

Date: Sum/74

Intvr: Champagne, Jane

Topic: Electronic music; Teaching

List: N

Biog: N

Source: CC "A composer-teacher makes music on the west coast." 94 (Nov. 1974): 4-11

Lang: ENG, FRE

563 Koprowski, Peter Paul, 1947-

Intvr: Kieser, Karen

Topic: Creative process; Philosophy & aesthetics

Works: Canzona; Music for strings, percussion and celesta; Quartet, string
List: N
Biog: Y
Source: MUSCAN "Words about music: A series of ...." 33 (Oct. 1977): 22-23
Lang: ENG, FRE

564 Kotoński, Wlodzimierz, 1925-
Date: 2/74, Mexico
Topic: Poland
List: N
Biog: N
Source: HETEROFONIA "Entrevista a Vladimir Kotonski." 35 (Mar.-Apr. 1974): 16-17
Lang: SPA

565 Kox, Hans, 1930-
Intvr: Jurres, André; Wouters, Jos
Topic: Audiences; Pijper, Willem, 1894-1947; Rhythm; Stravinsky, Igor, 1882-1971
List: N
Biog: Y
Source: WOUTERS F, pp. 60-77
Lang: ENG, GER
Notes: Ton de Leeuw also participated in the interview.

566 Kraft, William, 1923-
Intvr: Wilson, Patrick
Topic: Audiences; Conducting
List: N
Biog: N
Source: S MAG "W. Kraft on conducting, performance, and new music." 37/6 (1986): 18-20, 69, 71
Lang: ENG

567 Krauze, Zygmunt, 1938-
Intvr: Montague, Stephen
Topic: Composers–Social conditions; Composers as performers
List: N
Biog: Y
Source: CONTACT "Interview with Zygmunt Krauze." 19 (Sum. 1978): 8-10
Lang: ENG

568 Krauze, Zygmunt, 1938-
Intvr: Michalski, Grzegorz
Topic: Composition–Technique; Music & literature; Opera
Works: The star
List: N
Biog: N
Source: PM "With Zygmunt Krauze on his opera 'The Star.'" 20/3-4 (1985): 43-51
Lang: ENG, GER

569 Křenek, Ernst, 1900-1991.
Date: 7/70
Intvr: Ogdon, Will
Topic: Opera; Serialism
List: N
Biog: N
Source: PNM "Conversation with Ernst Křenek." 10/2 (Spr.-Sum. 1972): 102-110
Lang: ENG

570 Křenek, Ernst, 1900-1991.
Intvr: Antoniou, Theodore
List: N
Biog: N
Source: MUSICA "Das Interview: Theodore Antoniou im Gespräch

mit Ernst Křenek." 34 (Mar.-Apr.
1980): 145-47
Lang: GER

571 Křenek, Ernst, 1900-1991.
Intvr: Varga, Bálint András
Topic: Composition–Influences; Sound;
Style (Individual)
List: N
Biog: N
Source: NHQ   "Three questions on
music: Extracts from a book of
interviews in the making." 93
(Spr. 1984): 197-202
Lang: ENG

572 Křenek, Ernst, 1900-1991.
Intvr: Scherzer, Ernst
Topic: Composition–Technique; Cre-
ativity
Works: Karl V
List: Y
Biog: N
Source: NZ "Das aktuelle Porträt: Gehrt,
doch unbegehrt. Der Komponist
Ernst Křenek im Gespräch."
147/2 (Feb. 1986): 26-29
Lang: GER

573 Kunad, Rainer, 1936-
Date: 10/77
Intvr: Sturzbecher, Ursula
Topic: Chamber music; Composers–
Social conditions; Composition–
Technique; Opera; Philosophy &
aesthetics
List: Y
Biog: Y
Source: STURZ K, pp. 108-27
Lang: GER

574 Kupkovič Ladislav, 1936-
Intvr: Lichtenfeld, Monika
Topic: Composers–Social conditions;
Composition–Technique; Exper-
imental music
Works: Concours; R-Musik
List: N
Biog: N
Source: MELOS   "Begegnung mit
Ladislav Kupkovič." 41/1
(1974): 5-10
Lang: GER

575 Küpper, Leo
Topic: Computer music; Voice
Works: *Public-Computer-Music (Pro-*
ject)
List: N
Biog: N
Source: MUSWORKS "Computers and
voices: An interview with Leo
Küpper." 23 (Spr. 1983): 17-20
Lang: ENG

576 La Barbara, Joan, 1947-
Date: N.Y.
Intvr: Zimmermann, Walter
Topic: Experimental music; Harmony;
Vocal music
List: N
Biog: N
Source: ZIMMER D, pp. 149-62
Lang: ENG

577 La Barbara, Joan, 1947-
Intvr: Nielsen, Anne Kirstine
Topic: Minimal music; Women com-
posers
List: N
Biog: N

Source: MUSTEXTE "Von den Pyg-
mäen lernen: Joan La Barbara
im Gespräch." 7 (Dec. 1984):
5-8

Lang: GER

578 Lachenmann, Helmut, 1935-
Intvr: Konold, Wulf
Topic: Style (Individual)
Works: Accanto for clarinet and orches-
tra
List: N
Biog: N
Source: MUSICA "Wulf Konold: Distanz
wegen Nähe: Gespräch mit dem
Komponisten Helmut Lachen-
mann." 30 (Nov.-Dec. 1976):
481-84
Lang: GER

579 Laderman, Ezra, 1924-
Intvr: Ericson, Raymond
Topic: Incidental music
List: N
Biog: N
Source: NYT "A composer's double mu-
sical life." 25 May 1980, sec. 2,
p. 19
Lang: ENG

580 Laganà, Ruggero
Date: 7/17/82, Italy
Intvr: Failla, Salvatore Enrico
Topic: Careers in music; Philosophy &
aesthetics
List: N
Biog: N
Source: FAILLA M "Intervista a Rug-
gero Laganà: Mercato mangia
note." pp. 85-93
Lang: ITA

581 Landowski, Marcel, 1915-
Intvr: Walter, Edith
Topic: Arts & politics; Boulez, Pierre,
1925-; Composers–Economic
conditions; Composers–Political
conditions; Concerts & recitals;
Cultural affairs–France; Dance;
Education; Education–France;
Festival d'automne à Paris; Fes-
tival d'Orange; Festival inter-
national d'Aix-en-Provence;
Festivals; Orchestre de Paris;
Schools of music; Symphony
orchestras; Theater–France
List: N
Biog: N
Source: LAND B
Lang: FRE

Landré, Guillaume, 1905-
See no. 374.

582 Langlais, Jean, 1907-
Date: 5/14/86, Paris, France
Intvr: Thomerson, Kathleen
Topic: Vocal music
List: Y
Biog: Y
Source: THOM J "Interview with Jean
Langlais." pp. 17-20
Lang: ENG, FRE

583 Lansky, Paul, 1944-
Date: 3/14/83, Cambridge, Mass.
Intvr: Roads, Curtis B.
Topic: Computer music
Works: As if
List: Y
Biog: N

Source: CMJ "Interview with Paul Lansky." 7/3 (Fall 1983): 16-24

Lang: ENG

584 Lauber, Anne, 1943-
Intvr: Plamondon, Christiane
Topic: Creative process
Works: Cinq pièces pour orgue; Diver-
timento pour cordes; Poème pour
une métamorphose; Sonata, viola,
piano, no. 2
List: N
Biog: Y
Source: MUSCAN "Centrepiece." 41
(Wint. 1979-80): 17-18
Lang: ENG, FRE

585 Lavista, Mario, 1943-
Date: 1981
Intvr: Angeles González, María
Topic: Careers in music; Composers–
Relations with performers; Com-
position–Technique; Electronic
music; Form; Improvisation;
Notation; Performance practice;
Quotations, Musical; Sound;
Style (Individual); Wagner,
Richard, 1813-1883
Works: Contrapunto; Diacronia; Fic-
ciones para orquesta; Lyhannh;
Pieza para un(a) pianista y un
piano
List: Y
Biog: N
Source: ANGELES M, pp. 112-39
Lang: SPA

586 Lees, Benjamin, 1924-
Intvr: Schneider, Steve
Works: Concerto, piano, violoncello

List: N
Biog: N
Source: NYT "Communicating with a
concerto." 7 Nov. 1982, sec. 21,
p. 25
Lang: ENG

Leeuw, Reinbert de, 1938-
See no. 13.

Leeuw, Ton de, 1926-
See no. 565.

587 Leon, Bayani Mendoza de, 1942-
Intvr: Samson, Helen F.
Topic: Orchestral music
List: Y
Biog: N
Source: SAMSON C, pp. 100-8
Lang: ENG

588 Leon, Felipe Padilla de, 1912-
Intvr: Samson, Helen F.
Topic: Careers in music
List: Y
Biog: N
Source: SAMSON C, pp. 109-26
Lang: ENG

589 Leon, Rodolfo C. de, 1931-
Intvr: Samson, Helen F.
List: Y
Biog: N
Source: SAMSON C, pp. 127-35
Lang: ENG

590 Lesser, Wolfgang, 1923-
Intvr: Dasche, Michael
Topic: Sociology
List: N

Biog: N
Source: MG "Für die Entfaltung von Phantasie und Schöpferkraft." 35 (Apr. 1985): 186-91
Lang: GER

591 Letourneau, Omer, 1891-
Date: 7/78, Québec, Canada
Intvr: Huot, Cécile
Topic: Canada–Québec; Careers in music; Composers as performers; Education; Societies, associations, etc.–Canada–Québec
List: Y
Biog: N
Source: HUOT E
Lang: FRE

592 Lieber, Edvard, 1948-
Intvr: Harrison, Helen A.
Topic: De Kooning, Willem, 1904-; Music & art
List: N
Biog: N
Source: NYT "De Kooning's art inspires composer." 18 Mar. 1979, sec. 21, p. 7
Lang: ENG

593 Liebermann, Rolf, 1910-
Intvr: Geitel, Klaus
Topic: Performance practice–Opera
List: N
Biog: N
Source: MELOS "Rolf Liebermann: Pierre Boulez, her mit Ihrer Oper!" 34/12 (Dec. 1967): 438-40
Lang: GER
Notes: Previously published in *Die Welt* (12 Oct. 1967).

594 Lifchitz, Max, 1948-
Intvr: Pulido, Esperanza
Topic: Careers in music; Composers as performers
List: N
Biog: N
Source: HETEROFONIA "Con Max Lifchitz en Nueva York." 65 (Mar.-Apr. 1979): 26-28
Lang: SPA

595 Ligeti, György, 1923-
Date: 1968; 12/14/69
Intvr: Häusler, Josef
Topic: Chamber music; Electronic music; Form; Harmony; Orchestral music; Tone color
Works: Apparitions; Atmosphères; Lontano; Quartet, string, no. 2; Volumina
List: Y
Biog: Y
Source: LIGETI G, pp. 83-110
Lang: ENG
Notes: 1968 and 1969 interviews were originally published separately in *Györy Ligeti: Eine Monographie* (Mainz: Schott's, 1971). The first interview was previously published in *Melos* 37/12 (Dec. 1970): 496-507; Italian translation in *Notiziario* (Apr. 1971): 5-18; French translation in *Musique en Jeu* 15 (Sept. 1974): 110-119.

596 Ligeti, György, 1923-
Date: 1972, Stuttgart, Germany
Intvr: Gottwald, Clytus
Topic: Mahler, Gustav. Symphonies; Spatiality in composition

List: N

Biog: N

Source: NZ "Gustav Mahler und die musikalische Utopie: 1. Musik und Raum–ein Gespräch zwischen György Ligeti und Clytus Gottwald." 135/1 (Jan. 1974): 7-11

Lang: GER

597 Ligeti, György, 1923-

Date: 1972, Stuttgart, Germany

Intvr: Gottwald, Clytus

Topic: Collage in music; Mahler, Gustav. Symphonies

List: N

Biog: N

Source: NZ "Gustav Mahler und die musikalische Utopie: 2. Collage–ein Gespräch zwischen György Ligeti und Clytus Gottwald." 135/5 (May 1974): 288-91

Lang: GER

598 Ligeti, György, 1923-

Date: 1973, Stuttgart, Germany

Intvr: Gottwald, Clytus

Topic: Composers–United States–California

List: N

Biog: N

Source: MELOS/NZ "Tendenzen der Neuen Musik in den USA. György Ligeti im Gespräch mit Clytus Gottwald." 1/4 (July-Aug. 1975): 266-72

Lang: GER

Notes: Originally broadcast 1973 on South German Radio.

599 Ligeti, György, 1923-

Date: 5/74, England

Intvr: Jack, Adrian

Topic: Composition–Technique; Creative process; Opera

List: N

Biog: N

Source: MM "Ligeti talks to Adrian Jack." 263 (July 1974): 24-30

Lang: ENG

600 Ligeti, György, 1923-

Intvr: Lesle, Lutz

Topic: Composition–Technique; Computers

List: N

Biog: N

Source: M MED "Computer-Musik als kreativer Dialog zwischen Musiker und Machine? Gespräch mit dem Komponisten György Ligeti." 2/5 (1976): 43-45

Lang: GER

601 Ligeti, György, 1923-

Date: 10/23/78

Intvr: Sabbe, Herman

Topic: Composition–Technique; Creative process

Works: Le grand Macabre

List: N

Biog: N

Source: INTERFACE "György Ligeti–illusions et allusions." 8 (1979): 11-34

Lang: FRE

Notes: Abstract and summary of the interview in English.

602 Ligeti, György, 1923-
Date: 1978
Intvr: Várnai, Péter
Topic: Composition–Influences; Composition–Technique; Electronic music; Mahler, Gustav. Symphonies; Notation; Style (Individual); Teaching; Tone color
Works: Apparitions; Artikulation; Atmosphères; Aventures; Chamber concerto; Clocks and clouds; Concerto, violoncello; Continuum; Le grand Macabre; Lontano; Quartets, string, nos. 1, 2; Requiem; San Francisco Polyphony; Ten pieces
List: Y
Biog: Y
Source: LIGETI G, pp. 13-82
Lang: ENG
Notes: Originally published in Péter Várnai, *Beszelgetesek Ligeti Gyorggyel* (Budapest: Zenemukiadó Vállalat, 1979).

603 Ligeti, György, 1923-
Date: 5/10/81, Munich, Germany
Intvr: Lichtenfeld, Monika
Topic: Creative process
List: N
Biog: N
Source: NZ "Musik mit schlecht gebundener Krawatte." 142/5 (Sept.-Oct. 1981): 271-73
Lang: GER

604 Ligeti, György, 1923-
Date: 1981
Intvr: Samuel, Claude
Topic: Creative process; Libretto; Opera–Influences

Works: Le grand Macabre
List: N
Biog: N
Source: LIGETI G, pp. 111-23
Lang: ENG
Notes: Originally published in *Le Grand Macabre 'Entretien avec György Ligeti'* (Paris: Hubschmid & Bouret, 1981).

605 Ligeti, György, 1923-
Date: 12/1/82
Intvr: Griffiths, Paul
Topic: Composers–Political conditions; Electronic music; Style (Individual)
List: Y
Biog: Y
Source: GRIFFITHS G "Part one: East. Interview with the composer." pp. 13-26
Lang: ENG

606 Ligeti, György, 1923-
Date: 5/18/83, Stuttgart, Germany
Intvr: Lichtenfeld, Monika
Topic: Creative process; Style (Individual)
List: N
Biog: N
Source: NZ "Gespräch mit György Ligeti." 145/1 (Jan. 1984): 8-11
Lang: GER
Notes: French translation published in *Contrechamps* 3 (Sept. 1984): 44-49.

607 Ligeti, György, 1923-
Date: 7/83, Hamburg, Germany
Intvr: Bouliane, Denys

Topic: Choral music; Educational materials; Style (Individual)
List: N
Biog: N
Source: NEULAND "György Ligeti im Gespräch mit Denys Bouliane." 5 (1984-85): 72-90
Lang: GER

608 Ligeti, György, 1923-
Intvr: Borio, Gianmario
Topic: Bartók, Béla, 1881-1945; Folk music–Hungary; Folk music–Rumania; Form; Opera
List: N
Biog: N
Source: MR "Interventi: A colloquio con György Ligeti." 13 (Apr. 1984): 5-9
Lang: ITA

609 Ligeti, György, 1923-
Intvr: Szigeti, István
Topic: Composers–Social conditions; Style (Individual)
List: N
Biog: N
Source: NHQ "Musical life." 94 (Sum. 1984): 205-10
Lang: ENG

610 Ligeti, György, 1923-
Intvr: Klüppelholz, Werner
Topic: Community relations; Composers–Relations with audiences; Composition–Influences; Creativity; Philosophy & aesthetics; Style (Individual); 20th-century music
List: N

Biog: N
Source: KLUP W, pp. 66-75
Lang: GER

611 Ligeti, György, 1923-
Intvr: Politi, Edna
Topic: Composition–Technique; Opera; Style (Individual)
Works: Aventures et nouvelles aventures; Le grand Macabre; La tempête
List: N
Biog: N
Source: CONTRECHAMPS "Entretien avec Ligeti." 4 (Apr. 1985): 123-27
Lang: FRE

612 Lindgren, Pär, 1952-
Intvr: Brunson, William; Lunell, Hans
Topic: Computers; Electronic music; Elektro-akustisk Musik i Sverige (EMS); Festivals
List: N
Biog: N
Source: NUTIDA "Datorer-hjälpmedel eller fetisch?" 29/1 (1985-86): 18-22
Lang: SWE
Notes: Bo Rydberg also participated in the interview.

613 List, Garrett, 1943-
Intvr: Zimmermann, Walter
Topic: Composers, American; Composition–Influences; Concerts & recitals; Jazz
Works: Three processes
List: N
Biog: N

95

Source: ZIMMER D, pp. 287-97
Lang: ENG

614 Litwinski, Mieczylaw
Intvr: Hayman, Richard Perry
Topic: Composers as performers
List: N
Biog: N
Source: EAR "Mieczylaw Litwinski."
12/4 (June 1987): 20-21
Lang: ENG

615 Loevendie, Theo, 1930-
Intvr: Koning, Renske
Topic: Creative process
Works: Naima
List: N
Biog: N
Source: KN "Free individual versus traditional institution: Theo Loevendie's first steps in the New World and the world of opera." 20 (Dec. 1984): 16-17
Lang: ENG

616 Long, Zigmund
List: N
Biog: N
Source: CONTACT "Interview with Zigmund Long." 5 (Fall 1972): 30-31
Lang: ENG

617 Lorentzen, Bent, 1935-
Date: 4/73, Calif.
Intvr: Pooler, Frank
Topic: Choral music–20th-century; Commissions; Denmark
List: Y
Biog: N

Source: CJ "In quest of answers." 14/2 (Oct. 1973): 8-10
Lang: ENG

618 Lotring, I Wajan, ca. 1897-
Date: 8/72
Intvr: Mâche, François-Bernard
Topic: Bali; Creative process
List: N
Biog: Y
Source: RM "Les mal entendus. Compositeurs des années 70." 314-15 (1978): 79-85
Lang: FRE

Loudová, Ivana, 1941-
See no. 372.

619 Lucier, Alvin, 1931-
Intvr: Simon, Douglas
Works: Hartford memory space
List: N
Biog: N
Source: SOURCE "Alvin Lucier: Hartford memory space." 5/2 (1971): 98-102
Lang: ENG

620 Lucier, Alvin, 1931-
Intvr: Zimmermann, Walter
Topic: Sound, Environmental
Works: Gentle fire; I am sitting in a room; Vespers
List: N
Biog: N
Source: ZIMMER D, pp. 137-48
Lang: ENG

621 Lucier, Alvin, 1931-
Intvr: Means, Loren

Topic: Composition–Technique; Space
Works: I am sitting in a room
List: N
Biog: N
Source: COMP(CA) "An interview with Alvin Lucier." 9 (1977-78): 6-12
Lang: ENG

622 Lucier, Alvin, 1931-
Intvr: Simon, Douglas
Topic: Aleatory music; Composers–Relations with performers; Musique concrète; Sound
Works: Bird and person dying; Chambers; Gentle fire; The Duke of York; Hartford memory space; I am sitting in a room; Music for solo performer; Music on a long thin wire; Outlines; Quasimodo the great lover; The queen of the South; etc.
List: N
Biog: N
Source: SIMON C
Lang: ENG
Notes: Several interviews were previously published in similar or different form in *Arts in Society; Big Deal; The Painted Bride Quarterly ; Parachute; Pieces 3; The Something Else Yearbook; Source Magazine;* and *Post-Movement Art in America,* edited by Alan Sondheim (New York: E. P. Dutton, 1977).

623 Lucier, Alvin, 1931-
Intvr: Margolin, Arthur
Topic: Composers, American; Philosophy & aesthetics

Works: Music for solo performer; Music on a long thin wire
List: N
Biog: N
Source: PNM "Conversation with Alvin Lucier." 20 (Fall-Sum. 1981-82): 50-58
Lang: ENG

624 Lucier, Alvin, 1931-
Intvr: Gronemeyer, Gisela
Topic: Experimental music; Sound
List: N
Biog: N
Source: MUSTEXTE "Nachdenken, wie man zuhört: Alvin Lucier im Gespräch." 16 (Oct. 1986): 32-35
Lang: GER

Luening, Otto, 1900-
See no. 424.

625 Luening, Otto, 1900-
Date: 8/70
Intvr: Wuorinen, Charles
Topic: Amateur composers; Teaching
List: N
Biog: N
Source: PNM "Conversation with Otto Luening." 9/2-10/1 (1971): 200-8
Lang: ENG

626 Luening, Otto, 1900-
Intvr: Rockwell, John
Topic: Philosophy & aesthetics
List: N
Biog: N

Source: NYT "An influential musician at 80." 15 June 1980, sec. 2, pp. 27, 30

Lang: ENG

627 Luening, Otto, 1900-
Topic: Busoni, Ferruccio Benvenuto, 1866-1924; Composers as performers; Electronic music; Style (Individual); Tape recorders
List: N
Biog: N
Source: TW "Otto Luening's tape music." 1/2 (1983)
Lang: ENG
Notes: Sound recording.

628 Luening, Otto, 1900-
Intvr: Grimes, Ev
Topic: Audiences; Education; Philosophy & aesthetics; Teaching
List: N
Biog: Y
Source: MEJ "Conversations with American composers." 72/5 (Jan. 1986): 24-29
Lang: ENG

629 Lutosławski, Witold, 1913-
Intvr: Rich, Alan
Topic: Poland; Teaching
List: N
Biog: N
Source: NYT "Poland's far-out is finding an audience at Tanglewood." 12 Aug. 1962, sec. 2, p. 9
Lang: ENG

630 Lutosławski, Witold, 1913-
Date: 3/12/73-3/16/73, Warsaw, Poland

Intvr: Varga, Bálint András
Topic: Aleatory music; Audiences; Classicism; Composers–20th-century; Conducting; Creative process; Folk music; Performance practice; Poland; Theory; Vocal music
Works: Funeral music; Libre pour orchestre; Quartet, string; Symphonic variations; Symphonies, nos. 1, 2; Trois poèmes d'Henri Michaux
List: N
Biog: N
Source: VARGA L
Lang: ENG

631 Lutosławski, Witold, 1913-
Date: 1963-69, 1976?, Warsaw, Poland
Intvr: Kaczynski, Tadeusz
Topic: Aleatory music; Composers–Relations with performers; Composition–Technique; Festivals; Form; Sound; Style (Individual); Text setting; Warsaw Autumn
Works: Concerto, violoncello; Les espaces du sommeil; Livre pour orchestre; Mi-parti; Paroles tissées; Quartet, string; Symphony, no. 2; Trois poèmes d'Henri Michaux
List: N
Biog: N
Source: KAC C
Lang: ENG

632 Lutosławski, Witold, 1913-
Date: 1983
Works: Symphony, no. 3
List: N

Biog: N
Source: PM "Symphony no. 3 by Witold
Lutosławski. Conversation with
the composer." 18/3-4 (1983):
3-8
Lang: ENG, GER

633 Lutyens, Elisabeth, 1906-1983.
Intvr: Schafer, Raymond Murray
Topic: Creative process; Painting;
Women composers
Works: The symphonies for solo piano,
wind, harp and percussion
List: N
Biog: Y
Source: SCHAFER B, pp. 103-12
Lang: ENG

634 Lyne, Peter Howord, 1946-
Intvr: Tobeck, Christina
Topic: Sociology; Vocal music
Works: Conflict; Contrasts; Fern hill
List: N
Biog: N
Source: NUTIDA "Jag känner mig
hemma när jag skriver för
rösten." 23/4 (1979-80): 18-21
Lang: SWE

McCauley, William Alexander, 1917-
See no. 388.

635 Maceda, José, 1917-
Intvr: Samson, Helen F.
Topic: Philippine music
List: Y
Biog: N
Source: SAMSON C, pp. 136-43
Lang: ENG

636 McGuire, John
Date: 3/10/77
Intvr: Volans, Kevin
Topic: Style (Individual)
List: N
Biog: N
Source: FP "Interview with John
McGuire." 14 (Sept. 1977): 3-7
Lang: ENG

637 Mâche, François-Bernard, 1935-
Intvr: Adam, Elisabeth
Topic: Legends & myths; Philosophy
& aesthetics
Works: La traversée de l'afrique
List: N
Biog: N
Source: SILENCES "La musique égale
du mythe." 1 (1985): 143-48
Lang: FRE

638 MacKenzie, Ichabod Angus, 1894-
Date: 12/28/63
Intvr: Cope, David Howell
Topic: Experimental music
List: N
Biog: N
Source: COMP(CA) "Chronicle of a
cause: I. A. MacKenzie." 1/1
(June 1969): 35-42
Lang: ENG

639 MacKenzie, Robin
Topic: Bagpipe; Creative process
Works: Circular road
List: N
Biog: N
Source: MUSWORKS "Bagpipes, voices
and ocean: A talk with Robin

MacKenzie." 24 (Sum. 1983): 12-14
Lang: ENG

640 Maderna, Bruno, 1920-1973.
Date: 1/23/70, Chicago, Ill.
Intvr: Stone, George; Stout, Alan
Topic: Audiences; Composers as conductors; Concerts & recitals–20th-century music; Conductors; Germany; Interpretation; Malipiero, Gian Francisco–Influences; Scherchen, Tona, 1938-; Serial music; Symphony orchestras; 12-tone system
Works: Odekaton; Requiem
List: Y
Biog: Y
Source: MADERNA D "Quattro interviste radiofoniche." pp. 89-101
Lang: ITA

641 Maderna, Bruno, 1920-1973.
Date: 5/28/70, Saarbrücken, Germany
Intvr: Bitter, Christof
Topic: Composers–Relations with performers; Composers as conductors; Concerto–Style
Works: Concerto, violin; Hyperion
List: Y
Biog: Y
Source: MADERNA D "Quattro interviste radiofoniche." pp. 102-5
Lang: ITA
Notes: Theo Olof, violinist, also participated in the interview.

642 Maderna, Bruno, 1920-1973.
Date: 10/31/71, Saarbrücken, Germany
Intvr: Bitter, Christof

Topic: Cathedrals–Design & construction; Magnificat; Music & art–Italy–15th-century; Orchestration–15th-century music; Realizations & reconstructions; Stravinsky, Igor. Arrangements
List: Y
Biog: Y
Source: MADERNA D "Quattro interviste radiofoniche." pp. 106-10
Lang: ITA

643 Maderna, Bruno, 1920-1973.
Date: 3/72, Hilversum, Netherlands
Topic: Music & politics; Opera; Text setting
Works: Satyrikon
List: Y
Biog: Y
Source: MADERNA D "Quattro interviste radiofoniche." pp. 111-14
Lang: ITA

644 Maderna, Bruno, 1920-1973.
Date: 12/72, Milan, Italy
Intvr: Pinzauti, Leonardo
Topic: Cage, John, 1912-1992; Composers–20th-century; Composers, German; Conductors; Music & politics; Nono, Luigi, 1924-; Orchestras; 16th-century music; Socialism; Stockhausen, Karlheinz, 1928-; Theater–Italy; 20th-century music
List: N
Biog: N
Source: PINZAUTI M, pp. 203-12
Lang: ITA
Notes: Previously published in *Nuova Rivista Musicale Italiana* 6 (Oct.-Dec. 1972): 545-52.

645 Maderna, Bruno, 1920-1973.
Date: 5/7/73, Saarbrücken, Germany
Intvr: Bitter, Christof
Topic: Collage in music; Music & psychology; Stockhausen, Karlheinz, 1928-; Style (Individual)
Works: Tempo libero
List: Y
Biog: Y
Source: MADERNA D "Quattro interviste radiofoniche." pp. 115-18
Lang: ITA

646 Maiguashca, Mesias
Date: 4/26/84, Baden, Austria
Intvr: Barlow, Klarenz
Topic: Electronic music studios
List: N
Biog: N
Source: MUSTEXTE "Willkommen in BYTEschland." 6 (Oct. 1984): 31
Lang: GER

647 Malec, Ivo, 1925-
Date: 7/75
Intvr: Mâche, François-Bernard
Topic: Composers–Social conditions; Electronic music
List: N
Biog: Y
Source: RM "Les mal entendus. Compositeurs des années 70." 314-15 (1978): 87-94
Lang: FRE

Malec, Ivo, 1925-
See no. 254

648 Malipiero, Gian Francesco, 1882-1973.
Date: Spr/67
Intvr: Pinzauti, Leonardo
Topic: Composers–Influences; Composition–Technique; Monteverdi, Claudio, 1567-1643; Opera; Style (Individual); 20th-century music
Works: Don Tartufo bacchettone; Orfeide
List: N
Biog: N
Source: PINZAUTI M, pp. 11-17
Lang: ITA
Notes: Previouly published in *Nuova Rivista Musicale Italiana* 1 (Mar.-June 1967): 120-24

649 Mannino, Franco, 1924-
Date: 4/30/82, Italy
Intvr: Failla, Salvatore Enrico
Topic: Composers as performers; Conductors–Social conditions; Creativity; Opera; Style (Individual); Wagner, Richard, 1818-1913
List: N
Biog: N
Source: FAILLA M "Intervista a Franco Mannino: Inventare la comunicazione." pp. 39-49
Lang: ITA

Mariétan, Pierre, 1935-
See no. 244.

650 Maros, Miklós, 1943-
Intvr: Bodin, Lars-Gunnar; Johnson, Bengt Emil
Topic: Folk music; Hungary; Style (Individual); Sweden
List: N
Biog: N

Source: NUTIDA "Det är inte nöd-
vändigt att alla blir tonsättare!"
20/2 (1976-77): 4-7

Lang: SWE

651 Martinez Galnarez, Francisco

Date: 5/17/79

Intvr: Pulido Silva, Alberto

Topic: Schools of music–Mexico; Teaching

List: N

Biog: N

Source: HETEROFONIA "Entrevista
concertada por el Dr. Alberto
Pulido Silva, con el señor direc-
tor de la Escuela Nacional de
Musica de la UNAM, Prof. Lic.
Francisco Martinez Galnares ...."
66 (May-Aug. 1979): 28-29; 67
(Sept.-Dec. 1974): 23-25

Lang: SPA

652 Mather, Bruce, 1939-

Intvr: Robinow, Richard F.

Topic: Composers–Economic conditions

List: N

Biog: N

Source: CC "Meet your fellow members,
no. 2: The 20th century is not
too bad ...." 2 (Aug. 1965): 8-9,
38-40

Lang: ENG, FRE

653 Mather, Bruce, 1939-

Topic: 20th-century music

List: Y

Biog: Y

Source: MUSCAN "Bruce Mather, a portrait." 11 (May 1968): [8-9]

Lang: ENG, FRE

654 Mathews, Max V.

Date: 6/80, Cambridge, Mass.

Intvr: Roads, Curtis B.

Topic: Computer music; Computers–
Programs

List: N

Biog: Y

Source: CMJ "Interview with Max
Mathews." 4/4 (Wint. 1980):
15-22

Lang: ENG

655 Mathias, William, 1934-1991.

Intvr: Dawney, Michael

Topic: Composers–Political conditions;
Composers–Social conditions;
Welsh language

List: N

Biog: N

Source: COMP(LONDON) "Composer
speaks–6. William Mathias in
conversation with Michael
Dawney." 52 (Sum. 1974): 19-
22

Lang: ENG

656 Mathias, William, 1934-1991.

Date: 1975, St. Louis, Mo.

Intvr: Lamb, Gordon Howard

Topic: Choral directors–United States;
Choral music; Commissions;
Conducting; Education

Works: This world of joie

List: N

Biog: Y

Source: CJ "Interview with William
Mathias." 16/3 (Nov. 1975):
13-18

Lang: ENG

657 Matthews, Colin, 1946-
Intvr: Griffiths, Paul
Topic: Composition–Influences; Creative process; Symphony
List: Y
Biog: Y
Source: GRIFFITHS N, pp. 100-5
Lang: ENG

658 Matthews, David, 1943-
Intvr: Griffiths, Paul
Topic: Composers–Economic conditions; Style (Individual)
Works: Concerto, violin
List: Y
Biog: Y
Source: GRIFFITHS N, pp. 93-99
Lang: ENG

659 Matthus, Siegfried, 1934-
Date: 4/1/67
Intvr: Grabs, Manfred
Topic: Eisler, Hanns, 1898-1962; Teaching
Works: Grigorsk 42
List: Y
Biog: N
Source: GRABS H "Interviews mit Eisler-Schülern." pp. 201-3
Lang: GER

660 Matthus, Siegfried, 1934-
Date: 9/77
Intvr: Stürzbecher, Ursula
Topic: Eisler, Hanns, 1898-1962; Opera; Tonality
Works: Lazarillo vom Tormes; Der letzte Schuss
List: Y
Biog: Y

Source: STURZ K, pp. 218-44
Lang: GER

661 Matthus, Siegfried, 1934-
Intvr: Lange, Wolfgang
Topic: Opera–20th-century; Performance
List: N
Biog: Y
Source: MDB "Opera im Gespräch." 19/1 (1982): 34-38
Lang: GER

662 Matton, Roger, 1929-
Topic: Canada; 20th-century music
List: Y
Biog: Y
Source: MUSCAN "Roger Matton, a portrait." 16 (Dec. 1968): [8-9]
Lang: ENG, FRE

663 Maw, Nicholas, 1935-
Intvr: Griffiths, Paul
Topic: Creativity; Opera; Performance practice; Text setting; Tonality
Works: Scenes and arias
List: Y
Biog: Y
Source: GRIFFITHS N, pp. 166-78
Lang: ENG

664 Mayr, Albert
Date: 7/4/78, Florence, Italy
Intvr: Bouliane, Yves
Topic: Performance practice; Sound, Environmental
List: N
Biog: N
Source: MUSWORKS "Interview with Albert Mayr." 7 (Spr. 1979): 17
Lang: ENG

665 Mayr, Albert
Date: 11/84, Toronto, Canada
Intvr: Pearson, Tina
Topic: Experimental music; Time
List: N
Biog: N
Source: MUSWORKS "The music of times and tides: Albert Mayr." 29 (Fall 1985): 3-6
Lang: ENG

666 Medek, Tilo, 1940-
Date: 11/76
Intvr: Stürzbecher, Ursula
Topic: Audiences–20th-century music; Children, Music for; Creative process; Incidental music; Philosophy & aesthetics; Vocal music
Works: Concerto, marimba
List: Y
Biog: Y
Source: STURZ K, pp. 60-84
Lang: GER

667 Méfano, Paul, 1937-
Date: 3/70, France
Intvr: Bosseur, Jean-Yves
Topic: Composition–Influences
List: N
Biog: N
Source: M JEU "Dix jeunes compositeurs." 1 (Nov. 1970): 78-79
Lang: FRE

668 Méfano, Paul, 1937-
Date: 3/72
Intvr: Mâche, François-Bernard
Topic: Style (Individual)

List: N
Biog: Y
Source: RM "Les mal entendus. Compositeurs des années 70." 314-15 (1978): 95-101
Lang: FRE

Méfano, Paul, 1937-
See no. 254

669 Mengelberg, Misha, 1935-
Intvr: Koopmans, Rudy
Topic: Baaren, Kees van, 1906-1970
List: N
Biog: N
Source: KN "Keep things moving: Interview with Misha Mengelberg." 4 (Dec. 1976): 27-28
Lang: ENG

670 Mengelberg, Misha, 1935-
Date: 10/80, Toronto, Canada
Intvr: Timar, Andrew
Topic: Improvisation; Societies, associations, etc.
List: N
Biog: Y
Source: MUSWORKS "Misha Mengelberg: Interview by Andrew Timar." 14 (Wint. 1981): 1-2, 17-20
Lang: ENG

Mengelberg, Misha, 1935-
See no. 13.

671 Menotti, Gian Carlo, 1911-
Intvr: Taylor, William A.
Topic: Commissions; Television opera
Works: Irene and the Gypsies

List: N
Biog: N
Source: MC "Menotti tells about his video opera commissioned by NBC-TV." 139 (1 May 1949): 8
Lang: ENG

672 Menotti, Gian Carlo, 1911-
Date: Sum/63
Intvr: Chotzinoff, Samuel
Topic: Composers as theater directors; Festival of Two Worlds; Festivals; Opera
Works: Amelia; The island god; The medium
List: N
Biog: N
Source: CHOT L, pp. 53-70
Lang: ENG

673 Menotti, Gian Carlo, 1911-
Date: 1970
Intvr: Pinzauti, Leonardo
Topic: Composers–Influences; Music & politics; Opera; Popular music; Sociology
List: N
Biog: N
Source: PINZAUTI M, pp. 151-60
Lang: ITA
Notes: Previouly published in *Nuova Rivista Musicale Italiana* 4 (July-Aug. 1970): 712-20.

674 Messiaen, Olivier, 1908-1992.
Topic: Theory
List: N
Biog: N
Source: MELOS "Gespräch mit Olivier Messiaen." 16/4 (Apr. 1949): 101-4
Lang: GER

675 Messiaen, Olivier, 1908-1992.
Intvr: Goléa, Antoine
List: N
Biog: N
Source: GOLEA M
Lang: FRE

676 Messiaen, Olivier, 1908-1992.
Date: 2/61, Paris, France
Intvr: Gavoty, Bernard
Topic: Rhythm
Works: Bird songs
List: N
Biog: N
Source: TEMPO "Who are you, Olivier Messiaen?" 58 (Sum. 1961): 33-36
Lang: ENG
Notes: Also published in *Journal Musical Français* (1961).

677 Messiaen, Olivier, 1908-1992.
Intvr: Samuel, Claude
List: Y
Biog: Y
Source: SAMUEL C
Lang: ENG

678 Messiaen, Olivier, 1908-1992.
Intvr: Samuel, Claude
List: Y
Biog: N
Source: MESSIAEN M
Lang: FRE
Notes: This is a newly updated and expanded version of the 1967 ed. See also no. 677.

679 Messiaen, Olivier, 1908-1992.
Date: 5/17/71
Intvr: Pinzauti, Leonardo
Topic: Composers–20th-century; Music
        & religion
List: N
Biog: N
Source: PINZAUTI M, pp. 187-93
Lang: ITA
Notes: Previouly published in *Nuova
        Rivista Musicale Italiana* 5
        (Nov.-Dec. 1971): 1028-33;
        German translation published
        in *Melos* 39/5 (Sept.-Oct. 1972):
        270-73.

680 Messiaen, Olivier, 1908-1992.
Intvr: Nichols, Roger
Topic: Sound
List: N
Biog: N
Source: MM "Messiaen: Roger Nichols
        talks to the composer, who is 70
        on December 10." 316 (Dec.
        1978): 20-22
Lang: ENG

681 Messiaen, Olivier, 1908-1992.
Date: 1978
Intvr: Watts, Harriet
Topic: Creativity
Works: From the canyons to the stars
List: N
Biog: N
Source: TEMPO "Canyons, colours and
        birds: An interview with Olivier
        Messiaen." 128 (Mar. 1979): 2-8
Lang: ENG

682 Messiaen, Olivier, 1908-1992.
Intvr: Lyon, Raymond
Topic: Meter; Religion; Tone color
Works: Bird songs
List: N
Biog: N
Source: HETEROFONIA "Entrevista de
        Raymond Lyon con Olivier Mes-
        siaen." 66 (May-Aug. 1979): 13-
        18
Lang: SPA
Notes: Previously published in *Le
        Courier Musical de France*, no.
        64.

683 Messiaen, Olivier, 1908-1992.
Date: 5/85
Intvr: Margles, Pamela
Topic: Composition–Technique; Music
        & religion; Teaching
List: N
Biog: Y
Source: M MAG "Messiaen's reflec-
        tions on nature and religion."
        9/1 (Jan.-Feb. 1986): 11-13, 19
Lang: ENG

Miereanu, Costin, 1943-
See no. 242.

684 Milhaud, Darius, 1892-1974.
Date: 11/13/50
Topic: First performances
Works: Les choephores
List: N
Biog: N
Source: NYT   "Belated premiere of
        Milhaud's 'Choephores' to be
        played by Philharmonic on

Thursday." 14 Nov. 1950, sec. 1,
p. 38
Lang: ENG

685 Milhaud, Darius, 1892-1974.
Intvr: Chamfray, Claude
Topic: Electronic music; Genre
List: N
Biog: N
Source: MELOS "Gespräch mit Darius
Milhaud." 28/1 (Jan. 1961): 1-3
Lang: GER

686 Milhaud, Darius, 1892-1974.
Intvr: Rostand, Claude
Topic: Sociology
List: N
Biog: N
Source: RUFER B "Darius Milhaud."
pp. 267-70
Lang: GER

687 Molina, Antonio J., 1894-
Intvr: Samson, Helen F.
List: Y
Biog: N
Source: SAMSON C, pp. 144-55
Lang: ENG

688 Monach, Greta
Date: 6/11/86, Utrecht, Netherlands
Intvr: Escot, Pozzi
Topic: Pitch; Poetry; Sound
List: N
Biog: N
Source: SONUS "A poet of music: An
interview with Greta Monach."
8/2 (Spr. 1988): 47-55
Lang: ENG
Notes: Transcribed from the original
tape by Andrea Steinberg.

689 Monahan, Gordon
Intvr: Hayman, Richard Perry
Topic: Experimental music
List: N
Biog: Y
Source: EAR "Meet The Composer: Gor-
don Monahan." 12/4 (June 1987):
16-18
Lang: ENG

690 Monk, Meredith J., 1942-
Date: 12/4/79
Intvr: Garland, David
Topic: Philosophy & aesthetics
Works: Recent ruins
List: N
Biog: N
Source: EAR "Interview with Meredith
Monk." 5/4 (Feb.-Mar. 1980):
1, 8-9
Lang: ENG

691 Monk, Meredith J., 1942-
Date: 2/28/81, N.Y.
Intvr: Greenwald, Jan
Topic: Sexism; Style (Individual)
List: N
Biog: N
Source: EAR "Interview: Meredith
Monk." 6/3 (Apr.-May 1981): 5
Lang: ENG

692 Monk, Meredith J., 1942-
Intvr: Ortiz, Pablo
Topic: Vocal music
List: N
Biog: N
Source: CONTRECHAMPS "Entretien
avec Meredith Monk." 6 (Apr.
1986): 186-90
Lang: FRE

693 Monk, Meredith J., 1942-
Intvr: Ryan, Christina
Topic: Composition–Technique; Sound
recordings; Vocal music
Works: Do you be; Dolmen music
List: N
Biog: N
Source: EAR "Meet The Composer:
Meredith Monk." 12/8 (Nov.
1987): 16-19
Lang: ENG

694 Montgomery, James
Intvr: Lake, Larry
Topic: Canada; Philosophy & aesthetics
List: N
Biog: Y
Source: MUSCAN "Words about music:
A series of ...." 37 (Nov. 1978):
18-19
Lang: ENG, FRE

695 Moore, Carman Leroy, 1936-
Intvr: Henahan, Donal
Topic: Commissions; Philosophy & aes-
thetics
Works: Gospel fuse; Wild fires and field
songs
List: N
Biog: N
Source: NYT "This week's most wanted
composer: Carman Moore." 19
Jan. 1975, sec. 2, pp. 1, 17
Lang: ENG

696 Moore, Undine Smith, 1904-1989.
Intvr: Harris, Carl Gordon
Topic: Black music; Commissions
List: N
Biog: Y

Source: BPM "Conversation with Undine
Smith Moore, composer and master teacher." 13 (Spr. 1985): 79-
90
Lang: ENG

697 Morawetz, Oskar, 1917-
Topic: Composition–Influences
List: Y
Biog: Y
Source: MUSCAN "Oskar Morawetz, a
portrait." 25 (Dec. 1969): [8-9]
Lang: ENG, FRE

698 Morawetz, Oskar, 1917-
Intvr: Schulman, Michael
Topic: Concerts & recitals; Creativity
List: N
Biog: N
Source: CC "Oskar Morawetz: Canada's
celebrated composer ...." 226
(Dec. 1987): 6-11, 30-31
Lang: ENG, FRE

699 Morrill, Dexter G., 1938-
Date: 8/27/86, Cambridge, Mass.
Intvr: Roads, Curtis B.
Topic: Computer music
Works: Chowning; Getz variations;
Quartet, strings
List: Y
Biog: Y
Source: CMJ "Interview with Dexter
Morrill." 11/3 (Fall 1987): 11-
16
Lang: ENG

700 Morrow, Charles Geoffrey, 1942-
Intvr: Zimmermann, Walter
Topic: Indian music, American; Sing-
ing–Breathing; Voice

Works: Breath chant
List: N
Biog: N
Source: ZIMMER D, pp. 269-85
Lang: ENG

701 Morthenson, Jan Wilhelm, 1940-
Date: 12/19/73
Intvr: Bergendal, Göran
Topic: Church music; Composition–Technique; Military music; Philosophy & aesthetics
Works: Alla marcia; Sensory project I-III
List: N
Biog: N
Source: NUTIDA "Jan W. Morthenson–på marsch." 17/4 (1973-74): 11-16
Lang: SWE

702 Muldowney, Dominic, 1952-
Intvr: Griffiths, Paul
Topic: Composition–Influences; Style (Individual)
List: Y
Biog: Y
Source: GRIFFITHS N, pp. 160-65
Lang: ENG

703 Mumma, Gordon, 1935-
Intvr: Schrader, Barry
Topic: Composers–Relations with audiences; Composers–Relations with performers; Electronic music; Sound recording & reproduction
Works: Cybersonic cantilevers
List: N
Biog: N

Source: SCHRADER I "20. Interview with Gordon Mumma: 'Cybersonic cantilevers.'" pp. 202-10
Lang: ENG

Murail, Tristan, 1947-
See no. 254

704 Murray, Lyn, 1909-1989.
Intvr: Ulrich, Allan
Topic: Motion picture music; Philosophy & aesthetics
Works: Energetically yours
List: Y
Biog: N
Source: ULRICH A, pp. 19-22
Lang: ENG

705 Mycielski, Zygmunt, 1907-
Intvr: Marek, Tadeusz
Topic: Style (Individual); Symphony
List: N
Biog: N
Source: PM "Composer's workshop. Zygmunt Mycielski." 47 (1977): 16-19
Lang: ENG, GER

706 Nagorcka, Ron, 1948-
Intvr: Gerrard, Graeme
Topic: Computer music; Philosophy & aesthetics
Works: Seven rare dreamings
List: N
Biog: N
Source: NMA "An interview with Ron Nagorcka." 1 (1983): 4-6
Lang: ENG

707 Nancarrow, Conlon, 1912-
Date: 7/12/75, Mexico City, Mexico
Intvr: Reynolds, Roger
Topic: Composition–Technique; Creative process; Player piano; Tempo
Works: Studies for player piano
List: N
Biog: Y
Source: AM "Conlon Nancarrow: Interviews in Mexico City and San Francisco." 2 (Sum. 1984): 1-21
Lang: ENG

708 Nancarrow, Conlon, 1912-
Date: 7/12/80, Mexico City, Mexico
Intvr: Caras, Tracy; Gagne, Cole
Topic: Creative process
Works: Blues; Prelude for piano; Septet; Sonatina for piano; Studies for player piano, nos. 39, 40, 41; Toccata; Trio, piano, clarinet, bassoon
List: Y
Biog: Y
Source: GAGNE S, pp. 281-303
Lang: ENG

709 Nancarrow, Conlon, 1912-
Date: 6/14/81, San Francisco, Calif.
Intvr: Reynolds, Roger
Topic: Player piano; Tempo
Works: Studies for player piano
List: N
Biog: N
Source: AM "Conlon Nancarrow: Interviews in Mexico City and San Francisco." 2 (Sum. 1984): 21-24
Lang: ENG

710 Nancarrow, Conlon, 1912-
Date: 5/84, Mexico; 6/26/87, Amsterdam, Netherlands
Intvr: Fürst-Heidtmann, Monika
Topic: Mechanical instruments; Sound
Works: Studies for player piano
List: N
Biog: N
Source: MUSTEXTE "'Ich bin beim Komponieren nur meinen Wünschen gefolgt.' Conlon Nancarrow im Gespräch." 21 (Oct. 1987): 29-32
Lang: GER
Notes: A letter dated 10 Aug. 1987 is also included in the article.

711 Nancarrow, Conlon, 1912-
Intvr: Kuhl, Christopher
Topic: Composition–Influences; Composition–Technique; Improvisation; Performance; Player piano
List: N
Biog: N
Source: COMP(GA) "A conversation with composer Conlon Nancarrow." 2/1 (Fall 1987): 3-8
Lang: ENG

712 Nanes, Richard, 1939-
Intvr: Klein, Alvin
Topic: Careers in music; Concerts & recitals
List: N
Biog: N
Source: NYT "Executive returns to music." 13 Nov. 1983, sec. 11, p. 18
Lang: ENG

713 Nanes, Richard, 1939-
  Intvr: Finn, Terri Lowen
  Topic: Concerts & recitals
  List: N
  Biog: N
  Source: NYT "Kean narrating Copland piece." 6 May 1984, sec. 11, p. 36
  Lang: ENG

714 Narayan, Pondit Ram, 1927-
  Date: 9/75
  Intvr: Mâche, François-Bernard
  Topic: India; Music & religion; Teaching
  List: N
  Biog: Y
  Source: RM "Les mal entendus. Compositeurs des années 70." 314-15 (1978): 103-7
  Lang: FRE

715 Neikrug, Marc, 1946-
  Intvr: Holland, Bernard P.
  Topic: Composers as performers
  List: N
  Biog: N
  Source: NYT "Neikrug juggling careers as pianist and composer." 17 Aug. 1987, sec. 3, p. 15
  Lang: ENG

716 Neuhaus, Max, 1939-
  Intvr: Feldman, David
  Topic: Electronic music
  Works: Radio net; Times Spuare piece
  List: N
  Biog: N
  Source: EAR "Max Neuhaus interview." 5/5 (Apr.-May 1980): 8-9
  Lang: ENG

717 Niblock, Phill, 1933-
  Intvr: Stidfole, Arthur
  Topic: Motion picture music
  List: N
  Biog: N
  Source: EAR "Interview with Phill Niblock: 'That's your problem, not mine.'" 9/5-10/1 (Fall 1985): 20, 35
  Lang: ENG

718 Nilsson, Bo, 1937-
  Intvr: Rying, Matts
  Topic: Criticism
  Works: Nazm
  List: N
  Biog: N
  Source: NUTIDA "Det finns saker och ting son man inte talar om." 16/3 (1972-73): 34-36
  Lang: SWE

719 Nono, Luigi, 1924-1990.
  Date: 4/5/69-4/6/69, Venice, Italy
  Intvr: Pauli, Hansjörg
  Topic: Culture–Cuba; Music & politics; Philosophy & aesthetics; Political songs; Politics; Style (Individual); Vocal music
  List: N
  Biog: Y
  Source: PAULI F, pp. 106-27
  Notes: Originally done for a series of a radio program of Hessischer Radiofunk Frankfurt.

720 Nono, Luigi, 1924-1990.
  Date: 1/14/70, Venice, Italy
  Intvr: Pinzauti, Leonardo

111

Topic: Creativity; Music & politics; Opera; Sociology; South America; Stockhausen, Karlheinz, 1928-

Works: España en el corazón

List: N

Biog: N

Source: PINZAUTI M, pp. 119-32

Lang: ITA

Notes: Previouly published in *Nuova Rivista Musicale Italiana* 4 (Jan.-Feb. 1970): 69-81.

721 Nono, Luigi, 1924-1990.

Intvr: Bodenhöfer, Andreas; Vila, Cirilo

Topic: Collage in music; Culture; Philosophy & aesthetics; Sociology

List: N

Biog: Y

Source: RMC "Entrevista a Luigi Nono." 115-16 (July-Dec. 1971): 3-9

Lang: SPA

722 Nono, Luigi, 1924-1990.

Date: 5/86

Intvr: Dümling, Albrecht

Topic: Audiences–20th-century music; Philosophy & aesthetics; Sociology; Spatiality in composition

List: N

Biog: N

Source: NZ "Komponieren heute: 'Ich habe viel lieber die Konfusion.' Luigi Nonos Bekenntnis zu offenem Denken. Ein Gespräch." 148/2 (Feb. 1987): 22-28

Lang: GER

Nostrand, Burr van
See **Van Nostrand, Burr, 1945-.**

Nowak, Lionel, 1911-
See no. 145.

723 Nunes, Emmanuel, 1941-

Date: 1979

Intvr: Faust, Wolfgang Max

Topic: Composers–Social conditions; Creative process

List: N

Biog: N

Source: MUSTEXTE "Auf ein komplexes rhythmisches Urprinzip bezogen: Emmanuel Nunes im Gespräch (1979)." 15 (July 1986): 5-8

Lang: GER

724 Núñez, Francisco, 1945-

Intvr: Saavedra, Leonora

Topic: Composers–Influences; Composition–Technique; Culture–Mexico; Mexico; Musique concrète; Theory; Tonality; 20th-century music

List: Y

Biog: N

Source: ANGELES M, pp. 140-74

Lang: SPA

725 Ohana, Maurice, 1914-

Date: 11/71

Intvr: Mâche, François-Bernard

Topic: Philosophy & aesthetics

List: N

Biog: Y

Source: RM "Les mal entendus. Compositeurs des années 70." 314-15 (1978): 109-15

Lang: FRE

726 Olive, Vivienne, 1950-
 Intvr: Matthei, Renate; Sonntag, Brun-
    hilde
 Topic: Careers in music; Composition–
    Influences; Performance; Women
    composers
 List: N
 Biog: N
 Source: SONNTAG A, v. 2, pp. 55-64
 Lang: GER

727 Oliver, Stephen Michael Harding, 1950-
 Intvr: Griffiths, Paul
 Topic: Commissions; Libretto; Opera
 List: Y
 Biog: Y
 Source: GRIFFITHS N, pp. 140-47
 Lang: ENG

728 Oliveros, Pauline, 1932-
 Intvr: Zimmermann, Walter
 Topic: Experimental music; Physiology
 Works: Crow two, a ceremonial opera;
    Link; Sonic meditations
 List: N
 Biog: N
 Source: ZIMMER D, pp. 163-82
 Lang: ENG

729 Oliveros, Pauline, 1932-
 Date: 5/21/77, Bonn, Germany
 Topic: Experimental music
 List: N
 Biog: N
 Source: FP "Interview with Pauline Oli-
    veros." 14 (Sept. 1977): 8-9
 Lang: ENG

730 Oliveros, Pauline, 1932-
 Date: 11/79, Toronto, Canada

 Intvr: Timar, Andrew
 Topic: Electronic music; Performance
 Works: El relicario de los animales
 List: N
 Biog: N
 Source: MUSWORKS "Talk with
    Pauline Oliveros." 10 (Wint.
    1980): 16-18
 Lang: ENG

731 Oliveros, Pauline, 1932-
 Date: 11/80, Bonn, Germany
 Intvr: Hays, Doris Ernestine
 Topic: Sexism; Women in music
 List: N
 Biog: N
 Source: EAR "Women and music festi-
    val, Bonn 1980. Interview." 6/3
    (Apr.-May 1981): 10-12
 Lang: ENG
 Notes: Barbara Heller-Reichenbach
    and Candace Natvig also
    participated in the interview.

732 Oliveros, Pauline, 1932-
 Intvr: Anderson, Beth
 Topic: Experimental music; Teaching
 List: N
 Biog: N
 Source: EAR "Interview with Pauline
    Oliveros." 6/2 (Feb.-Mar. 1981):
    12-13
 Lang: ENG

733 Oliveros, Pauline, 1932-
 Intvr: Schrader, Barry
 Topic: Composition–Technique; Elec-
    tronic music
 Works: I of IV
 List: N

Biog: N
Source: SCHRADER I "17. Interview with Pauline Oliveros: 'I of IV.'" pp. 184-87
Lang: ENG

734 Oliveros, Pauline, 1932-
Date: 2/27/85, Austin, Tex.
Intvr: Girouard, Tina; Hay, Deborah
Topic: Multi-media compositions; Performance practice
List: N
Biog: N
Source: MUSWORKS "Tasting the blaze: A conversation in a park; Tina Girouard, Pauline Oliveros, Deborah Hay ...." 33 (Wint. 1985-86): 8-12
Lang: ENG

735 Oliveros, Pauline, 1932-
Intvr: Pearson, Tina
Topic: Religion
Works: Angels and demons
List: N
Biog: N
Source: MUSWORKS "Angels and demons and Pauline Oliveros." 31 (Spr. 1985): 3-5
Lang: ENG

736 Oliveros, Pauline, 1932-
Intvr: Wachtel, Peggy Ann
Topic: Accordion; Sound; Teaching
List: N
Biog: N
Source: EAR "Meet The Composer: Pauline Oliveros." 12/9 (Dec.-Jan. 1987-88): 24-26
Lang: ENG

737 Orff, Carl, 1895-1982.
Intvr: Seifert, Wolfgang
Topic: Incidental music
Works: Carmina burana
List: N
Biog: Y
Source: NZ "'... auf den Geist kommt es an': Carl Orff zum 75. Geburtstag–Kommentar und Gespräch." 131/7-8 (1970): 370-77
Lang: GER

738 Ornstein, Leo, 1892-
Topic: Composers as performers; Cubism; Futurist music
List: N
Biog: N
Source: NYT "A musical futurist rediscovered." 14 Mar. 1976, sec. 2, p. 15
Lang: ENG

739 Ornstein, Leo, 1892-
Date: 6/15/83
Intvr: O'Grady, Terence J.
Topic: Composition–Technique; Philosophy & aesthetics; Style (Individual)
Works: Dance sauvage
List: N
Biog: N
Source: PNM "A conversation with Leo Ornstein." 23/1 (Fall-Wint. 1984): 126-33
Lang: ENG

740 Osborne, Nigel, 1948-
Intvr: Griffiths, Paul
Topic: Creativity; Music & literature; Philosophy & aesthetics

List: Y
Biog: Y
Source: GRIFFITHS N, pp. 125-32
Lang: ENG

741 Otte, Hans, 1926-
Intvr: Gronemeyer, Gisela;
         Oehlschlägel, Reinhard
Topic: Composition–Technique; Orchestration; Sound
List: N
Biog: N
Source: MUSTEXTE "Warten auf die eigenen Klänge: Hans Otte im Gespräch." 17 (Dec. 1986): 24-31
Lang: GER

742 Pablo, Luis de, 1930-
Date: 4/73
Intvr: Mâche, François-Bernard
Topic: Ethnic music; Sociology; Style (Individual)
List: N
Biog: Y
Source: RM "Les mal entendus. Compositeurs des années 70." 314-15 (1978): 117-23
Lang: FRE

743 Paik, Nam June, 1932-
Date: 9/24/82-9/25/82, Paris, France
Intvr: Weiss, Jason
Topic: Music & art
List: N
Biog: Y
Source: EAR "Nam June Paik interview." 9/5-10/1 (Fall 1985): 11, 36-37
Lang: ENG

744 Pajaro, Eliseo M., 1915-
Intvr: Samson, Helen F.
Topic: Careers in music
List: Y
Biog: N
Source: SAMSON C, pp. 156-72
Lang: ENG

745 Palestine, Charlemagne, 1945-
Date: 11/28/72
Intvr: Garland, Peter
Topic: Sound
List: N
Biog: N
Source: SOUNDINGS "Charlemagne Palestine–talking: A conversation with Peter Garland." 6 (Spr. 1973): 31-36
Lang: ENG

746 Palestine, Charlemagne, 1945-
Intvr: Zimmermann, Walter
Topic: Harmony
List: N
Biog: N
Source: ZIMMER D, pp. 257-68
Lang: ENG

747 Palmer, Robert, 1915-
Intvr: Blackburn, Robert T.; Risenhoover, Morris
Topic: Colleges & universities–Faculty; Teaching
List: N
Biog: Y
Source: RISEN A, pp. 104-10
Lang: ENG

748 Papineau-Couture, Jean, 1916-
Topic: Education

Works: Concerto, piano; Fantasie for woodwind quintet; Pièces concertantes, nos. 1, 5; Psaume clarinet; Suite, violin
List: Y
Biog: Y
Source: MUSCAN "Jean Papineau-Couture; a portrait." 3 (July 1967): [8-9]
Lang: ENG, FRE

749 Parsons, Michael, 1938-
Date: 1/74, England
Intvr: Potter, Keith
Topic: Composition–Technique; Experimental music–England
List: N
Biog: Y
Source: CONTACT "Some aspects of an experimental attitude." 8 (Sum. 1974): 20-25
Lang: ENG

750 Pauk, Alex, 1945-
Intvr: Kieser, Karen
Topic: Community relations
List: N
Biog: Y
Source: MUSCAN "Words about music: A series of interviews with Canadian composers." 30 (Nov. 1976): 15
Lang: ENG, FRE

751 Penderecki, Krzystof, 1933-
Date: 1967, Perugia, Italy
Intvr: Pinzauti, Leonardo
Topic: Composers–Influences; Composers, Russian; Music & religion; Style (Individual)

Works: Dies irae; Passio et mors domini nostri Jesu Christi secundum Lucam
List: N
Biog: N
Source: PINZAUTI M, pp. 43-53
Lang: ITA
Notes: Previouly published in *Nuova Rivista Musicale Italiana* 1 (Nov.-Dec. 1967): 776-84.

752 Penderecki, Krzystof, 1933-
Intvr: Henahan, Donal
Topic: Composers, Polish; Religion
Works: Passio et mors domini nostri Jesu Christi secundum Lucam
List: N
Biog: N
Source: NYT "Religiously, a free spirit. Politically?" 23 Feb. 1969, sec. 2, pp. 19-20
Lang: ENG

753 Penderecki, Krzystof, 1933-
Intvr: Orga, Ateş
Topic: Creative process
Works: Symphony, no. 1
List: N
Biog: Y
Source: MM "Krzysztof Penderecki: Ateş Orga talks to the composer ...." 254 (Oct. 1973): 38-41
Lang: ENG

754 Penderecki, Krzystof, 1933-
Date: 3/31/77, Cincinnati, Ohio
Intvr: Felder, David; Schneider, Mark
Topic: Composition–Technique; Style (Individual)
Works: Paradise lost; Passio et mors

domini nostri Jesu Christi secundum Lucam

List: N

Biog: N

Source: COMP(CA) "An interview with
Krzysztof Penderecki." 8 (1976-
77): 8-20

Lang: ENG

755 Penderecki, Krzystof, 1933-

Intvr: Grzenkowicz, Izabella

Topic: Composers as conductors; Philosophy & aesthetics; Program
music

Works: Jacob's awakening

List: N

Biog: N

Source: PM "Conversation with
Krzysztof Penderecki." 46
(1977): 24-30; 47 (1977):
10-14

Lang: ENG, GER

756 Penderecki, Krzystof, 1933-

Intvr: Margles, Pamela

Topic: Church music; Composers–
Political conditions

List: N

Biog: Y

Source: M MAG "Krzystof Penderecki.
His passion and politics." 7/5
(Nov.-Dec. 1984): 10-13

Lang: ENG

757 Penderecki, Krzystof, 1933-

Intvr: Holland, Bernard P.

Topic: Music & religion

List: N

Biog: N

Source: NYT "Penderecki is retrogress-
ing now–on purpose." 12 Jan.
1986, sec. 2, p. 25

Lang: ENG

758 Pennisi, Francesco, 1934-

Date: 3/26/82, Italy

Intvr: Failla, Salvatore Enrico

Topic: Audiences–Italy; Community
relations; Composers–Relations
with audiences; Gruppo Nuova
Consonanza; Philosophy & aesthetics; Societies, associations,
etc.; Teaching; 20th-century
music

Works: Carteggio; Sylvia simplex

List: N

Biog: N

Source: FAILLA M "Intervista a Francesco Pennisi: Odissea nelle
note." pp. 9-17

Lang: ITA

759 Pentland, Barbara, 1912-

Topic: Canada

List: Y

Biog: Y

Source: MUSCAN "Barbara Pentland,
a portrait." 21 (July-Aug. 1969):
[8-9]

Lang: ENG, FRE

760 Pentland, Barbara, 1912-

Intvr: Adames, John

Topic: Composers–Relations with audiences; Composition–Influences;
Serial music

List: N

Biog: Y

117

Source: PAC "The art of composition."
20/3 (Fall 1983): 38-42
Lang: ENG

761 Pépin, Clermont, 1926-
Topic: Composers–Economic conditions
List: Y
Biog: Y
Source: MUSCAN "Clermont Pépin, a portrait." 2 (June 1967): 8-9
Lang: ENG, FRE

762 Perkinson, Coleridge-Taylor, 1932-
Intvr: Baker, David N., et al.
Topic: Black composers; Composers–Influences; Composition–Technique; Performance; Style (Individual)
Works: Attitudes; Commentary
List: Y
Biog: Y
Source: BAKER B, pp. 239-76
Lang: ENG

763 Persichetti, Vincent, 1915-1987.
Intvr: Shackelford, Rudy
Topic: Philosophy & aesthetics; Religion; Teaching; 12-tone system
List: N
Biog: N
Source: PNM "Conversation with Vincent Persichetti." 20 (Fall-Sum. 1981-82): 104-33
Lang: ENG

Persson, Mats, 1943-
See no. 246.

764 Petrassi, Goffredo, 1904-
Intvr: Briggs, John
Topic: Style (Individual)
List: N
Biog: N
Source: NYT "Composer with style: Goffredo Petrassi, visitor from Italy, explains his aims and methods." 18 Dec. 1955, sec. 2, p. 9
Lang: ENG

765 Petrassi, Goffredo, 1904-
Date: 2/6/68
Intvr: Pinzauti, Leonardo
Topic: Electronic music; 17th-century music; Stockhausen, Karlheinz, 1928-; 20th-century music
List: N
Biog: N
Source: PINZAUTI M, pp. 67-79
Lang: ITA
Notes: Previously published in *Nuova Rivista Musicale Italiana* 2 (Mar.-June 1968): 482-93.

766 Petrassi, Goffredo, 1904-
Date: 11/77-Sum/78, Rome, Italy
Intvr: Lombardi, Luca
Topic: Cage, John, 1912-1992; Chamber music; Critics; Electronic music; Kagel, Mauricio, 1931-; Motion picture music; Music & art; Schoenberg, Arnold, 1874-1951; Teaching; Text setting; 20th-century music–Style
Works: Concerto, orchestra; Coro di morti; Partita; Salmo IX
List: N
Biog: Y
Source: LOM C

Lang: ITA
Notes: Extracts in German published in *Neue Zeitschrift für Musik* 147/3 (Mar. 1986): 21-25.

767 Petrassi, Goffredo, 1904-
Date: 5/8/82, Italy
Intvr: Failla, Salvatore Enrico
Topic: Composition–Technique; Concerto; Creativity; Form; Italy–20th-century; Motion picture music; Music & literature; Style (Individual); Symphony
Works: Concerto, orchestra
List: N
Biog: N
Source: FAILLA M "Intervista a Goffredo Petrassi: Non c'è pace tra le note." pp. 51-60
Lang: ITA

768 Pfrengle, Roland, 1945-
Date: 5/10/84, Berlin, Germany
Intvr: Barlow, Klarenz
Topic: Computer music
List: N
Biog: N
Source: MUSTEXTE "Willkommen in BYTEschland! ...." 6 (Oct. 1984): 35-36
Lang: GER

769 Phillips, Tom
Date: 6/23/76, London, England
Intvr: Bryars, Gavin; Orton, Fred
Topic: Music & art; Notation, Graphic
List: N
Biog: N
Source: SI "Tom Phillips: Interview by Fred Orton and Gavin Bryars." 984 (Nov.-Dec. 1976): 290-96
Lang: ENG

770 Pisk, Paul Amadeus, 1893-1990.
Date: 11/72
Intvr: Smith, Joan Allen, et al.
Topic: Performance; Schoenberg, Arnold, 1874-1951
List: N
Biog: N
Source: SMITH S, pp. 90, 110-4, 180
Lang: ENG

771 Pisk, Paul Amadeus, 1893-1990.
Intvr: Antokoletz, Elliott
Topic: Schoenberg, Arnold, 1874-1951; Societies, associations, etc.–Austria
List: N
Biog: Y
Source: TEMPO "A survivor of the Vienna Schoenberg circle: An interview with Paul A. Pisk." 154 (Sept. 1985): 15-21
Lang: ENG

772 Piston, Walter, 1894-1976.
Intvr: Westergaard, Peter
Topic: Performance; Philosophy & aesthetics; Teaching
List: N
Biog: N
Source: PNM "Conversation with Walter Piston." 7/1 (Fall-Wint. 1968): 3-17
Lang: ENG

773 Pope, Stephen
Date: 4/28/84

Intvr: Barlow, Klarenz
Topic: Computer music; Electronic music studios
List: N
Biog: N
Source: MUSTEXTE "Willkommen in BYTEschland! ...." 6 (Oct. 1984): 32-33
Lang: GER

774 Poulenc, Francis, 1899-1963.
Date: 1953; 1955-62
Intvr: Audel, Stéphane
Topic: Church music; Composers, French–20th-century; Éluard, Paul, 1895-1952; Falla, Manuel de, 1876-1946; Jacob, Max, 1876-1944; Prokofiev, Sergey, 1891-1953; Stravinsky, Igor, 1882-1971; Vocal music
List: N
Biog: N
Source: AUDEL P
Lang: ENG

775 Pousseur, Henri, 1929-
Intvr: Wolf, Muriel Hebert
Topic: Opera; Text setting
Works: Votre Faust
List: N
Biog: N
Source: OJ "Notre Faust is 'Votre Faust': Conversation with Michel Butor and Henri Pousseur." 1/2 (Spr. 1968): 13-19
Lang: ENG

776 Powell, Melvin, 1923-
Date: Fall/82, Calif.
Intvr: Robins, Reid

Topic: Education; Style (Individual); Theory
List: N
Biog: N
Source: MQ "An interview with Mel Powell." 72 (1986): 476-93
Lang: ENG

Puig, Michel, 1930-
See no. 244.

777 Quintanar, Héctor, 1936-
Intvr: Pulido, Esperanza
Topic: Electronic music; Electronic music studios; Live performance
List: N
Biog: N
Source: HETEROFONIA "Conversación con Héctor Quintanar. Director del Laboratorio de Música Electrónica del Conservatorio." 18 (May-June 1971): 21-22, 40
Lang: SPA

778 Radauer, Irmfried, 1928-
Date: 4/29/84, Salzburg, Germany
Intvr: Barlow, Klarenz
Topic: Computers
List: N
Biog: N
Source: MUSTEXTE "Willkommen in BYTEschland! ...." 6 (Oct. 1984): 33
Lang: GER

Radig, Éliane
See **Radigue, Éliane.**

779 Radigue, Éliane
Intvr: Haessig, Georges
Topic: Electronic music

List: N
Biog: N
Source: M JEU "... dans la réalité." 8
(Sept. 1972): 69-70
Lang: FRE

Radique, Éliane
See no. 242.

780 Raecke, Hans-Karsten, 1941-
Date: 12/76
Intvr: Stürzbecher, Ursula
Topic: Composers–Influences; Jazz–
Style; Sound
Works: Klangwerkstatt; Temperamente
List: Y
Biog: Y
Source: STURZ K, pp. 332-48
Lang: GER

781 Raksin, David, 1912-
Intvr: Ulrich, Allan
Topic: Motion picture music; Philoso-
phy & aesthetics
Works: The bad and the beautiful; Force
of evil; Forever amber; Giddyap;
Laura; A unicorn in the garden
List: Y
Biog: N
Source: ULRICH A, pp. 23-28
Lang: ENG

782 Randall, James Kirtland, 1929-
Intvr: Kovacic, William
Topic: Computer music
List: N
Biog: N
Source: NYT "Now it's music by com-
puter." 24 Sept. 1972, sec. 1,
p. 113
Lang: ENG

783 Rands, Bernard, 1935-
Intvr: Rockwell, John
Topic: Contests & awards; Pulitzer
prizes
Works: Canti del sole
List: N
Biog: N
Source: NYT "Composer sees Pulitzer
as a long-term benefit." 8 May
1984, sec. 3, p. 11
Lang: ENG

784 Reed, Alfred, 1921-
List: N
Biog: Y
Source: ACCENT "Meet The Composer:
An interview with Alfred Reed."
2/1 (Sept.-Oct. 1976): 22-23
Lang: ENG

785 Reibel, Guy, 1936-
Date: 6/73
Intvr: Mâche, François-Bernard
Topic: Computers; Electronic music–
Notation; Experimental music
List: N
Biog: Y
Source: RM "Les mal entendus. Com-
positeurs des années 70." 314-
15 (1978): 125-34
Lang: FRE

786 Reich, Steve, 1936-
Date: Sum/70, London, England
Intvr: Nyman, Michael
Topic: Electronic music; Instrumental
music
Works: Come out to show them; Phase
patterns
List: N

Biog: Y
Source: MT "Steve Reich. An interview with Michael Nyman." 1537 (Mar. 1971): 229-31
Lang: ENG
Notes: A part of the interview was published in Steve Reich, *Writings about Music* (N.Y.: Universal Edition, 1974).

787 Reich, Steve, 1936-

Intvr: Wasserman, Emily
Topic: African music; Composition–Technique; Electronic music; Performance
List: N
Biog: N
Source: ARTFORUM "An interview with composer Steve Reich." 10/9 (May 1972): 44-48
Lang: ENG
Notes: A part of the interview was published in Steve Reich, *Writings about Music* (N.Y.: Universal Edition, 1974).

788 Reich, Steve, 1936-

Date: 6/26/76-6/27/76, La Rochelle, France
Intvr: Nyman, Michael
Topic: Composition–Technique; LeWitt, Sol, 1928-; Philosophy & aesthetics
Works: Drumming; Music for 18 musicians; Pendulum music
List: N
Biog: N
Source: SI "Steve Reich. Interview by Michael Nyman." 984 (Nov.-Dec. 1976): 300-7
Lang: ENG

789 Reich, Steve, 1936-

Date: 6/77
Intvr: Nyman, Michael
Topic: Composition–Technique
Works: Music for 18 musicians
List: N
Biog: N
Source: MM "Steve Reich." 293 (Jan. 1977): 18-19
Lang: ENG

790 Reich, Steve, 1936-

Date: 4/13/80, New York City, N.Y.
Intvr: Caras, Tracy; Gagne, Cole
Topic: Creative process
Works: Come out; Music for a large ensemble; Octet; Piano phase; Reed phase; Variations for winds, strings and keyboards; Violin phase
List: Y
Biog: Y
Source: GAGNE S, pp. 305-17
Lang: ENG
Notes: Excerpts published in *Music Magazine* 6/3 (May-June 1983): 16-19.

791 Reich, Steve, 1936-

Intvr: Varga, Bálint András
Topic: Composition–Influences; Sound; Style (Individual)
List: N
Biog: N
Source: NHQ "Three questions on music: Extracts from a book of interviews in the making." 93 (Spr. 1984): 197-202
Lang: ENG

792 Reich, Steve, 1936-
Intvr: Dery, Mark
Topic: Minimal music
Works: The desert music
List: N
Biog: N
Source: HP "Steve Reich." 28 (1984): 52-55, 95
Lang: ENG

793 Reich, Steve, 1936-
Intvr: Page, Tim
Topic: Concerts & recitals; Minimal music
List: N
Biog: N
Source: NYT "Composer to perform." 3 Aug. 1986, sec. 21, p. 15
Lang: ENG

794 Reich, Steve, 1936-
Intvr: Lohner, Henning
Topic: Composition–Technique; Minimal music; Popular music–United States
Works: The desert music
List: N
Biog: Y
Source: NZ "Komponieren heute: 'Musik ist immer ethnische Musik.' Ein Gespräch mit Steve Reich." 147/10 (Oct. 1986): 22-27
Lang: GER

795 Reich, Steve, 1936-
Intvr: Strickland, Edward
Topic: Composition–Technique; Jewish music; 20th-century music
Works: The desert music
List: N
Biog: Y

Source: FANFARE "Downtown: An interview with Steve Reich." 10/4 (Mar.-Apr. 1987): 43-51
Lang: ENG

796 Reimann, Aribert, 1936-
Intvr: Burde, Wolfgang
Topic: Composers as performers
List: N
Biog: N
Source: NZ "... als Komponist und Interpret: Interview mit Aribert Reimann." 141/6 (Nov.-Dec. 1980): 535-36
Lang: GER

797 Reith, Dirk
Date: 6/10/84, Essen, Germany
Intvr: Barlow, Klarenz
Topic: Computers
List: N
Biog: N
Source: MUSTEXTE "Willkommen in BYTEschland! ...." 6 (Oct. 1984): 37
Lang: GER

798 Reynolds, Roger, 1934-
Date: 1973
Intvr: Kobrin, Ed; Mizelle, Dary John
Topic: Experimental music
List: N
Biog: N
Source: IAIMR "Interview with Roger Reynolds." 11 (1975): 157-67
Lang: ENG

799 Reynolds, Roger, 1934-
Date: 6/9/80, N.Y.
Intvr: Caras, Tracy; Gagne, Cole

Topic: Creative process; Performance
Works: Again; Ambages; Blind men; Compass; The emperor of ice cream; I/O; Masks; A merciful coincidence; Ping; Quick are the mouths of earth; Shadowed narrative; Threshold; Voicespace
List: Y
Biog: Y
Source: GAGNE S, pp. 319-36
Lang: ENG

800 Reynolds, Roger, 1934-
Date: 3/9/84, San Diego, Calif.
Intvr: Boulanger, Richard
Topic: Electronic music; Music & science; Sound
Works: Transfigured wind; Voicespace
List: N
Biog: N
Source: CMJ "Interview with Roger Reynolds, Joji Yuasa, and Charles Wuorinen." 8/4 (Wint. 1984): 45-54
Lang: ENG
Notes: Charles Wuorinen and Jōji Yuasa were also interviewed.

801 Richardson, Dana, 1953-
Intvr: Kleege, Stephen
Topic: Creative process
Works: Fantasy and fugue
List: N
Biog: N
Source: NYT "Composing without hearing the music." 7 Nov. 1982, sec. 21, p. 25
Lang: ENG

802 Ridout, Godfrey, 1918-
Topic: Canada
Works: Ascension; Fall fair; Two etudes for strings
List: Y
Biog: Y
Source: MUSCAN "Godfrey Ridout, a portrait." 12 (June-July 1968): [8-9]
Lang: ENG, FRE

803 Ridout, Godfrey, 1918-
Intvr: Hatton, Helen
Topic: Composers–Social conditions; Creativity; Style (Individual)
List: N
Biog: N
Source: CC "Interview! Godfrey Ridout." 93 (Sept. 1974): 4-13
Lang: ENG, FRE

804 Riehm, Rolf, 1937-
Intvr: Leukert, Bernd
Topic: Composition–Technique; Philosophy & aesthetics; Wind instrument music
List: Y
Biog: N
Source: MUSTEXTE "Splitter zerbrochener Zeit: Ein Gespräch mit dem Komponisten Rolf Riehm." 6 (Oct. 1984): 43-53
Lang: GER

805 Rieti, Vittorio, 1898-
Date: Wint/85, N.Y.
Intvr: Ricci, Franco Carlo
Topic: Artists–20th-century; Musicians–20th-century; Poets–20th-century
List: Y

Biog: N
Source: RICCI V "I. Conversazioni con Vittorio Rieti: Testimonianze sui contemporanei." pp. 227-71
Lang: ITA

806 Rihm, Wolfgang, 1952-
Intvr: Lombardi, Luca
Topic: Style (Individual)
Works: Klavierstück, no. 6; Symphony, no. 3
List: N
Biog: N
Source: MR "Ritorno al disordine. Conversazione con Wolfgang Rihm." 2 (Aug. 1980): 91-101
Lang: ITA

807 Rihm, Wolfgang, 1952-
Date: 5/4/85, Berlin, Germany
Intvr: Jungheinrich, Hans-Klaus
Topic: Composers–Social conditions; Culture–Germany, West (former); Philosophy & aesthetics; Style (Individual); 20th-century music
List: N
Diog: N
Source: JUNG L "Einer an und für sich? Zwölf Fragen an Wolfgang Rihm." pp. 13-23
Lang: GER

808 Riley, Terry, 1935-
Topic: Electronic music; Electronic music synthesizers; Harmony; Indian music–Influences; Style (Individual)
List: N
Biog: N

Source: TW "Terry Riley's electronic mantra." 1/15 (1983)
Lang: ENG

809 Riley, Terry, 1935-
Intvr: Amirkhanian, Charles
Topic: Experimental music; Indian music; Performance practice
Works: In C
List: N
Biog: N
Source: MUSTEXTE "A channel for some higher energy: Terry Riley im Gespräch." 7 (Dec. 1984): 35-41
Lang: GER

810 Risset, Jean-Claude, 1938-
Intvr: Lynner, Doug; Quesada, Virginia
Topic: Computers; Institut de Recherche et de Coordination Acoustique-Musique (IRCAM)
List: N
Biog: N
Source: SYNAPSE "Jean-Claude Risset." 2/5 (Mar.-Apr. 1978): 26 31
Lang: ENG

811 Risset, Jean-Claude, 1938-
Intvr: Schrader, Barry
Topic: Computer music; Electronic music; Form; Style (Individual); Tone color
Works: Mutations I
List: N
Biog: N
Source: SCHRADER I "19. Interview with Jean-Claude Risset: 'Mutations I.'" pp. 194-201
Lang: ENG

812 Rochberg, George, 1918-
Intvr: Blackburn, Robert T.; Risen-
hoover, Morris
Topic: Colleges & universities– Faculty;
Composers–Economic condi-
tions; Teaching
List: N
Biog: Y
Source: RISEN A, pp. 123-32
Lang: ENG

813 Rochberg, George, 1918-
Intvr: Ericson, Raymond
Works: Concord quartets
List: N
Biog: N
Source: NYT "Rochberg writes quartets
by threes." 21 Jan. 1979, sec. 2,
pp. 15, 28
Lang: ENG

814 Rochberg, George, 1918-
Date: 3/16/80, Newton Square, Penn.
Intvr: Caras, Tracy; Gagne, Cole
Topic: Philosophy & aesthetics
Works: Apocalyptica; Black sounds;
Contra mortem et tempus; Elec-
trikaleidoscope; Music for the
magic theater; Octet; Quintet,
piano, string; Ricordanza;
Twelve bagatelles
List: Y
Biog: Y
Source: GAGNE S, pp. 337-54
Lang: ENG

815 Rochberg, George, 1918-
Intvr: Grimes, Ev
Topic: Culture; 18th-century music;
19th-century music; Teaching

List: N
Biog: Y
Source: MEJ "Conversations with
American composers." 73/1
(Sept. 1986): 42-44, 46-48
Lang: ENG

Roquin, Louis
See no. 244.

Rorem, Ned, 1923-
See no. 424.

816 Rorem, Ned, 1923-
Intvr: Gruen, John
Topic: Composers as authors; Contests
& awards; Pulitzer prizes; Vocal
music
List: N
Biog: N
Source: NYT "'Now I can die offi-
cial,' says Pulitzer-winner Ned
Rorem." 30 May 1976, sec. 2,
p. 12
Lang: ENG

817 Rorem, Ned, 1923-
Intvr: Gruen, John
List: N
Biog: N
Source: ASCAP "Ned Rorem." 9/1 (Spr.
1978): 14-16
Lang: ENG
Notes: Reprinted from *New York Times*,
1977.

818 Rorem, Ned, 1923-
Intvr: Davis, Deborah
Topic: Choral music; Composition–
Technique

List: N
Biog: N
Source: MQ "An interview about choral music with Ned Rorem." 68 (July 1982): 390-97
Lang: ENG

819 Rorem, Ned, 1923-
Intvr: Peyser, Joan
Topic: 20th-century music
List: N
Biog: N
Source: NYT "Ned Rorem delivers a solo on the state of music." 3 May 1987, sec. 2, p. 21
Lang: ENG

820 Rosenboom, David, 1947-
Intvr: Henahan, Donal
Topic: Experimental music
List: N
Biog: N
Source: NYT "Music draws strains direct from brains." 25 Nov. 1970, sec. 1, p. 24
Lang: ENG

821 Rosenboom, David, 1947-
Intvr: Zimmermann, Walter
Topic: Experimental music; Physiology
List: N
Biog: N
Source: ZIMMER D, pp. 183-92
Lang: ENG

822 Rosenboom, David, 1947-
Date: 11/6/82
Intvr: Siddall, John; Timar, Andrew
Topic: Computers; Culture
List: N
Biog: N

Source: MUSWORKS "In conversation: David Rosenboom and Richard Teitelbaum." 21 (Fall 1982): 12-14
Lang: ENG
Notes: Richard Teitelbaum was also interviewed.

823 Rosenboom, David, 1947-
Intvr: Polansky, Larry
Topic: Computer music; Sound recordings; Style (Individual)
List: N
Biog: N
Source: CMJ "Interview with David Rosenboom." 7/4 (Wint. 1983): 40-44
Lang: ENG

824 Rota, Nino, 1911-1979.
Date: 1/71, Rome, Italy
Intvr: Pinzauti, Leonardo
Topic: Church music; Composers–Influences; Motion picture music
List: N
Biog: N
Source: PINZAUTI M, pp 175-86
Lang: ITA
Notes: Previously published in *Nuova Rivista Musicale Italiana* 5 (Jan.-Feb. 1971): 74-83.

825 Rózsa, Miklós, 1907-
Intvr: Wheelwright, D. Sterling
Topic: Motion picture music; Sound recordings
List: N
Biog: N
Source: MN "An interview with Miklós Rózsa." 44 (Oct. 1952): 15
Lang: ENG

826 Rubbra, Edmund, 1901-1986.
Intvr: Schafer, Raymond Murray
Topic: Creativity; Criticism; Form;
Symphony
List: N
Biog: N
Source: SCHAFER B, pp. 64-72
Lang: ENG

827 Rubbra, Edmund, 1901-1986.
Date: 3/76
Intvr: Fawkes, Richard
List: N
Biog: Y
Source: MM "Edmund Rubbra talks to
Richard Fawkes." 285 (May
1976): 22-23
Lang: ENG

828 Rubio, Hilarion F., 1902-
Intvr: Samson, Helen F.
Topic: Composers as conductors
List: Y
Biog: N
Source: SAMSON C, pp. 173-81
Lang: ENG

829 Rudhyar, Dane, 1895-1985.
Date: 5/19/75; 5/23/75; 6/1/75; 3/27/76
Intvr: Rayner, Sheila Finch, et al.
Topic: Astrology; Buddhism; Cosmol-
ogy; New Music Society; Paint-
ing; Performance practice; Philos-
ophy & aesthetics; Theosophy;
Time
Works: Four pentagrams; Granites;
Mosaic; Paens; Tetragrams;
Three poems; Thresholds
List: N
Biog: N

Source: RAYNER D
Lang: ENG
Notes: Recorded on 5 tapes.

Ruyneman, Daniël, 1886-1963.
See no. 12.

830 Ruzicka, Peter, 1948-
Intvr: Krellmann, Hanspeter
Topic: Composers–Relations with audi-
ences; Style (Individual)
List: N
Biog: N
Source: MUSICA "Komposition als
Moment der Verweigerung.
Gespräch mit dem Komponisten
Peter Ruzicka." 30 (Mar.-Apr.
1976): 122-27
Lang: GER

831 Ruzicka, Peter, 1948-
Date: 11/28/76
Intvr: Konold, Wulf
Topic: Copyright; Gesellschaft zur
Wahrnehmung von Urheber-
rechten (GEMA)
List: N
Biog: N
Source: FP "Interview mit Peter Ruzicka
über seine GEMA-Initiative." 13
(June 1977): 30-31
Lang: GER
Notes: Previously published in *Hifi-
Stereophonie* 4 (1977).

Rydberg, Bo
See no. 612.

832 Rzewski, Frederic, 1938-
Intvr: Zimmermann, Walter

Topic: Political songs; Wolff, Christian,
1934-
Works: Apolitical intellectuals; It's com-
ing together; The people united
will never be defeated
List: N
Biog: N
Source: ZIMMER D, pp. 299-325
Lang: ENG

833 Rzewski, Frederic, 1938-
Intvr: Pestalozza, Luigi
Topic: Cardew, Cornelius, 1936-1981;
Electronic music
List: N
Biog: N
Source: MR "Colloquio con Rzewsky
su Cornelius Cardew." 8 (Aug.
1982): 37-52
Lang: ITA

834 Saariaho, Kaija
Intvr: Nieminen, Risto
Topic: Computer music
Works: Berglendungen
List: N
Biog: N
Source: FMQ "An interview with Kaija
Saariaho." 1/3-4 (1985): 22-27
Lang: ENG

835 Sacramento, Lucino T., 1908-
Intvr: Samson, Helen F.
Works: Concerto, piano, no. 2 ("Mahar-
like")
List: Y
Biog: N
Source: SAMSON C, pp. 182-90
Lang: ENG

836 Salzedo, Leonard Lopes, 1921-
Intvr: Knight, Judyth
Topic: Dance music
Works: Hazard; Realms of choice; The
travellers; The witch boy
List: N
Biog: N
Source: COMP(LONDON) "Music for
dance." 40 (Sum. 1971): 15-17
Lang: ENG

837 Samter, Alice, 1908-
Intvr: Matthei, Renate; Sonntag, Brun-
hilde
Topic: Commissions; Sexism; Women
composers
List: N
Biog: Y
Source: SONNTAG A, v. 1, pp. 27-34
Lang: GER

838 San Pedro, Lucio D., 1913-
Date: 1973
Intvr: Samson, Helen F.
List: Y
Biog: N
Source: SAMSON C, pp. 191-201
Lang: ENG
Notes: Previously published in *Bulletin
Today* (29 Nov. 1973): 1.

839 Sandström, Jan, 1954-
Intvr: Karkoff, Maurice Ingvar
Topic: Composition–Technique
Works: Format mirrors
List: Y
Biog: Y
Source: NUTIDA "Jan Sandströms 'Fro-
mat Mirrors': En upptäktsresa i

språket, en vaggvisa full av vrede." 29/1 (1985-86): 4-5

Lang: SWE

840 Sandström, Sven-David, 1942-
Intvr: Rying, Matts
Works: Requiem, de ur alla minnen fallna
List: N
Biog: N
Source: NUTIDA "'Inga leksaker fick tas med på den långa resan.'" 25/3 (1981-82): 9-11
Lang: SWE
Notes: Poet Tobias Berggren was also interviewed.

841 Sandström, Sven-David, 1942-
Intvr: Tobeck, Christina
Topic: Creative process; Opera; Orchestral music
Works: Through and through
List: N
Biog: N
Source: NUTIDA "Musik är känsla." 29/4 (1985-86): 21-28
Lang: SWE

842 Santos, Ramon, Pagayon, 1941-
Intvr: Samson, Helen F.
Topic: Experimental music
List: Y
Biog: N
Source: SAMSON C, pp. 202-11
Lang: ENG

843 Sapieyevski, Jerzy, 1945-
Date: 2/23/85, Washington, D.C.
Intvr: Gamarekian, Barbara
Topic: Community relations

List: N
Biog: N
Source: NYT "Her words, his music." 24 Feb. 1985, sec. 1, p. 49
Lang: ENG
Notes: Poet Anne Morrow Lindbergh was also interviewed.

844 Sauer, Arthur, 1962-
Intvr: Baartman, Nicoline
Topic: Style (Individual)
List: N
Biog: Y
Source: KN "'I could just as well have been a criminal.'" 24 (1987): 41-42
Lang: ENG

845 Sauguet, Henri, 1901-1989.
Intvr: Downes, Olin
Topic: Philosophy & aesthetics
List: N
Biog: N
Source: NYT "French composer: Henri Sauguet, visiting America, talks about his life, art and philosophy." 19 Apr. 1953, sec. 2, p. 7
Lang: ENG

846 Sauguet, Henri, 1901-1989.
Date: 5/29/70, Florence, Italy
Intvr: Pinzauti, Leonardo
Topic: Ansermet, Ernest, 1883-1969; Composers–20th-century; Composers, Italian; Conducting; Debussy, Claude, 1862-1918; Messiaen, Olivier, 1908-1992; Style (Individual)
List: N
Biog: N

Source: PINZAUTI M, pp. 143-50
Lang: ITA
Notes: Previously published in *Nuova Rivista Musicale Italiana* 4 (Mar.-June 1970): 482-87.

847 Saxton, Robert, 1953-
Intvr: Griffiths, Paul
Topic: Composers–Influences; Electronic music; Music & Literature; Style (Individual)
List: Y
Biog: Y
Source: GRIFFITHS N, pp. 179-85
Lang: ENG

848 Schaeffer, Pierre, 1910-
Intvr: Bayle, François
Topic: Henry, Pierre, 1927-
List: N
Biog: N
Source: RM "Pierre Schaeffer parle de Pierre Henry avec François Bayle." 265-66 (1968): 109-13
Lang: FRE

849 Schaeffer, Pierre, 1910-
Intvr: Pierret, Marc
Topic: Composers as authors; Composition–Technique; Education; Electronic music; Electronic musical instruments; Henry, Pierre, 1927-; Music & language; Musique concrète; Sociology; Sound; Stochastic theory
Works: Clotaire Nicole; Monsieur Gurdjieff; Opéra de minuit; Symphonie pour un homme seul
List: Y
Biog: Y

Source: PIERRET E
Lang: FRE

850 Schaeffer, Pierre, 1910-
Intvr: Lyon, Raymond
Topic: Electro-acoustics; Electronic music; Musique concrète; Philosophy & aesthetics; Teaching
List: N
Biog: N
Source: CMF "Entretien avec Pierre Schaeffer." 52 (1975): 132-35
Lang: FRE

851 Schaeffer, Pierre, 1910-
Topic: Composition–Technique; Electro-acoustics; France–20th-century; Musique concrète; Philosophy & aesthetics
List: N
Biog: N
Source: TW "French musique concrète: Pierre Schaeffer & Pierre Henry." 2/3 (1985)
Lang: ENG

Schaeffer, Pierre, 1910-
See no. 462.

852 Schafer, Raymond Murray, 1933-
Topic: Composers–Economic conditions
Works: Loving/Toi; Patria
List: Y
Biog: Y
Source: MUSCAN "R. Murray Schafer, a portrait." 15 (Oct. 1968): [8-9]
Lang: ENG, FRE

853 Schafer, Raymond Murray, 1933-
Date: 5/75, England
Intvr: Potter, Keith; Shepherd, John
Topic: Composers–Canada
Works: Patria; *Soundscape project*
List: N
Biog: N
Source: CONTACT "Interview with Murray Schafer." 13 (Spr. 1976): 3-10
Lang: ENG

854 Schafer, Raymond Murray, 1933-
Date: 1/17/81, Vancouver, Canada
Intvr: Westerkamp, Hildegard
Topic: Sound, Environmental
Works: Music for wilderness lake
List: N
Biog: N
Source: MUSWORKS "Wilderness lake." 15 (Spr. 1981): 20-21
Lang: ENG

855 Schafer, Raymond Murray, 1933-
Topic: Audiences–20th-century music; Legends & myths; Sound, Environmental
Works: Patria; Princess of the stars; Ra
List: N
Biog: N
Source: MUSWORKS "Beyond Ra: R. Murray Schafer in conversation." 25 (Fall 1983): 3-11
Lang: ENG

Schat, Peter, 1935-
See no. 547.

856 Schat, Peter, 1935-
Intvr: Koopmans, Rudy
Topic: Baaren, Kees van, 1906-1970; Composers–Political conditions
List: N
Biog: N
Source: KN "The revolution has returned to Europe: Interview with Peter Schat." 4 (Dec. 1976): 29-32
Lang: ENG

857 Schenker, Friedrich, 1942-
Date: 6/77
Intvr: Stürzbecher, Ursula
Topic: Composers as performers; Eisler, Hanns, 1898-1962; Instrumental music; Jazz
List: Y
Biog: Y
Source: STURZ K, pp. 246-67
Lang: GER

858 Schickele, Peter, 1935-
Date: 3/22/75, Cambridge, Mass.
Intvr: Everett, Thomas G.
Topic: Bach, P.D.Q., 1807-1742?
List: N
Biog: N
Source: MEJ "An interview with Peter Schickele." 62/6 (Feb. 1976): 76-78
Lang: ENG

859 Schickele, Peter, 1935-
Intvr: Blau, Eleanor
Topic: Bach, P.D.Q., 1807-1742?
List: N
Biog: N
Source: NYT "P.D.Q. is back for another season's musical Mayhem." 24 Dec. 1976, sec. 3, p. 11
Lang: ENG

860 Schickele, Peter, 1935-
Intvr: Kozinn, Allan
Topic: Bach, P.D.Q., 1807-1742?; Concerts & recitals
List: N
Biog: N
Source: NYT "Peter Schickele versus P. D.Q. Bach." 25 Dec. 1977, sec. 2, pp. 17, 20
Lang: ENG

861 Schickele, Peter, 1935-
Intvr: Colgrass, Ulla
Topic: Bach, P.D.Q., 1807-1742?
List: N
Biog: N
Source: M MAG "P.D.Q. strikes again!" 1/4 (July-Aug. 1978): 25-28
Lang: ENG

862 Schickele, Peter, 1935-
Intvr: Blau, Eleanor
Topic: Bach, P.D.Q., 1807-1742?
List: N
Biog: N
Source: NYT "P.D.Q. Bach's 'Liebeslieder Polkas' is unearthed." 28 Dec. 1979, sec. 3, p. 8
Lang: ENG

863 Schickele, Peter, 1935-
Intvr: Bennetts, Leslie
Topic: Bach, P.D.Q., 1807-1742?
List: N
Biog: N
Source: NYT "Surprises for fans of P. D.Q. Bach." 25 Dec. 1987, sec. 3, p. 3
Lang: ENG

Schmid, Erich, 1907-
See no. 544.

864 Schmidt, Christfried, 1932-
Date: 4/77
Intvr: Stürzbecher, Ursula
Topic: Chamber music; Choral music; Style (Individual)
Works: Psalm 21
List: Y
Biog: Y
Source: STURZ K, pp. 44-59
Lang: GER

865 Schmidt, Christfried, 1932-
Intvr: Kühn, Georg-Friedrich
Topic: Style (Individual); Teaching
List: N
Biog: Y
Source: MUSTEXTE "Unbefangen, ungebärdig, in die Extreme des Ausdrucks; Glied der musikalischen Gesellschaft: Christfried Schmidt." 4 (Apr. 1984): 18-21
Lang: GER

866 Schnebel, Dieter, 1930-
Date: 10/30/69, 11/16/69, Frankfurt, Germany
Intvr: Pauli, Hansjörg
Topic: Community relations; Composers–Relations with audiences; Composition–Influences; Composition–Technique; Concerts & recitals–20th-century music; Music & politics; Philosophy & aesthetics; Popular music; Style (Individual); 20th-century music–Style
List: N

Biog: Y
Source: PAULI F, pp. 11-36
Lang: GER
Notes: Originally done for a series of a radio program of Hessischer Rundfunk Frankfurt.

867 Schnebel, Dieter, 1930-
Intvr: Lichtenfeld, Monika
Topic: Creative process; Performance
Works: Thanatos-Eros
List: N
Biog: N
Source: NZ "Thanatos-Eros: Liebe und Tod/Sterben und Leben. Gespräch mit Dieter Schnebel." 140/5 (Sept.-Oct. 1979): 482-86
Lang: GER

868 Schnitke, Alfred, 1934-
Date: 5/21/84, Moscow, USSR (former)
Intvr: Polin, Claire C. J.
Topic: Style (Individual)
List: N
Biog: N
Source: TEMPO "Interviews with Soviet composers. I: Alfred Schnitke." 151 (Dec. 1984): 10-13
Lang: ENG

869 Schönberg, Arnold, 1874-1951.
Date: 7/49, Brentwood, Calif.
Intvr: Stevens, Halsey
Topic: Music & art; Painting
List: N
Biog: N
Source: SCHON G "Schoenberg talks about his paintings." pp. 109-11
Lang: ENG

Notes: Previously published in *The Composer Magazine* 5/1 (Fall-Wint. 1973): 18-21. French translation in *Musique en Jeu* 16 (Nov. 1974): 70-71. Also recorded on *Columbia Masterworks: The Music of Arnold Schoenberg,* v. 3 (Columbia M2S709: Side 4, Bd. 4).

Schönberger, Elmer, 1950-
See no. 15.

870 Schoener, Eberhard
Topic: Electronic music; Gamelan
List: N
Biog: N
Source: TW "Trans-world synthesis. Part 1: John Hassell & Eberhard Schoener." 2/5 (1985)
Lang: ENG

871 Schuller, Gunther, 1925-
Intvr: Gratovich, Eugene
Topic: Commissions; Jazz ; Musicians–Training; Orchestras; Violin music
Works: Little blue devil; The power within us; Seven studies on themes of Paul Klee
List: N
Biog: N
Source: MJ "Should orchestras become museums?" 30/9 (Nov. 1972): 9, 42-43, 50, 58
Lang: ENG

872 Schuller, Gunther, 1925-
Date: 12/7/77, Ann Arbor, Mich.
Intvr: Harvith, John; Harvith, Susan Edwards

Topic: Sound recording & reproduction
List: N
Biog: Y
Source: HARVITH E, pp. 396-408
Lang: ENG

873 Schuller, Gunther, 1925-
Intvr: Ericson, Raymond
Topic: Composers–Relations with audiences
List: N
Biog: N
Source: NYT "New encounters of the Schuller kind." 3 Feb. 1978, sec. 3, p. 11
Lang: ENG

874 Schuller, Gunther, 1925-
Date: 6/21/85
Intvr: Hoffmann, James Avery; Maneri, Joseph Gabriel
Topic: Conducting; Teaching
List: N
Biog: N
Source: PNM "A conversation with Gunther Schuller." 24/2 (Spr.-Sum. 1986): 242-49
Lang: ENG

875 Schuller, Gunther, 1925-
Date: 12/17/85, New Orleans, La.
Intvr: Carnovale, Norbert
Topic: Composers as authors; Concerto; Creativity; History–Evaluation; Manuscripts–Preparation; Orchestra musicians; Performance practice
Works: Concerto, viola; *Musings; Nobody gives a damn about the composer*

List: Y
Biog: Y
Source: CARNOVALE G "Interview." pp. 37-64
Lang: ENG

876 Schuman, William, 1910-1992.
Intvr: Ericson, Raymond
Topic: Concerts & recitals
List: N
Biog: N
Source: NYT "Schuman: No pessimist he." 19 Jan. 1969, sec. 2, pp. 13, 23
Lang: ENG

877 Schuman, William, 1910-1992.
Intvr: Rockwell, John
Topic: Composers, American; Style (Individual)
List: N
Biog: N
Source: NYT "William Schuman–'the continuum has been composition.'" 3 Aug. 1980, sec. 2, pp. 19, 22
Lang: ENG

878 Schuman, William, 1910-1992.
Date: 12/15/80, N.Y.
Intvr: Clark, John W.
Topic: Symphony
List: N
Biog: N
Source: AM "William Schuman on his symphonies: An interview." 4 (Fall 1986): 328-36
Lang: ENG

879 Schuman, William, 1910-1992.
Intvr: Grimes, Ev
Topic: Education; Philosophy & aesthet-
ics; Teaching
List: N
Biog: N
Source: MEJ "Conversations with
American composers." 72/8
(Apr. 1986): 46-47, 50-54
Lang: ENG

880 Sciarrino, Salvatore, 1947-
Date: Spr/77, Florence, Italy
Intvr: Pinzauti, Leonardo
Topic: Bussotti, Sylvano, 1931-; Com-
posers–Influences; 19th-century
music; Opera; Philosophy & aes-
thetics; Stockhausen, Karlheinz,
1928-; 20th-century music
List: N
Biog: N
Source: PINZAUTI M, pp. 221-30
Lang: ITA
Notes: Previously published in *Nuova
Rivista Musicale Italiana* 11
(Jan.-Mar. 1977): 50-57.

881 Sciarrino, Salvatore, 1947-
Date: 4/14/82, Italy
Intvr: Failla, Salvatore Enrico
Topic: Concerts & recitals; Drama–
Style; Education; Incidental mu-
sic; Settimane di Nuova Musica;
Style (Individual)
Works: Trachinie
List: N
Biog: N
Source: FAILLA M "Intervista a Salva-
tore Sciarrino: Prima nota, l'essen-
zialità." pp. 29-38
Lang: ITA

882 Searle, Humphrey, 1915-1982.
Intvr: Schafer, Raymond Murray
Topic: Serialism; Tonality; 12-tone sys-
tem; Webern, Anton von, 1883-
1945
Works: The gold coast customs
List: N
Biog: Y
Source: SCHAFER B, pp. 125-36
Lang: ENG

883 Searle, Humphrey, 1915-1982.
Date: 10/73
Intvr: Smith, Joan Allen, et al.
Topic: 12-tone system; Webern, Anton
von, 1883-1945
List: N
Biog: N
Source: SMITH S, pp. 214-17
Lang: ENG

884 Seeger, Charles Louis, 1886-1979.
Date: 3/70
Intvr: Perlis, Vivian
List: N
Biog: N
Source: SOUNDINGS "Charles Seeger/
Vivian Perlis." 10 (1976), part 3
Lang: ENG

885 Seeger, Charles Louis, 1886-1979.
Date: 4/6/76-4/8/76, Conn.
Intvr: Dunaway, David King
Topic: Composers' Collective; Folk
music; Musicology; Performance
practice; Workers music
List: N
Biog: N
Source: ETHMUS "Charles Seeger and

Carl Sands: 'Composers' Collective years.'" 24 (1980): 159-68
Lang: ENG

886 Sessions, Roger, 1896-1985.
Date: 6/16/65
Intvr: Cone, Edward T.
Topic: Bloch, Ernest, 1880-1959; Composition–Technique; Parker, Horatio William, 1863-1919; Teaching; 12-tone system
List: N
Biog: N
Source: PNM "Conversation with Roger Sessions." 4/2 (Spr.-Sum. 1966): 29-46
Lang: ENG

887 Sessions, Roger, 1896-1985.
Date: 11/19/75, N.Y.
Intvr: Caras, Tracy; Gagne, Cole
Topic: Electronic music
Works: Idyll of Theocritus; Montezuma
List: Y
Biog: Y
Source: GAGNE S, pp. 355-65
Lang: ENG

888 Sessions, Roger, 1896-1985.
Date: 1/29/80, N.Y.
Intvr: LaBrecque, Rebecca
Topic: Creative process; Interpretation
Works: Sonatas, piano, nos. 1, 2
List: N
Biog: N
Source: SESSION T, Side 4, Bd. 2
Lang: ENG
Notes: Notes relating to the dialog (1 leaf) laid in container.

889 Sessions, Roger, 1896-1985.
Intvr: Rockwell, John
Topic: Composition–Technique
List: N
Biog: N
Source: NYT "Roger Sessions, nearing 85, is still a maverick composer." 22 Mar. 1981, sec. 2, pp. 17-18
Lang: ENG

890 Settles, Roberta
Intvr: Sundin, Nils-Göran
Topic: Television music
Works: Isolation-Meinhof in memoriam 12'14"
List: N
Biog: N
Source: NUTIDA "Isolation-Meinhof in memoriam 12'14"." 23/1 (1979-80): 23
Lang: SWE

891 Shapey, Ralph, 1921-
Date: 2/18/80, N.Y.
Intvr: Caras, Tracy; Gagne, Cole
Topic: Creative process; Philosophy & aesthetics
Works: Convocation; Discourse; Ontogeny; Praise; Rituals; Songs of Eros
List: Y
Biog: Y
Source: GAGNE S, pp. 367-82
Lang: ENG

892 Shapey, Ralph, 1921-
Intvr: Rockwell, John
List: N
Biog: N
Source: NYT "Ralph Shapey at 60–he

137

defied neglect." 10 May 1981, sec. 2, p. 17

Lang: ENG

893 Shapey, Ralph, 1921-
Date: 4/84, Boston, Mass.
Intvr: Cogan, Robert David
Topic: Composition–Technique; Philosophy & aesthetics
List: N
Biog: N
Source: SONUS "Thou shalt make graven images: An interview with Ralph Shapey." 5/1 (Fall 1984): 1-13
Lang: ENG

894 Shchedrin, Rodion Konstantinovich, 1932-
Intvr: Holland, Bernard P.
Topic: Union of Soviet Socialist Republics (former)
List: N
Biog: N
Source: NYT "Russian composer in New York." 13 Jan. 1986, sec. 3, p. 13
Lang: ENG

895 Shifrin, Seymour, 1926-1979.
Intvr: Blackburn, Robert T.; Risenhoover, Morris
Topic: Colleges & universities–Faculty; Teaching
List: N
Biog: Y
Source: RISEN A, pp. 153-62
Lang: ENG

896 Shostakovich, Dmitriĭ Dmitrievich, 1906-1975.
Date: 1959

Topic: 12-tone system; 20th-century music; Warsaw Autumn
List: N
Biog: N
Source: MDB "Eine Mode ohne Zukunft: Schostakowitsch über den 'Warschauer Herbst.'" 10/2 (Feb. 1960): 74-76
Lang: GER

897 Shostakovich, Dmitriĭ Dmitrievich, 1906-1975.
Intvr: Markowski, Liesel; Schaefer, Hansjürgen
Topic: Program music
Works: Symphony, no. 12
List: N
Biog: N
Source: MDB "Gespräch mit Dmitri Schostakowitsch." 11/12 (Dec. 1961): 706-8
Lang: GER

898 Shostakovich, Dmitriĭ Dmitrievich, 1906-1975.
Intvr: Rubin, Stephen E.
Topic: Composers–Political conditions
List: N
Biog: N
Source: NYT "Shostakovich: 'If my dreams cease ....'" 24 June 1973, sec. 2, pp. 1, 10
Lang: ENG

899 Siegmeister, Elie, 1909-1991.
Intvr: Ericson, Raymond
Topic: Fellowships & scholarships; Guggenheim fellowship
List: N
Biog: N

Source: NYT "Awards for Siegmeister at 70." 7 Jan. 1979, sec. 2, pp. 15, 20

Lang: ENG

900 Siegmeister, Elie, 1909-1991.

Intvr: Delatiner, Barbara

Topic: Philosophy & aesthetics

List: N

Biog: N

Source: NYT "What they always ask the composer." 23 Nov. 1980, sec. 21, p. 19

Lang: ENG

901 Silvestrov, Valentin, 1937-

Intvr: Nikolayev, Ivan

Topic: 20th-century music

List: N

Biog: N

Source: SL "Avant-garde eruption is not unlike the outburst of the romanticists." 149 (Feb. 1969): 14-15

Lang: ENG

Notes: Previously published in *Yunost*.

902 Simó, Manuel, 1916-

Intvr: Pierret-Villanueva, Florencia

Topic: Schools of music–Dominican Republic; Style (Individual); Symphony orchestras; Teaching

List: N

Biog: N

Source: RMC "Entrevista. Manuel Simó, compositor y director de la Orquesta Sinfonica Nacional." 134 (Apr.-Sept. 1976): 118-23

Lang: SPA

903 Singer, Jeanne, 1924-

Intvr: Van Gelder, Lawrence

List: N

Biog: N

Source: NYT "Her music and cats are a perfect mix." 25 Oct. 1981, sec. 21, p. 2

Lang: ENG

904 Singleton, Alvin, 1940-

Date: 5/21/82, Houston, Tex.

Intvr: Wyatt, Lucius Reynolds

Topic: Black composers

Works: Calm sea; Dream sequence '76; Extension of a dream; Kwitana; A yellow rose petal

List: N

Biog: Y

Source: BPM "Conversation with ... Alvin Singleton, composer." 11 (Fall 1983): 178-89

Lang: ENG

Sjöstrand, Östen, 1925-
See no. 49.

905 Slonimsky, Nicolas, 1894-

Intvr: Grimes, Ev

Topic: Composers–Economic conditions; Teaching

List: N

Biog: Y

Source: MEJ "Conversation with American composers." 72/7 (Mar. 1986): 40-43

Lang: ENG

Smirnov, Dmitri, 1948-
See no. 372.

906 Smith, Hale, 1925-

Intvr: Baker, David N., et al.

Topic: Black composers; Composers–
Influences; Composition–Tech-
nique; Jazz; Performance; Style
(Individual)
List: Y
Biog: Y
Source: BAKER B, pp. 313-36
Lang: ENG

907 Smith, William Overton, 1926-
Intvr: Meyer, Neal
Topic: Audiences; Improvisation
Works: Eye music; Outrage; Re-mi vari-
ations
List: N
Biog: N
Source: PNM "An interview with Stuart
Dempster and William O. Smith."
24/2 (Spr.-Sum. 1986): 190-223
Lang: ENG

908 Somers, Harry (Stewart), 1925-
Topic: 20th-century music
List: Y
Biog: Y
Source: MUSCAN "Harry Somers, a
portrait." 4 (Sept. 1967): 8-9
Lang: ENG, FRE

909 Souster, Tim, 1943-
Intvr: Griffiths, Paul
Topic: Electronic music; Popular music;
Stockhausen, Karlheinz, 1928-;
Tonality
List: Y
Biog: Y
Source: GRIFFITHS N, pp. 133-39
Lang: ENG

910 Sowande, Olufela ("Fela"), 1905-1987.
Date: Spr/75, N.Y.
Intvr: Southern, Eileen
Topic: African music; Philosophy &
aesthetics
List: N
Biog: Y
Source: BPM "Conversations with Fela
Sowande, high priest of music."
4 (Spr. 1976): 90-104
Lang: ENG

911 Spiegel, Laurie, 1945-
Topic: Occupational songs
List: N
Biog: N
Source: EAR "Dialogue with Laurie
Spiegel." 2/7 (Nov. 1976): [5-6]
Lang: ENG

912 Spinner, Leopold, 1906-
Intvr: Drew, David
Topic: Webern, Anton von, 1883-1945
List: Y
Biog: N
Source: TEMPO "Twelve questions for
Leopold Spinner." 99 (1972):
14-17
Lang: ENG

913 Steiner, Frederick, 1923-
Intvr: Ulrich, Allan
Topic: Motion picture music; Philoso-
phy & aesthetics
Works: Merry-go-round in the jungle;
Run for the sun; The St. Valen-
tine's Day massacre
List: N
Biog: N
Source: ULRICH A, pp. 29-34
Lang: ENG

914 Steuermann, Edward, 1892-1964.
Intvr: Schuller, Gunther
Topic: Performance; Schoenberg,
Arnold, 1874-1951
List: N
Biog: Y
Source: PNM "A conversation with
Steuermann." 3/1 (Fall-Wint.
1964): 22-35
Lang: ENG

915 Steven, Donald, 1945-
Intvr: Kieser, Karen
Topic: Composition–Influences; Edu-
cation
Works: Crossroads; The transient
List: N
Biog: Y
Source: MUSCAN "Words about music:
A series of interviews with Cana-
dian composers." 31 (Feb. 1977):
17-19
Lang: ENG, FRE

916 Stevens, Halsey, 1908-1989.
Intvr: Cope, David Howell
Topic: Audiences–20th-century music;
Popular music; 20th-century
music–Style
List: N
Biog: N
Source: COMP(CA) "An interview with
Halsey Stevens." 5/1 (Fall-Wint.
1973): 28-41
Lang: ENG

917 Still, William Grant, 1895-1978.
Intvr: Southern, Eileen
Topic: Black composers
List: N

Biog: N
Source: BPM "Conversation with...
William Grant Still." 3 (May
1975): 165-76
Lang: ENG
Notes: Also published in *ASCAP Today*
7/2 (Wint. 1975): 18–22.

918 Stockhausen, Karlheinz, 1928-
Date: 4/22/60, Hesse, Germany
Intvr: Adorno, Theodor Wiesengrund
Topic: Sociology; 20th-century music
List: N
Biog: N
Source: NEULAND "Der Widerstand
gegen die neue Musik. Diskus-
sion zwischen Theodor W.
Adorno und Karlheinz Stock-
hausen." 5 (1984-85): 7-23
Lang: GER
Notes: Danish translation published in
Dansk Musiktidsskrift 60 (1985-
86): 138-46.

Stockhausen, Karlheinz, 1928-
See no. 29.

919 Stockhausen, Karlheinz, 1928-
Date: 12/67, Rome, Italy
Intvr: Pinzauti, Leonardo
Topic: Composers–Influences; Criticism
List: N
Biog: N
Source: PINZAUTI M, pp. 55-65
Lang: ITA
Notes: Previously published in *Nuova
Rivista Musicale Italiana* 2
(Jan.-Feb. 1968): 96-104.

920 Stockhausen, Karlheinz, 1928-
Date: 2/71, N.Y.
Intvr: Cott, Jonathan
Topic: Philosophy & aesthetics; Style
           (Individual)
Works: Hymnen; Kurzwellen; Spiral
List: N
Biog: Y
Source: RS "Talking (whew) to Stock-
           hausen." 8 July 1971, pp. 36-40
Lang: ENG
Notes: Also published in Jonathan Cott,
           *Stockhausen: Conversations with
           the Composer* (N.Y.: Simon &
           Schuster, 1973), part 1.

921 Stockhausen, Karlheinz, 1928-
Intvr: Heyworth, Peter
Topic: Concerts & recitals; Philosophy
           & aesthetics
Works: Hymnen
List: N
Biog: N
Source: NYT "Stockhausen: Is he the
           way and the light?" 21 Feb.
           1971, sec. 2, pp. 13, 26
Lang: ENG

922 Stockhausen, Karlheinz, 1928-
Intvr: Heyworth, Peter
Topic: Composers–Relations with per-
           formers; Performance practice
List: N
Biog: N
Source: MM "Spiritual dimensions." 19/9
           (May 1971): 32-39
Lang: ENG

923 Stockhausen, Karlheinz, 1928-
Date: 2/71, N.Y.; 9/71, Cologne, Ger-
           many

Intvr: Cott, Jonathan
Topic: Composition–Technique; Cre-
           ative process; Philosophy & aes-
           thetics; Style (Individual)
List: Y
Biog: Y
Source: COTT S
Lang: ENG

924 Stockhausen, Karlheinz, 1928-
Date: 6/2/73, Germany
Intvr: Pit, Hugo, et al.
Topic: Education; Interpretation; Jazz
           & popular music; Music thera-
           py; Philosophy & aesthetics;
           Schoenberg, Arnold, 1874-1951;
           Socialism & culture; Webern,
           Anton von, 1883-1945
Works: Für kommende Zeiten
List: N
Biog: N
Source: STOCK G, pp. 1-33
Lang: ENG, GER

925 Stockhausen, Karlheinz, 1928-
Date: 6/23/73, Germany
Intvr: Pit, Hugo, et al.
Topic: Composers–Relations with audi-
           ences; Composition–Technique;
           Philosophy & aesthetics
Works: Aus den sieben Tagen; Für kom-
           mende Zeiten
List: N
Biog: N
Source: STOCK G, pp. 34-51
Lang: GER

926 Stockhausen, Karlheinz, 1928-
Intvr: Albet, Montserrat
Topic: Aleatory music; Composition–

Technique; Computer music; Expressionism; Form; Futurist music; Impressionism; Performance practice; Philosophy & aesthetics; Popular music; 20th-century music

Works: Ceylon
List: N
Biog: Y
Source: ALBET M, pp. 7-21
Lang: GER
Notes: Originally published in *La música contemporánea* (Barcelona, Spain: Salvat Editores, S. A., 1973).

927 Stockhausen, Karlheinz, 1928-
Intvr: Oesch, Hans
Topic: Intuition
List: N
Biog: N
Source: MELOS/NZ "Interview mit Karlheinz Stockhausen." 1/6 (Nov.-Dec. 1975): 456-60
Lang: GER

928 Stockhausen, Karlheinz, 1928-
Date: 7/15/76, Washington, D.C.
Intvr: Felder, David
Topic: Musique concrète; Sound
Works: Aus den sieben Tagen; Inori; Sirius
List: N
Biog: N
Source: PNM "An interview with Karlheinz Stockhausen." 16/1 (Fall-Wint. 1977): 85-101
Lang: ENG

929 Stockhausen, Karlheinz, 1928-
Date: 8/11/76, Germany
Intvr: Faas, Ekbert
Topic: Aleatory music; Cage, John, 1912-1992; Electronic music; Music & science; Oriental music
List: N
Biog: N
Source: INTERFACE "Interview with Karlheinz Stockhausen held August 11, 1976." 6/3-4 (Dec. 1977): 187-204
Lang: ENG
Notes: Also published in *Feedback Papers* 16 (Aug. 1978): 23-34.

930 Stockhausen, Karlheinz, 1928-
Date: 4/77, Cologne, W. Germany
Intvr: Danielson, Janet Henshaw
Topic: Concerts & recitals; Creative process; Electronic music; Sound
Works: Inori
List: N
Biog: N
Source: SYNAPSE "Karlheinz Stockhausen: The search for control." 2/3 (Nov.-Dec. 1977): 26-29; 2/4 (Jan.-Feb. 1978): 32-35
Lang: ENG

931 Stockhausen, Karlheinz, 1928-
Date: 11/79-4/81, Rome, etc., Italy; Paris, France
Intvr: Tannenbaum, Mya
Topic: Acoustics; Community relations; Creativity; Electronic music; Form; Incidental music; Mathematics; Philosophy & aesthetics
Works: Licht
List: Y

Biog: Y
Source: TANNEN C
Lang: ENG
Notes: Previously published in Italian as Mya Tannenbaum, *Intervista sul Genio Musicale* (Roma: Laterza, 1985).

932 Stockhausen, Karlheinz, 1928-
Date: 12/5/83
Intvr: Hintzenstern, Michael von
Topic: Performance practice
List: N
Biog: N
Source: NEULAND "Sind wir es oder sind wir es nicht: Knechte Stockhausens? Aus der Arbeit des 'Ensembles für intuitive Musik Weimar.'" 5 (1984-85): 27-29
Lang: GER

933 Stockhausen, Karlheinz, 1928-
Topic: Electronic music; Religion
List: N
Biog: N
Source: TW "I sing the body electric." 1/1 (1983)
Lang: ENG

934 Stockhausen, Karlheinz, 1928-
Topic: Composers–Relations with audiences; Composition–Technique; Electronic music; Electronic music synthesizers; Philosophy & aesthetics; Sound
Works: Hymnen
List: N
Biog: N
Source: TW "Stockhausen." 1/5 (1983)
Lang: ENG

935 Stockhausen, Karlheinz, 1928-
Date: 3/8/84, Ann Arbor, Mich.
Intvr: Udow, Michael
Topic: Orchestration; Percussion instruments; Percussion music; Performance practice
Works: Gruppen for three orchestras; Kontakte; Licht; Zyklus
List: N
Biog: N
Source: PN "An interview with Karlheinz Stockhausen" 23/6 (Sept. 1985): 4-47
Lang: ENG

936 Stockhausen, Karlheinz, 1928-
Date: 5/31/84; 6/2/84, Milan, Italy
Intvr: Kohl, Jerome
Topic: Opera–Analysis; Performance
Works: Licht
List: N
Biog: N
Source: PNM "Stockhausen on opera: Karlheinz Stockhausen in conversation with Jerome Kohl." 23/2 (Spr.-Sum. 1985): 24-39
Lang: ENG

937 Stockhausen, Karlheinz, 1928-
Topic: Death; Opera
Works: Licht
List: N
Biog: N
Source: NZ "Musik und Tod: Ein Gespräch mit Guido Canella und Luigi Ferrari über 'Samstag' aus *Licht*." 148/5 (May 1987): 16-22
Lang: GER
Notes: Previously published in *Hinterland* 7/29-30 (1984).

938 Stockhausen, Karlheinz, 1928-
Intvr: Riccardi, Fulvia
Topic: Nature; Style (Individual)
Works: Licht
List: N
Biog: N
Source: RASS MC "Intervista a Karlheinz Stockhausen." 38/3 (Sept. 1985): 11-14
Lang: ITA

939 Stranz, Ulrich, 1946-
Intvr: Kühn, Clemens
Topic: Style (Individual)
List: N
Biog: N
Source: MUSICA "Das Interview: Clemens Kühn im Gespräch mit Ulrich Stranz." 32 (Jan.-Feb. 1973): 34-36
Lang: GER

940 Stravinsky, Igor, 1882-1971.
Date: 1935, Copenhagen, Denmark
Topic: Composers–Relations with audiences
List: N
Biog: N
Source: M MAG "A talk with Stravinsky at 53." 5/3 (May-June 1982): 18
Lang: ENG
Notes: Reprinted from *Politiken* (14 Oct. 1935).

941 Stravinsky, Igor, 1882-1971.
Date: 9/11/51, Venice, Italy
Intvr: Zanetti, Emilia
Topic: Opera
Works: The rake's progress

List: N
Biog: N
Source: MZ "'The rake's progress' Stravinsky hat gesagt ...." 1 (1952): 41-44
Lang: GER

942 Stravinsky, Igor, 1882-1971.
Intvr: Craft, Robert
List: N
Biog: N
Source: WM "An interview with Igor Stravinsky." 2 (Oct. 1957): 1-2
Lang: ENG

943 Stravinsky, Igor, 1882-1971.
Date: 9/57-10/57
Intvr: Craft, Robert
Topic: Composers–Relations with artists; Composition–Technique; 20th-century music
List: N
Biog: N
Source: STRA C
Lang: ENG
Notes: German translation of part of the conversations published in *Melos* 28/12 (Dec. 1961): 385-403.

944 Stravinsky, Igor, 1882-1971.
Intvr: Craft, Robert
Topic: Artists; Composition–Technique; Creative process; Performance
List: N
Biog: N
Source: MELOS "Neue Dialoge: Igor Strawinsky–Robert Craft." 25/9 (Sept. 1958): 261-93
Lang: GER

945 Stravinsky, Igor, 1882-1971.
Intvr: Craft, Robert
List: N
Biog: N
Source: STRA M
Lang: ENG
Notes: German translation of part of the conversations published in *Melos* 28/12 (Dec. 1961): 385-403.

946 Stravinsky, Igor, 1882-1971.
Intvr: Craft, Robert
Topic: Composition–Technique; Style (Individual)
Works: Apollo; Octet; Perséphone; Scènes de ballet; Symphony of Psalms
List: N
Biog: N
Source: PNM "A quintet of dialogues." 1/1 (Fall 1962): 7-17
Lang: ENG

947 Stravinsky, Igor, 1882-1971.
Intvr: Craft, Robert
Topic: Composers, American; Composition–Technique; Creative process
List: N
Biog: N
Source: STRA E
Lang: ENG

948 Stravinsky, Igor, 1882-1971.
Date: 1962
Intvr: Craft, Robert
Topic: Creative process; Debussy, Claude, 1862-1918
List: N

Biog: N
Source: M MAG "Craft and Stravinsky." 5/3 (May-June 1982): 19-21
Lang: ENG

949 Stravinsky, Igor, 1882-1971.
Intvr: Craft, Robert
Topic: Authors; Creative process
List: N
Biog: N
Source: STRA D
Lang: ENG
Notes: Includes interviews previously published in journals and newspapers.

950 Stravinsky, Igor, 1882-1971.
Date: 1/64, N.Y.
Topic: Menotti, Gian Carlo. *Le dernier sauvage*; Opera audiences
List: N
Biog: N
Source: STRA T "In the name of Jan-Jacques!" pp. 97-101
Lang: ENG
Notes: Previously published in *Show* (Apr. 1964).

951 Stravinsky, Igor, 1882-1971.
Date: 1/65, N.Y.
Topic: Criticism; Culture
List: N
Biog: N
Source: STRA T "A talk with Stravinsky." pp. 101-8
Lang: ENG
Notes: Previously published in the *New York Review of Books* (27 May 1965).

952 Stravinsky, Igor, 1882-1971.

Date: 11/5/65, Hollywood, Calif.

Topic: Auden, Wystan Hugh, 1907-1973; Text setting

List: N

Biog: N

Source: STRA T "Transcript of BBC Television interview." pp. 96-97

Lang: ENG

953 Stravinsky, Igor, 1882-1971.

Date: 11/5/65, Hollywood, Calif.

Topic: Criticism; Performance; Webern, Anton von, 1883-1945

List: N

Biog: N

Source: STRA T "A decade later." pp. 115-23

Lang: ENG

Notes: Previously published as the preface to *Anton von Webern: Perspectives* (University of Washington Press, 1966).

954 Stravinsky, Igor, 1882-1971.

Topic: Audiences; Careers in music

List: N

Biog: N

Source: STRA T "A perfect total." pp. 108-14

Lang: ENG

Notes: Previously published in *Seventeen* (Aug. 1966).

955 Stravinsky, Igor, 1882-1971.

Topic: Composers–Political conditions; 20th-century music

List: N

Biog: N

Source: MELOS "Wo ist dein Stachel?" 36/10 (Oct. 1969): 401-9

Lang: GER

Notes: Translated from English into German by W. E. Süßkind. Previously published in the *New York Review of Books* (Apr. 1969); German translation in *Süddeutsche Zeitung* (17-18 May 1969).

956 Stravinsky, Igor, 1882-1971.

List: N

Biog: N

Source: MELOS "Das neueste Interview." 37/2 (Feb. 1970): 33-35

Lang: GER

Notes: Previously published in English in the *New York Review of Books* (1969); German translation in *Die Welt* (6 Dec. 1969).

957 Stravinsky, Igor, 1882-1971.

List: N

Biog: N

Source: STRA R, pp. 13-101

Lang: ENG

Notes: Reprinted from interviews in *The New York Times,* the *New York Review of Books, Commentary,* and *Harper's Magazine,* 1966 to 1969.

958 Stravinsky, Igor, 1882-1971.

List: N

Biog: N

Source: TEMPO "Stravinsky in interview." 97 (1971): 6-9

Lang: ENG

Notes: Extracts from interviews in *Daily Mail* (13 Feb. 1913) and *Beaux Arts* (28 Feb. 1936).

959 Subotnick, Morton, 1933-
Intvr: Schrader, Barry
Topic: Electronic music; Philosophy &
       aesthetics; Tone color
Works: Silver apples of the moon; Touch;
       Until spring; The wild bull
List: N
Biog: N
Source: SCHRADER I "18. Interview
       with Morton Subotnick: 'Until
       spring.'" pp. 188-93
Lang: ENG

Sutermeister, Heinrich, 1910-
See no. 116.

960 Swanson, Howard, 1907-1978.
Intvr: Ericson, Raymond
Topic: Black composers
List: N
Biog: N
Source: NYT "Tribute to Howard Swan-
       son." 10 June 1977, sec. 3, p. 23
Lang: ENG

961 Swanson, Howard, 1907-1978.
Intvr: Smith, Hale
Topic: Black composers; Composers–
       Influences; Composition–Tech-
       nique; Performance; Text setting
List: Y
Biog: Y
Source: BAKER B, pp. 337-55
Lang: ENG

962 Tabachnik, Michel, 1942-
Intvr: Jameux, Dominique
Topic: Boulez, Pierre, 1925-; Com-
       posers as conductors
List: N

Biog: N
Source: M JEU "Débat avec Michel
       Tabachnik. À propos du film
       'Boulez chef d'orchestre.'" 16
       (Nov. 1974): 31-32
Lang: FRE

963 Taira, Yoshihisa, 1938-
Date: 3/75
Intvr: Mâche, François-Bernard
Topic: Japanese music; Style (Indi-
       vidual)
List: N
Biog: Y
Source: RM "Les mal entendus. Com-
       positeurs des années 70." 314-15
       (1978): 135-40
Lang: FRE

964 Takemitsu, Tōru, 1930-
Intvr: Hall, Robert
Topic: Japan; Orchestration
List: N
Biog: Y
Source: CONTACT "Contemporary
       Japanese music and interview
       with Toru Takemitsu." 7 (Wint.
       1973-74): 20-26
Lang: ENG

965 Takemitsu, Tōru, 1930-
Intvr: Rockwell, John
Topic: Japanese music; Motion picture
       music; Style (Individual)
List: N
Biog: N
Source: NYT "2 worlds of Takemitsu,
       Japan's leading composer." 13
       Feb. 1981, sec. 3, p. 8
Lang: ENG

966 Talma, Louise, 1906-
Intvr: Ericson, Raymond
Topic: Teaching
List: N
Biog: N
Source: NYT "Celebrating Louise Talma." 4 Feb. 1977, sec. 3, p. 22
Lang: ENG

967 Tavener, John Kenneth, 1944-
Intvr: Griffiths, Paul
Topic: Modes; Music & religion
List: Y
Biog: Y
Source: GRIFFITHS N, pp. 106-112
Lang: ENG

968 Tcherepnin, Alexander, 1899-1977.
Date: 9/77, N.Y.
Topic: Performance
Works: Concerto, piano, no. 6
List: N
Biog: N
Source: M ART "Tcherepnin piano concerto premiered in Lucerne." 5/4 (Sept.-Oct. 1972): 20
Lang: ENG

969 Teitelbaum, Richard, 1939-
Intvr: Zimmermann, Walter
Topic: Electronic music; Performance practice; Physiology; Sound, Environmental
Works: Threshold music
List: N
Biog: N
Source: ZIMMER D, pp. 193-206
Lang: ENG

Teitelbaum, Richard, 1939-
See no. 822.

970 Tenney, James C., 1934-
Intvr: Zimmermann, Walter
Topic: Composers–20th-century–Influences; Computer music; Instrumental music
List: N
Biog: N
Source: ZIMMER D, pp. 221-32
Lang: ENG

971 Tenney, James C., 1934-
Date: 1983
Intvr: Kasemets, Udo, et al.
Topic: Culture; Music & science; Sound
List: N
Biog: N
Source: MUSWORKS "A tradition of experimentation: James Tenney in conversation." 27 (Spr. 1984): 2-9, 20
Lang: ENG

972 Tenney, James C., 1934-
Intvr: Monahan, Gordon; Pearson, Tina
Topic: Computer music
Works: Bridge
List: N
Biog: N
Source: MUSWORKS "Bridge." 27 (Spr. 1984): 10-13
Lang: ENG

973 Tenney, James C., 1934-
Date: 12/85, Toronto, Canada
Intvr: Belet, Brian
Topic: Composers–Social conditions; Composition–Technique; Philosophy & aesthetics
Works: Changes
List: N

Biog: N
Source: PNM "An interview with James Tenney." 25 (1987): 459-66
Lang: ENG

974 Theodorakis, Mikis, 1925-
Intvr: Heckman, Don
Topic: Composers–Political conditions
List: N
Biog: N
Source: NYT "Theodorakis: I am a symbol of power." 16 Aug. 1970, sec. 2, pp. 11, 14
Lang: ENG

975 Thiele, Siegfried, 1934-
Date: 1/78
Intvr: Stürzbecher, Ursula
Topic: Composers–Relations with audiences; 14th-century music; Text setting; 12-tone system
List: Y
Biog: Y
Source: STURZ K, pp. 294-309
Lang: GER

976 Thomson, Virgil, 1896-1989.
Date: New York
Topic: Criticism; Critics; Television opera; Television programs; United States
List: N
Biog: N
Source: BRAVO "Conversation piece: Virgil Thomson." 1961, pp. 16-19
Lang: ENG

977 Thomson, Virgil, 1896-1989.
Date: New York

Topic: Audiences–20th-century music
List: N
Biog: N
Source: BRAVO "Conversation piece: Virgil Thomson (II)." Feb. 1962, pp. 41-42
Lang: ENG

978 Thomson, Virgil, 1896-1989.
Intvr: Henahan, Donal
Topic: Composers, American; Style (Individual)
List: N
Biog: N
Source: NYT "And now, Virgil's odyssey." 21 Mar. 1971, sec. 2, pp. 15, 26
Lang: ENG

979 Thomson, Virgil, 1896-1989.
Intvr: Gent, George
Topic: Contests & awards; Handel Medallion
List: N
Biog: N
Source: NYT "Thomson is given city's top award: Hechscher presents Handel medal to composer-critic." 14 Nov. 1971, sec. 1, p. 79
Lang: ENG

980 Thomson, Virgil, 1896-1989.
Intvr: Gruen, John
Works: Lord Byron
List: N
Biog: N
Source: NYT "Virgil sings of 'Lord Byron.'" 9 Apr. 1972, sec. 2, pp. 17, 20
Lang: ENG

981 Thomson, Virgil, 1896-1989.
Intvr: Hughes, Allen
List: N
Biog: N
Source: NYT   "In Virgil Thomson's rooms, style reigns." 16 Apr. 1972, sec. 8, pp. 1, 6
Lang: ENG

982 Thomson, Virgil, 1896-1989.
Intvr: Wickes, George
Topic: Barney, Natalie Clifford, 1876-1972; Homosexuality
List: N
Biog: N
Source: PR "A Natalie Barney Garland." 61 (Spr. 1975): 113-18
Lang: ENG

983 Thomson, Virgil, 1896-1989.
Intvr: Alcaraz, José Antonio
Topic: Cage, John, 1912-1992; Critics; Music & language; Opera; Satie, Erik, 1866-1925
Works: Four saints in three acts
List: N
Biog: Y
Source: HETEROFONIA "Virgil Thomson, 'Leyenda Viviente.'" 49 (July-Aug. 1976): 24-29
Lang: SPA

984 Thomson, Virgil, 1896-1989.
Intvr: Rockwell, John
List: N
Biog: N
Source: NYT "Virgil Thomson vigorous at 80." 25 Nov. 1976, sec. 1, p. 38
Lang: ENG

985 Thomson, Virgil, 1896-1989.
Date: 4/6/77
Intvr: Rockwell, John
Topic: American music; Criticism; Style (Individual)
List: N
Biog: N
Source: THOMSON V "A conversation with Virgil Thomson." pp. 525-41
Lang: ENG
Notes: Previously published in *Parnassus: Poetry in Review* (Spr.-Sum. 1977).

986 Thomson, Virgil, 1896-1989.
Intvr: Horowitz, Joseph
Topic: 20th-century music
List: N
Biog: N
Source: NYT "Continuum salutes Virgil Thomson at Tully Hall." 5 Jan. 1979, sec. 3, p. 15
Lang: ENG

987 Thomson, Virgil, 1896-1989.
Intvr: Trilling, Diana
Topic: Composers–Political conditions; Composers–United States; Stein, Gertrude, 1874-1946
List: N
Biog: N
Source: THOMSON V   "An interview with Virgil Thomson." pp. 542-55
Lang: ENG
Notes: Previously published in *Partisan Review* 4 (1980).

988 Thomson, Virgil, 1896-1989.

Date: 1981-84, N.Y., Boston, Mass.
Intvr: Tommasini, Anthony Carl
Works: Portraits
List: N
Biog: N
Source: MQ "Musical portraits by Virgil Thomson." 70 (Spr. 1984): 234-47
Lang: ENG
Notes: Also published in *Virgil Thomson's Musical Portraits* (N.Y.: Pendragon Press, 1986).

989 Tiomkin, Dimitri, 1894-1979.

Intvr: Epstein, Dave A.
Topic: Motion picture music
List: N
Biog: N
Source: ETUDE "Back stage with the film composer: From an interview with Dimitri Tiomkin." 71 (Feb. 1953): 19, 60-61
Lang: ENG

990 Tippett, Michael Kemp, 1905-

Intvr: Schafer, Raymond Murray
Topic: Composers as authors; Composition–Technique; Music & art
Works: A child of our time; The midsummer marriage; *Moving into Aquarius*
List: N
Biog: Y
Source: SCHAFER B, pp. 92-102
Lang: ENG
Notes: Reprinted in *Music and Musicians* 13/6 (Feb. 1965): 24-26, 55.

991 Tippett, Michael Kemp, 1905-

Intvr: Woodward, Ian
Topic: Style (Individual)
Works: Child of our time; King Priam; Knot garden; The midsummer marriage
List: N
Biog: N
Source: MM "Tippett looks ahead: Ian Woodward talks to the composer." 17/7 (Mar. 1969): 32-34
Lang: ENG

992 Tippett, Michael Kemp, 1905-

Intvr: Northcott, Bayan
Topic: Style (Individual)
Works: Symphony, no. 3
List: N
Biog: N
Source: MM "Tippett's third symphony: Bayan Northcott talks to the composer about the work which will be first performed by the London Symphony under Colin Davis ...." 238 (June 1972): 30-32
Lang: ENG

993 Tippett, Michael Kemp, 1905-

Intvr: Edberg, Ulla-Britt
Topic: Opera; Symphony
Works: Songs for Dov; Symphony, no. 3
List: N
Biog: N
Source: NUTIDA "Michael Tippett." 22/1 (1978-79): 7-13
Lang: SWE

994 Toch, Ernst, 1887-1964.

Topic: Colleges & universities–United States; Composers–United States

List: N
Biog: N
Source: MELOS "Ein Interview: Ernst
         Toch in Europa." 17/9 (Sept.
         1950): 251-53
Lang: GER

Tredici, David Del
   See **Del Tredici, David, 1937-**.

995 Tremblay, Gilles Léonce, 1932-
List: N
Biog: N
Source: MUSCAN "Gilles Tremblay, a
         portrait." 24 (Nov. 1969): [8-9]
Lang: ENG, FRE

996 Trojahn, Manfred, 1949-
Date: 5/7/85, Hannover, Germany
Intvr: Konold, Wulf
Topic: Community relations; Compos-
         ers–Relations with audiences;
         Composers–Social conditions;
         Composers–20th-century; Com-
         position–Technique; Creativity;
         Darmstadt. Institut für Neue Mu-
         sik und Musikerziehung; Phi-
         losophy & aesthetics; Style (Indi-
         vidual); Symphony
List: N
Biog: Y
Source: JUNG L "Komponieren heute,"
         pp. 60-83
Lang: GER

997 Tudor, David, 1926-
Intvr: Fullemann, John David
Topic: Composition–Technique; Elec-
         tronic music; Spatiality in com-
         position

Works: Tonburst
List: N
Biog: N
Source: MUSTEXTE "Composer inside
         electronics: David Tudor im
         Gespräch." 15 (July 1986): 11-
         17
Lang: GER

998 Turner, Robert Comrie, 1920-
List: Y
Biog: Y
Source: MUSCAN "Robert Turner, a
         portrait." 29 (May 1970): [10-11]
Lang: ENG, FRE

999 Umali, Restituto, 1916-
Intvr: Samson, Helen F.
Topic: Motion picture music
List: Y
Biog: N
Source: SAMSON C, pp. 212-20
Lang: ENG

1000 Urreta, Alicia, 1935-1986.
Intvr: Saavedra, Leonora
Topic: Careers in music; Composers,
         Mexican; Incidental music; Mex-
         ico; Opera; Performance prac-
         tice; Schools of music–Curricu-
         lum; 20th-century music–Style
Works: Caperucita roja; Dialogo del
         amor con un viejo
List: Y
Biog: Y
Source: ANGELES M, pp. 88-111
Lang: SPA

1001 Ussachevsky, Vladimir, 1911-1990.
Intvr: Peyser, Joan

Topic: Computers
List: N
Biog: N
Source: NYT "Seven times the computer said no." 3 Mar. 1968, sec. 2, pp. 19, 28
Lang: ENG

1002 Ussachevsky, Vladimir, 1911-1990.
Intvr: Pulido, Esperanza; Vázquez, Alida
Topic: Composition–Technique; Electronic music
List: N
Biog: N
Source: HETEROFONIA "Con Vladimir Ussachevsky en Nueva York." 64 (Jan.-Feb. 1979): 24-26
Lang: SPA

1003 Vaggione, Horacio, 1943-
Intvr: Dehoux, Vincent; Stoïanova, Ivanka
Topic: Composition–Technique
Works: Le máquina de cantar
List: N
Biog: N
Source: M JEU "La máquina de cantar." 32 (Sept. 1978): 13-21
Lang: FRE

1004 Van de Vate, Nancy, 1930-
Intvr: Grimes, Ev
Topic: Community relations; Schools of music–Curriculum; Teaching
List: N
Biog: Y
Source: MEJ "Conversations with American composers." 73/2 (Oct. 1986): 52-56
Lang: ENG
Notes: Written in response to questions sent to the composer at her home in Jakarta, Indonesia.

1005 Van Nostrand, Burr, 1945-
Intvr: Cogan, Robert David
Topic: Composers–Influences; Composers–Social conditions; Style (Individual)
Works: Fantasy manual for urban survival–1972; Symphony nosferatu
List: N
Biog: N
Source: SONUS "Burr Van Nostrand: An interview by Robert Cogan." 4/1 (Fall 1983): 39-45
Lang: ENG

1006 Varèse, Edgar, 1883-1965.
Intvr: Schuller, Gunther
Topic: Electronic music; Music & architecture
List: N
Biog: N
Source: PNM "Conversation with Varèse." 3/2 (Spr.-Sum. 1965): 32-37
Lang: ENG
Notes: German translation by R. Riehn published in Heinz-Klaus Metzger, ed., *Edgar Varèse. Rückblick auf die Zukunft* (München: Edition Text und Kritik, 1978), pp. 46-51.

1007 Velarde, Miguel "Mike", Jr., 1913-
Intvr: Samson, Helen F.
Topic: Style (Individual); Vocal music

List: Y
Biog: N
Source: SAMSON C, pp. 221-32
Lang: ENG

1008 Velez, Glen
Intvr: Brooks, Iris
Topic: Improvisation; Percussionists
List: N
Biog: Y
Source: EAR "Meet The Composer: Glen Velez." 12/6 (Sept. 1987): 16-19
Lang: ENG

1009 Vivier, Claude, 1948-1983.
Date: Sum/81
Intvr: Frykberg, Susan
Topic: Style (Individual)
List: N
Biog: N
Source: MUSWORKS "Claude Vivier in conversation." 18 (Wint. 1982): 8-9
Lang: ENG

1010 Vlad, Roman, 1919-
Date: 1/20/83, Italy
Intvr: Failla, Salvatore Enrico
Topic: Audiences–Italy; Stravinsky, Igor, 1882-1971; Television programs
List: N
Biog: N
Source: FAILLA M "Intervista a Roman Vlad: Giù la maschera Igor." pp. 115-25
Lang: ITA

1011 Vlijmen, Jan van, 1935-
Intvr: Koopmans, Rudy

Topic: Teaching
Works: Reconstruction
List: N
Biog: N
Source: KN "A warning to begin with: Interview with Jan van Vlijmen." 4 (Dec. 1976): 32-34
Lang: ENG

1012 Vogel, Wladimir, 1896-1984.
Date: 6/81, Zurich, Switzerland
Intvr: Reininghaus, Frieder; Traber, Jürgen Habakuk
Topic: Composers–Political conditions; Style (Individual)
List: N
Biog: Y
Source: MUSTEXTE "Das Abseits als gesicherter Ort: Ein Gespräch mit und Anmerkungen zu Wladimir Vogel." 7 (Dec. 1984): 30-34
Lang: GER

1013 Volkonsky, Andrei, 1933-
Date: 5/31/73, Vienna, Austria
Intvr: Kamm, Henry
Topic: Composers–Political conditions–Union of Soviet Socialist Republics (former)
List: N
Biog: N
Source: NYT "Composer tells of artistic battle in Soviet." 5 June 1973, sec. 1, p. 14
Lang: ENG

1014 Wagemans, Peter-Jan, 1952-
Intvr: Beer, Roland de
Topic: Performance practice; Style (Individual)

Works: Muziek II
List: Y
Biog: Y
Source: KN "Peter-Jan Wagemans: 'We should turn music toward the people without falling in the neoromantic trap.'" 10 (Dec. 1979): 4-9
Lang: ENG

1015 Walker, George, 1922-
Intvr: Baker, David N., et al.
Topic: Black composers; Composers–Influences; Composition–Technique; Performance; Style (Individual)
List: Y
Biog: Y
Source: BAKER B, pp. 356-78
Lang: ENG

1016 Walker, George, 1922-
Intvr: Finn, Terri Lowen
Topic: Black musicians
List: N
Biog: N
Source: NYT "A serious composer talks about the path to success." 8 Feb. 1981, sec. 11, pp. 4-5
Lang: ENG

1017 Wall, Bengt V., 1916-
Intvr: Johnson, Bengt Emil
Topic: Creative process; Liturgical drama
List: N
Biog: N
Source: NUTIDA "Stockholms kyrkoopera." 17/1 (1973-74): 13-15
Lang: SWE

1018 Walton, William, 1902-1983.
Intvr: Downes, Olin
Topic: Atonality; Folk music
List: N
Biog: N
Source: NYT "Visiting composer: Sir William Walton, now in this country, discusses problems of modern musician." 16 Aug. 1953, sec. 2, p. 7
Lang: ENG

1019 Walton, William, 1902-1983.
Intvr: Schafer, Raymond Murray
Topic: Creative process; Criticism
Works: Façade
List: N
Biog: Y
Source: SCHAFER B, pp. 73-82
Lang: ENG

1020 Weinzweig, John, 1913-
Topic: Canada; Composition–Technique
Works: Suite, no. 1
List: Y
Biog: Y
Source: MUSCAN "John Weinzweig, a portrait." 9 (Mar. 1968): [8-9]
Lang: ENG, FRE

1021 Weinzweig, John, 1913-
Intvr: Champagne, Jane
Topic: Composition–Technique; Schools of music; Teaching; 12-tone system
Works: New homes for old; Quartet, string; Suite, piano
List: N
Biog: Y

Source: CC "Interview! John Weinzweig." 100 (Apr. 1975): 24-33,
43

Lang: ENG, FRE

1022 Weiss, Elliot

Intvr: Klein, Alvin

Topic: Musicals, revues, etc.

Works: Bittersuite

List: N

Biog: N

Source: NYT "A composer sets midlife
blues to music." 2 Aug. 1987,
sec. 21, p. 21

Lang: ENG

1023 Wellesz, Egon, 1885-1974.

Intvr: Schafer, Raymond Murray

Topic: Careers in music; Creative process; Creativity; Musicology; 12-
tone system

List: N

Biog: Y

Source: SCHAFER B, pp. 36-46

Lang: ENG

1024 Werle, Lars-Johan, 1926-

Intvr: Edberg, Ulla-Britt

Topic: Opera; Style (Individual)

Works: Titomara

List: N

Biog: N

Source: NUTIDA "Drömmen om Titomara." 16/2 (1972-73): 19-23

Lang: SWE

1025 Westerkamp, Hildegard

Intvr: Young, Gayle

Topic: Performance practice; Sound,
Environmental; Voice

Works: A walk through the city; Whis-
per study

List: N

Biog: N

Source: MUSWORKS "Composing
with environmental sound: An
interview with Hildegard Westerkamp." 26 (Wint. 1984): 4-8

Lang: ENG

1026 Wildberger, Jacques, 1922-

Date: 8/12/70, Poschiavo, Switzerland;
8/30/70, Basel, Switzerland

Intvr: Pauli, Hansjörg

Topic: Composition–Technique; Creative process; Philosophy & aesthetics; Style (Individual); 20th-
century music–Style

List: N

Biog: Y

Source: PAULI F, pp. 128-48

Lang: GER

Notes: Originally done for a radio program of Hessischer Rundfunk
Frankfurt.

1027 Williamson, Malcom, 1931-

Date: 5/5/84, Baltimore, Md.

Intvr: Franklin, Ben A.

Works: Mass of Christ the King

List: N

Biog: N

Source: NYT "Master of the Queen's
Music has two passions." 6 May
1984, sec. 1, p. 67

Lang: ENG

1028 Wilson, Olly, 1937-

Date: 5/22/74-5/26/74, N.Y.

Intvr: Southern, Eileen

Topic: Black composers; Electronic music; Jazz musicians; Philosophy & aesthetics; 12-tone system

Works: Prelude and line study; Three movements for orchestra

List: N

Biog: Y

Source: BPM "Conversation with Olly Wilson: The education of a composer." 5 (Spr. 1977): 90-103; 6/1 (Spr. 1978): 56-70

Lang: ENG

1029 Wilson, Olly, 1937-

Intvr: Baker, David N., et al.

Topic: Black composers; Composers–Influences; Composition–Technique; Performance; Text setting

Works: In memoriam, Martin Luther King, Jr.

List: Y

Biog: Y

Source: BAKER B, pp. 379-401

Lang: ENG

1030 Wolff, Christian, 1934-

Date: 9/72

Intvr: Ivanji, Ildi

Topic: Philosophy & aesthetics; Teaching

List: N

Biog: N

Source: SONUS "What are we doing? An interview with Christian Wolff." 5/2 (Spr. 1985): 20-29

Lang: ENG

1031 Wolff, Christian, 1934-

Intvr: Helms, Hans Günter

Topic: Cage, John, 1912-1992; Feldman, Morton, 1926-1987

List: N

Biog: N

Source: MBR "Conversation with John Cage, Christian Wolff, Hans G. Helms." Side 7, Bd. 2

Lang: ENG

1032 Wolff, Christian, 1934-

Intvr: Zimmermann, Walter

Topic: Composers–20th-century–Influences; Creative process

Works: Accompaniments; Burdocks; Duos; Quartet, string; Summer

List: N

Biog: N

Source: ZIMMER D, pp. 21-46

Lang: ENG

1033 Wolff, Christian, 1934-

Intvr: Daske, Martin

Topic: Composition–Technique; 12-tone system

Works: Burdocks; Edges; Flying or possibly sitting still or crawling; For 1, 2 or 3 people; Wobbly music

List: N

Biog: N

Source: MUSTEXTE "Eine Welt, die anders orientiert wäre: Christian Wolff im Gespräch mit Martin Daske." 4 (Apr. 1984): 40-51

Lang: GER

1034 Wolpe, Stefan, 1902-1972.

Intvr: Peyser, Joan

List: N

Biog: N

Source: NYT "Wolpe: A thoroughly modern maverick." 6 Feb. 1972, sec. 2, pp. 17, 20

Lang: ENG

1035 Wren, Brian A., 1936-
Date: 7/25/80, Oxford, England
Intvr: Eskew, Harry Lee
Topic: Hymns
List: N
Biog: Y
Source: HYMN "An interview with
        Brian Wren." 32/1 (Jan. 1981):
        25-29; 32/2 (Apr. 1981): 96-102
Lang: ENG

Wren, Brian A., 1936-
See no. 287.

1036 Wuensch, Gerhard, 1925-
Intvr: Adams, Stephen
Topic: Creative process; Theory
Works: Concerto, bassoon; Concerto,
        piano; Sonata, soprano saxo-
        phone
List: N
Biog: Y
Source: MUSCAN "Words about music:
        A series of ...." 34 (Jan. 1978):
        22-23
Lang: ENG, FRE

1037 Wüsthoff, Klaus, 1922-
Intvr: Molkow, Wolfgang
Topic: Singing commercials
List: N
Biog: N
Source: MUSICA "Das Interview: Wolf-
        gang Molkow im Gespräch mit
        Klaus Wüsthoff." 34 (Jan.-Feb.
        1980): 32-35
Lang: GER

1038 Wüsthoff, Klaus, 1922-
Intvr: Rummenhöller, Peter

Topic: Contests & awards; Forum
        Junger Deutscher Komponisten
        für Orchestermusik; Orchestral
        music
List: N
Biog: N
Source: MUSICA "Das Interview:
        'Forum junger deutscher Kom-
        ponisten für Orchestermusik
        1985.' Peter Rummenhöller im
        Gespräch mit Klaus Wüsthoff."
        38 (Mar.-Apr. 1984): 148-49
Lang: GER

1039 Wuorinen, Charles, 1938-
Date: 1962
Intvr: Childs, Barney
Topic: Audiences; Composers–Rela-
        tions with performers; Composi-
        tion–Technique; Critics; Europe–
        Influences; Gebrauchsmusik;
        Jazz; Webern, Anton von, 1883-
        1945
List: N
Biog: N
Source: SCHWARTZ C "An interview
        with Barney Childs, 1962." pp.
        367-75
Lang: ENG
Notes: Previously published in "What
        concerns me is music," *Genesis
        West* 1 (Fall 1962): 11-18.

1040 Wuorinen, Charles, 1938-
Date: 7/14/75, New York City, N.Y.
Intvr: Gagne, Cole
Topic: Creative process; Electronic
        music
Works: Reliquary; Ringing changes;
        Time's encomium

159

List: Y
Biog: Y
Source: GAGNE S, pp. 383-400
Lang: ENG

1041 Wuorinen, Charles, 1938-
Intvr: Peyser, Joan
Topic: Composers as conductors
List: N
Biog: N
Source: NYT "It's a big week for Wuorinen." 10 Apr. 1983, sec. 2, pp. 21, 24
Lang: ENG

Wuorinen, Charles, 1938-
See no. 800.
Works: Bamboula squared; Time's encomium

1042 Xenakis, Iannis, 1922-
Intvr: Rich, Alan
Topic: 20th-century music
List: N
Biog: N
Source: NYT "Best of two worlds: Greek composer finds career through combining music and architecture." 4 Aug. 1963, sec. 2, p. 9
Lang: ENG

1043 Xenakis, Iannis, 1992-
Date: 3/4/66
Intvr: Bois, Mario
Topic: Composers–Influences; Compsers–Relations with audiences; Composition–Technique; Creative process; Mathematics; Philosophy & aesthetics; Stochastic theory

Works: Metastasis; Teretektorh
List: Y
Biog: Y
Source: BOIS I "The Meeting of 4th March, 1966," pp. 5-22
Lang: ENG

1044 Xenakis, Iannis, 1922-
Intvr: Henahan, Donal
Topic: Computers; Music & science
List: N
Biog: N
Source: NYT "How one man defines man." 17 Mar. 1968, sec. 2, p. 19
Lang: ENG

1045 Xenakis, Iannis, 1922-
Date: 10/68
Intvr: Bourgeois, Jacques
Topic: Music & science; Philosophy & aesthetics; Serial music; Sound; Theory
List: N
Biog: N
Source: XENAKIS E
Lang: FRE

1046 Xenakis, Iannis, 1922-
Intvr: Perrot, Michel
Topic: Education; Form; Mathematics; Sociology; Stochastic theory
List: N
Biog: N
Source: RM "Entretien avec Iannis Xenakis." 265-66 (1968): 61-76
Lang: FRE

1047 Xenakis, Iannis, 1922-
Date: 1969, 1/31/70, Royan, France
Intvr: Durney, Daniel; Jameux, Dominique

Topic: Composers–Relations with audiences; Mathematics; Music & architecture
Works: Metastasis; Nuits; Perséphassa; Pithoprakta
List: N
Biog: N
Source: M JEU "Rencontres avec Iannis Xenakis." 1 (Nov. 1970): 46-65
Lang: FRE

1048 Xenakis, Iannis, 1922-
Date: 10/73
Intvr: Mâche, François-Bernard
Topic: Computer music; Philosophy & aesthetics
List: N
Biog: Y
Source: RM "Les mal entendus. Compositeurs des années 70." 314-15 (1978): 141-50
Lang: FRE

1049 Xenakis, Iannis, 1922-
Date: 5/75, Paris, France
Intvr: Zaplitny, Michael
Topic: Composition–Technique; Computers; Music & architecture
Works: Erikhthon; Gmeeoorh; Noomena; *Formalized Music*
List: N
Biog: N
Source: PNM "Conversation with Iannis Xenakis." 14/1 (1975): 86-103
Lang: ENG

1050 Xenakis, Iannis, 1922-
Intvr: Rockwell, John
Topic: Music & science
List: N

Biog: N
Source: NYT "In these equations lurks lush music." 21 Apr. 1976, sec. 1, p. 20
Lang: ENG

1051 Xenakis, Iannis, 1922-
Intvr: Emmerson, Simon
Topic: Composition–Technique
Works: Psappha
List: N
Biog: N
Source: MM "Xenakis talks to Simon Emmerson." 285 (May 1976): 24-26
Lang: ENG

1052 Xenakis, Iannis, 1922-
Date: 1978
Intvr: Bois, Mario
Topic: Aleatory music; Composers–Economic conditions; Composers–Relations with audiences; Composers, Polish; Composition–Technique; Culture–Greece; Folk music; Mathematics; Music & architecture; Music & art; Stochastic theory
Works: Akrata; Duel; Metastasis; Terretektorh
List: N
Biog: N
Source: HETEROFONIA "Una entrevista de Iannis Xenakis con Mario Bois." 64 (Jan.-Feb. 1979): 31-35; 65 (Mar.-Apr. 1979): 19-26; 66 (May-Aug. 1979): 19-24; and 67 (Sept.-Dec. 1979): 17-23
Lang: SPA

1053 Xenakis, Iannis, 1922-
Intvr: Baroni, Mario
Topic: Form; Serial music; Stochastic
theory
Works: Psappha
List: N
Biog: N
Source: MR "Problemi di un composi-
tore. Conversazione con Iannis
Xenakis." 3 (Dec. 1980): 127-43
Lang: ITA

1054 Xenakis, Iannis, 1922-
Intvr: L. B.
Topic: Composition–Technique; Com-
puters
List: N
Biog: N
Source: PNM "Xenakis on Xenakis. III.
Iannis Xenakis: Music and com-
puters." 25 (1987): 25-28
Lang: ENG
Notes: Previously pubilshed in *Pour
la Science* (Nov. 1982). This
article consists of 5 sections of
which secs.1 (see no. 1060) and
3 have interviews with the
composoer.

1055 Xenakis, Iannis, 1922-
Intvr: Loubet, Emmanuelle
Topic: Computers; Electronics; Mathe-
matics; Theory
List: N
Biog: N
Source: MUSICA "Das Interview: Iannis
Xenakis im Gespräch mit Em-
manuelle Loubet." 36 (Nov.-Dec.
1982): 525-30
Lang: GER

1056 Xenakis, Iannis, 1922-
Intvr: Krauze, Zygmunt
Topic: Teaching
List: N
Biog: N
Source: PM "Interview with Iannis
Xenakis in Kazimierz on the
Vistula." 19/3-4 (1984): 29-31
Lang: ENG, GER

1057 Xenakis, Iannis, 1922-
Date: 8/17/85, Delphi, Greece
Intvr: Lohner, Henning
Topic: Centre d'Études de Mathema-
tique et Automatique Musicales
(CEMAMu); Computers; Elec-
tronic music
List: N
Biog: N
Source: CMJ "Interview with Iannis
Xenakis." 10/4 (Wint. 1986):
50-55
Lang: ENG
Notes: German translation published
in Heinz-Klaus Metzger, ed.,
Iannis Xenakis (München: Edi-
tion Text und Kritik, 1987), pp.
83-90.

1058 Xenakis, Iannis, 1922-
Intvr: Dusapin, Pascal; Rey, Anne
Topic: Theory
List: N
Biog: N
Source: NUTIDA "Intervjuad av Pascal
Dusapin och Anne Rey." 28/3
(1984-85): 3-5
Lang: SWE
Notes: Previously published in *Le
Monde de la Musique* 11 (May
1979).

1059 Xenakis, Iannis, 1922-

Topic: Computers; Mathematics

List: N

Biog: N

Source: MUSTEXTE "'Schwieriger ist es nicht!' Zur musikalischen Informatik. 'Pour la science' im Gespräch mit Iannis Xenakis." 13 (Feb. 1986): 31-32

Lang: GER

Notes: Previously published in *Pour la Science* (Nov. 1982).

1060 Xenakis, Iannis, 1922-

Intvr: L. B.

Topic: Computer music; Music & architecture; Music & science; Style (Individual)

Works: Metastasis

List: Y

Biog: N

Source: PNM "Xenakis on Xenakis. I. Portrait of Iannis Xenakis." 25 (1987): 20-24

Lang: ENG

Notes: See *Notes* of no. 1054

1061 Young, Gayle

Date: 5/27/85, Ontario, Canada

Intvr: Pearson, Tina

Topic: Creative process; Philosophy & aesthetics

Works: Lunatic phases

List: N

Biog: N

Source: MUSWORKS "Lunatic phases: Gayle Young talks about her music." 31 (Spr. 1985): 14-17

Lang: ENG

1062 Young, La Monte, 1935-

Date: Sum/66

Intvr: Kostelanetz, Richard

Topic: Composition–Technique; Experimental music; Harmony; Performance practice; Serial music; Sound, Environmental; Theater

Works: Composition 1960, no. 9; Tortoise, his dreams and journeys; Vision

List: N

Biog: Y

Source: KOST T Part 2. "Conversations. 8–La Monte Young." pp. 183-218

Lang: ENG

1063 Young, La Monte, 1935-

Date: 5/72, Bremen, Germany

Intvr: Gligo, Nikša

Topic: Composition–Technique; Indian music; Sound

Works: The well-tuned piano

List: N

Biog: N

Source: MELOS "Ich sprach mit La Monte Young und Marian Zazeela." 40/6 (Nov.-Dec. 1973): 338-44

Lang: GER

1064 Young, La Monte, 1935-

Intvr: Reinhard, Johnny

Topic: Minimal music; Temperament

List: N

Biog: N

Source: EAR "A conversation with La Monte Young and Marian Zazeela." 7/5 (Nov.-Jan. 1982-83): 4-5

Lang: ENG

1065 Young, La Monte, 1935-
Intvr: Vidić, Ljerka
Topic: Style (Individual)
Works: The well-tuned piano
List: N
Biog: Y
Source: EAR "Meet The Composer: La Monte Young and Marian Zazeela." 12/3 (May 1987): 24-26
Lang: ENG

Yuasa, Jōji, 1929-
See no. 800.
Works: Beyond the midnight sun; Icon

1066 Yun, Isang, 1917-
Date: 1/77
Intvr: Kleinen, Günter; Kühn, Hellmut
Topic: Audiences–20th-century music; Composition–Influences; Ethnic music; Metamusik-Festival; Style (Individual); Teaching; Tonality
List: N
Biog: N
Source: ZM "Musik aus unserer Welt und doch nicht von hier." 2/3 (Apr. 1977): 3-7
Lang: GER

1067 Yun, Isang, 1917-
Intvr: Rinser, Luise
Topic: Acoustics; Buddhism; Composers–Political conditions; Composition–Technique; Creativity; Critics; Operas; Philosophy & aesthetics; Style (Individual)
List: Y
Biog: N

Source: RINSER V
Lang: GER

1068 Yun, Isang, 1917-
Date: 4/30/82, Frankfurt, Germany
Intvr: Gerhartz, Leo Karl
Topic: Style (Individual)
Works: Concerto, violin, no. 1
List: Y
Biog: Y
Source: HEISTER K "Zukunft soll ahnbar werden." pp. 260-62
Lang: GER

1069 Yun, Isang, 1917-
Date: 7/19/86, Kladow, Germany
Intvr: Sachtleben, Rainer; Winkler, Wolfgang
Topic: Composers–Political conditions; Culture, Asian–Influences; Music & politics; Philosophy & aesthetics
List: Y
Biog: Y
Source: HEISTER K "Gespräch mit Isang Yun." pp. 288-96
Lang: GER

1070 Zaimont, Judith Lang, 1945-
Intvr: Van Gelder, Lawrence
Topic: Composers as performers
List: N
Biog: N
Source: NYT "A medley of talent and 'responsibility.'" 1 Apr. 1979, sec. 21, p. 2
Lang: ENG

1071 Zechlin, Ruth, 1926-
Date: 4/77, Berlin, Germany

Intvr: Stürzbecher, Ursula
Topic: Composers–Influences; Music
& literature; Women in music
Works: Quartets, string
List: Y
Biog: Y
Source: STURZ K, pp. 150-70
Lang: GER

1072 Zechlin, Ruth, 1926-
Date: 1984
Intvr: Mainka, Annelore; Mainka,
Jürgen
Topic: Bach, Johann Sebastian, 1685-
1750; Composition–Technique;
Germany, East (former); Philos-
ophy & aesthetics; Teaching
Works: Canzoni alla notte
List: Y
Biog: Y
Source: MAINKA S "I. Gespräche/
Selbstzeugnisse." pp. 7-74
Lang: GER

1073 Zimmermann, Udo, 1943-
Intvr: Gojowy, Detlef
Topic: Composition–Technique; Music
& art; Opera; Style (Individual)
Works: Der Schuhu und die fliegende
Prinzessin
List: N
Biog: Y
Source: MUSICA "Affinität zu szenisch
gebundener Musik. Gespräch mit
dem Komponisten Udo Zimmer-
mann." 30 (1976): 384-91
Lang: GER

1074 Zimmermann, Udo, 1943-
Intvr: Stürzbecher, Ursula

Topic: Composition–Technique; Music
& literature; Opera; Style (Indi-
vidual); Theater
Works: Der Schuhu und die fliegende
Prinzessin; Die wundersame
Schustersfrau
List: Y
Biog: Y
Source: STURZ K, pp. 85-106
Lang: GER

1075 Zimmermann, Udo, 1943-
Intvr: Lange, Wolfgang
Topic: Composition–Technique; Opera
List: N
Biog: Y
Source: MDB "Oper im Gespräch." 19/1
(1982): 38-44
Lang: GER

1076 Zimmermann, Udo, 1943-
Intvr: Dümling, Albrecht
Topic: Church music
Works: Pax questuosa
List: N
Biog: N
Source: NZ "Komponieren heute: 'Ruhe
ist eines der kompliziertesten
Dinge.' Ein Gespräch mit dem
Dresdner Komponisten Udo Zim-
mermann." 145/11 (Nov. 1984):
20-24
Lang: GER

1077 Zimmermann, Walter, 1949-
Date: 5/5/70
Topic: Composition–Technique
List: Y
Biog: Y

Source: ZIMMER I "Komponieren kann jeder ...." pp. 13-14

Lang: GER

1078 Zimmermann, Walter, 1949-

Date: 3/1/77, Cologne, Germany

Intvr: Volans, Kevin

Topic: Creative process

Works: Beginner's mind

List: Y

Biog: Y

Source: FP "Conversation with Walter Zimmermann." 13 (June 1977): 25-28

Lang: ENG

1079 Zimmermann, Walter, 1949-

Intvr: Oehlschlägel, Reinhard

Topic: Composers as performers; Creativity; Folk music; Interpretation; Sociology; United States

Works: Akkordarbeit; Beginner's mind; Einer ist keiner; Lokale Musik; *Organ project*

List: Y

Biog: Y

Source: ZIMMER I "Nachwort: Von Anfang an auf der Suche. Reinhard Oehlschlägel im Gespräch mit Walter Zimmermann." pp. 519-46

Lang: GER

1080 Zimmermann, Walter, 1949-

Date: Sum/84, Darmstadt, Germany

Intvr: Volans, Kevin

Topic: Philosophy & aesthetics

List: N

Biog: N

Source: MUSTEXTE "Jenseits der Ich-bezogenheit: Walter Zimmermann in einem Darmstädter Gespräch." 12 (Dec. 1985): 25-29

Lang: GER

1081 Zorn, John

Intvr: Mandel, Howard

Topic: Improvisation

List: N

Biog: N

Source: EAR "Howard Mandel interviews John Zorn." 11/2 (Oct. 1986): 16-17

Lang: ENG

1082 Zwedberg, Tommy, 1946-

Intvr: Tobeck, Christina

Topic: Electronic music; Improvisation; Instrumental music

Works: Care of; Face the music; Like mother like child; Musik mellan raderna

List: N

Biog: Y

Source: NUTIDA "Jag ser ingen skillnad pa elektromusik och instrumentalmusik: Musik som musik." 23/1 (1979-80): 8-10

Lang: SWE

1083 Zwilich, Ellen Taaffe, 1939-

Intvr: Grimes, Ev

Topic: Audiences; Teaching

List: N

Biog: N

Source: MEJ "Conversations with American composers." 72/6 (Feb. 1986): 61-65

Lang: ENG

Interviewers

Subjects

Bibliography

Boston Public Library. *Dictionary Catalog of the Music Collection.* Boston, Mass.: G. K. Hall, 1972, 1977.

DIALOG Publications. Palo Alto, Calif.: Dialog Information Services.

Encyclopedia of Library and Information Science. 1977 ed. S.v. "Oral History," by Louis Starr.

Grele, Ronald J. *Envelopes of Sound.* Chicago, Ill.: Precedent Publishing, 1985.

Library of Congress Catalogs: Music, Books on Music and Sound Recordings. Washington, D. C.: Library of Congress, 1953-

Lindsey, Roberta Lewise. "A Thematic Annotated Bibliography of the Literary Works and Interviews of Aaron Copland from 1924-1964." Thesis (M.A.), Butler University, 1986.

The Music Index. Detroit: Information Coordinators Inc., 1949-

New York Public Library. *Bibliographic Guide to Music.* Boston, Mass.: G. K. Hall, 1964-

New York Times Index. N.Y.: The New York Times, September 1851-

Répertoire International de Littérature Musicale. *RILM Abstracts.* New York: RILM, 1967-

Research Libraries Information Network. Stanford, Calif.: Research Libraries Group.